Post Keynesian Price Theory

This book sets out the foundation of Post Keynesian price theory by developing an empirically grounded pricing model and production schema. The administered, normal cost, and mark up price doctrines are explained in parts I–III of the book, as many of their theoretical arguments are important for developing the subsequent foundation. The work of Gardiner Means, Philip Andrews, and Michal Kalecki is discussed, as well as that of the developers of the doctrines such as Edwin Nourse, Paolo Sylos Labini, Harry Edwards, Josef Steindl, and Alfred Eichner. Drawing upon the arguments and formal modeling offered by the doctrines in conjunction with empirical evidence from 100 studies on pricing and production, an empirically grounded pricing model and production schema are developed; it is then argued that the model and the schema together constitute the foundation for Post Keynesian price theory.

FREDERIC S. LEE is a Reader in Economics at De Montfort University. He has taught and researched at numerous institutions in both the United States and England. He received the Helen Potter Award in Social Economics in 1988.

Post Keynesian Price Theory

FREDERIC S. LEE

De Montfort University

338,528
247p

PUBLISHED BY THE PRESS SYNDICATE OF THE UNIVERSITY OF CAMBRIDGE
The Pitt Building, Trumpington Street, Cambridge CB2 1RP, United Kingdom

CAMBRIDGE UNIVERSITY PRESS
The Edinburgh Building, Cambridge, CB2 2RU, United Kingdom
  http://www.cup.cam.ac.uk
40 West 20th Street, New York, NY 10011-4211, USA   http://www.cup.org
10 Stamford Road, Oakleigh, Melbourne 3166, Australia

First published 1998

Printed in the United Kingdom at the University Press, Cambridge

Typeset in Times Roman   [CE]

A catalogue record for this book is available from the British Library

Library of Congress Cataloguing in Publication Data
Lee, Frederic S., 1949–
   Post Keynesian price theory / Frederic S. Lee.
      p.   cm.
   Includes bibliographical references and indexes.
   ISBN 0 521 32870 5 (hb)
   1. Prices.   2. Keynesian economics.   I. Title.
HB221.L45   1998
338.5′28–dc21   97-49242   CIP

ISBN 0 521 32870 5 hardback

JK

Contents

v

Figures and tables

Figures

Tables

Acknowledgments

I am grateful to L. Boggio, J. Carson, J. Davies, P. Earl, H. R. Edwards, G. Harcourt, J. King, J. Kregel, J. Irving-Lessmann, P. Reynolds, A. Robinson, R. Robinson, P. Skott, and I. Steedman for earlier comments on various chapters of the book. I would especially like to thank the former members of the Oxford Economists' Research Group whose reminiscences provided the initial impetus for the book. I would also like to thank the late Alfred S. Eichner for his support of my unfashionable interest in the non-Kaleckian contributions to Post Keynesian price theory. Earlier versions of several chapters have been published in academic journals and chapters in books: parts of chapter 1 in the *Journal of Economic Issues* and in the *Review of Social Economy*; an early version of chapter 2 in Arestis and Kitromilides (1990); parts of chapter 4 in Young and Lee (1993), in *Banca Nazionale del Lavoro Quarterly Review*, and in *Australian Economic Papers*; an early version of chapter 5 in *British Review of Economic Issues*; and parts of chapters 11 and 12 in *Review of Political Economy* and Groenewegen (1993).

Introduction

Poverty of Post Keynesian price theory

If one is going to write a book on Post Keynesian price theory, it would, from the reader's viewpoint, be nice to know what "Post Keynesian economics" is. However, this is the wrong way of looking at it. Post Keynesian economics is not a set creed which can be looked up in some dictionary of economic terms; nor can it be defined as simply as anything which is anti-neoclassical economics, for coherence does count. At the present time, Post Keynesian economics is rather what Post Keynesian economists say it is. Thus, whereas it would appear that Post Keynesian economics is in a state of anarchy, it is in fact not so, because Post Keynesian economists have a common reference point – that of engaging in work which

> moves the Keynesian analysis forward to encompass more realistic analyses of pricing, distribution, investment and dynamic growth paths, both long-run steady state and short-period disequilibrium, than are to be found within *The General Theory*; and the work of those post-Keynesian economists like yourself [Gardiner Means] can be distinguished from that of the pre-Keynesians who still posit 19th Century institutional arrangements and market processes. (Eichner, 1978a*m*, p. 2)

Surveyors of Post Keynesian economics have consequently concentrated on the contributions of specific individuals, the "paradigms" of ideas on which they draw, and their attempts to move the Keynesian analysis forward. Hence, when they cast their net widely, Post Keynesian economists include such individuals as Piero Sraffa, Joan Robinson, Paul Davidson, Piero Garegnani, Michal Kalecki, and Nicholas Kaldor and the paradigms of ideas which they draw upon have been identified as classical political economy, Marxism, Sraffian economics, Institutionalism, and Keynesian economics. On the other hand, when they draw their net rather narrowly then we have Post Keynesian economics vs.

1

Sraffian economics vs. Kaleckian economics. There have also been attempts to define a Post Keynesian theoretical core in terms of Keynes, Kalecki, and classical political economy so as to give it the appearance of coherence. But such endeavors have, ironically, actually undermined the name Post Keynesian economics; for if Marx, Kalecki, Sraffa, and Keynes are thought to provide the theoretical core of the Post Keynesian research program, then Post Classical economics would seem the more appropriate nomenclature.[1] Moreover, and germane to this book, these attempts at establishing a coherent theoretical core would likewise fail if the price-theoretic foundations of the Post Keynesian research program were not entirely found in the works of Marx, Kalecki, Sraffa, and Keynes (Eichner and Kregel, 1975; Sawyer, 1982b, 1991; Groenewegen, 1986; Reynolds, 1987, 1989; Hamouda and Harcourt, 1988; Arestis, 1990; Dow, 1991; Arestis and Chick, 1992; Lavoie, 1992a, and 1992b; Henry, 1993; Chick, 1995).

In surveys of Post Keynesian economics, attention was paid to its price-theoretic foundations; however, the discussion was usually restricted to the Kaleckian price tradition, to the Sraffian approach to prices, or to an integration of the two (see table IA.1, p. 11).[2] This restricted vision of Post Keynesian price theory followed largely from the strongly held view that macroeconomics determined its own price-theoretic foundations. Consequently, Post Keynesians have devoted relatively little energy towards articulating a consistent and realistic non-neoclassical theory of prices and little research effort has been made on such price-related themes and issues as the nature of the underlying schema of production, the nature of the business enterprise, costs, pricing, the organization of markets, structure of consumption, and the nature of competitive activities, power, co-ordination of economic activity, innovation, and technical change. As a result, there exists no well grounded cohesive and consistent body of economic analysis that can be referred to as Post Keynesian price theory.[3]

When considering macroeconomic or microeconomic issues, Post Keynesians have utilized three distinct pricing or price-setting procedures – mark up, normal cost, and target rate of return pricing procedures – in conjunction with three distinct production models –

---

[1] This suggestion has been made rather forcefully by Eichner (1985), Lavoie (1990u, 1992b), and Henry (1993).

[2] John King's interview survey of Post Keynesian economists (1995) carried out in 1992 revealed the same partiality for Kalecki.

[3] One interesting consequence of this is that Post Keynesian ideology and economic policy covers a wide range of political viewpoints – see Chernomas (1982), Arestis (1990), Dow (1991), Arestis and Sawyer (1993).

the Austrian production model, the Burchardt production model, and the circular production model – in their writings. However, most of them prefer mark up pricing procedures based on constant average direct costs and Austrian or Burchardt production models (see table IA.2, pp. 12–16). Yet, the empirical evidence shows (see part IV) that production is a circular process and that all three pricing procedures are used by business enterprises in industrial market economies, while some evidence suggests that enterprise size (as measured by sales) and degree of diversification plays an important role in determining which pricing procedure is used. Moreover, the empirical evidence (see Lee, 1986) on average direct costs and average direct labor costs shows that they cannot, as a general theoretical principle, be assumed constant. Consequently, in emphasizing a single pricing procedure in conjunction with constant average direct costs and Austrian and Burchardt production models in their research, Post Keynesians have clearly violated economic reality and undermined their defining characteristic of moving the Keynesian analysis forward to encompass more realistic analyses.

Compounding this is the habit of Post Keynesians to employ a chosen pricing procedure as a stylized fact without realizing that it has a number of inherent and associated properties which often makes it inconsistent with the research being done, and to ignore the theoretical contributions of other economists. The habit persists for two reasons: (1) because Post Keynesians are largely unaware of the vast number of empirical investigations on, or related to, pricing procedures, pricing objectives, prices, and mark ups for profit; and (2) because Post Keynesians have largely rejected or ignored the contributions of economists who happen to have resided outside of Cambridge (UK), to have political beliefs not consistent with those Cambridge economists, or to have carried out their work without giving slavish praise to Keynes and Kalecki. What passes for Post Keynesian price theory is not grounded in empirical reality and, moreover, is a stunted theoretical artifact which would benefit from the ideas coming from the works of Gardiner Means and Philip Andrews (see Eichner, 1978a*m*, 1978b*m*, 1978). Post Keynesian price theory has no real existence beyond the idiosyncratic writings of various Post Keynesian economists, its various renditions are theoretically incompatible to a lesser or greater degree, and it has not been entirely freed from neoclassical concepts and terminology. My objective in this book is to move Post Keynesian analysis forward towards a more comprehensive, coherent, realistic – and, indeed, believable – non-neoclassical theory of prices by setting out its non-neoclassical pricing foundation by developing an empirically grounded pricing model in conjunction with an empirically grounded production schema.[4]

Methodology

The methodology used to develop the pricing foundation of Post Keynesian price theory is derived from the grounded theory approach articulated by Barney Glaser and Anselm Strauss. The approach is a qualitative research method which inductively derives a theory or analytical story from a given set of comparable qualitative data and is therefore specific to the data. From an extensive and detailed collection of comparable qualitative data, the researcher isolates a range of specific categories or analytical concepts and their associative properties, and identifies the relationships between the concepts. With the concepts and relationships empirically grounded in detail, the researcher then develops a descriptive, narrative, and analytical story about the data's core concept(s) in which the secondary concepts and relationships are integrated.[5] An essential property of the story is that it explains why and how the sequence of events in the story take place. In constructing the empirically grounded theory, the researcher does not try to simplify, but endeavors to capture the complexity of the data by empirically establishing many different secondary concepts and relationships and weaving them together with the core concept(s), thereby ensuring that the theory is conceptually dense as well as having broad explanatory power. The establishment of the central analytical story brings to light secondary concepts and relationships which need further empirical grounding as well as suggesting purely analytical concepts and relationships which need empirical grounding if they are to be integrated into the theory. The researcher's immersion with the data is pre-dated with familiarity of but not dogmatically committed to the relevant theoretical literature that assists in approaching the data, establishing concepts, and developing the theory. Once the theory is developed, the researcher can then "test" it on additional data as well as hypothesize about potential situations. In this latter case, the hypothesized situation is subject to the same empirical grounding as the theory was (Glaser and Strauss, 1967; Glaser, 1978; Charmaz, 1983; Strauss, 1987; Strauss and Corbin, 1990).

---

[4] Since the development of a non-neoclassical pricing foundation is the book's objective, there will be little criticism aimed directly at neoclassical price theory.

[5] When constructing the story, the researcher generally finds that even the best empirically grounded concepts need better specific grounding, which requires both a finer analysis of the data and the introduction of additional comparable data.

Theoretical milieu of Post Keynesian price theory

The development of a pricing foundation for Post Keynesian price theory will take place in two stages. The first involves delineating the broad theoretical milieu from which a Post Keynesian theory might be extracted, while the second draws upon a part of the milieu to develop a grounded pricing foundation on which to develop a Post Keynesian theory of prices. As noted above, over the last 25 years much has been written on various aspects of Post Keynesian price theory, and yet there has been little movement to a core set of ideas and arguments.[6] This is not because Post Keynesians are theoretical individualists. Rather it is because they are unaware that the ideas they are working with can be located in three different but largely compatible price doctrines whose own development over time has been away from neoclassical price theory and towards a non-neoclassical theory of prices. The theoretical milieu of Post Keynesian price theory consists of ideas, arguments, statements, and explanations which make up the three price doctrines associated with Post Keynesian economics – the administered, the normal cost, and the mark up price doctrines. The beginnings of the doctrines date from the 1930s and the economic disaster of the Great Depression. Clearly, the initiators and developers of the doctrines were influenced by ideas which pre-date the 1930s – Michal Kalecki's and Josef Steindl's familiarity with Marxism via Rosa Luxemburg and Mikhail Tugan-Baranovsky (see Sawyer, 1985 and Steindl, 1952) and Philip Andrews' connection with Alfred Marshall through David MacGregor (see Lee, 1989) being the best known examples. However, those ideas, whether formulated in 1776, 1860, or 1890, had little direct impact upon the development of the doctrines, for a variety of reasons. The capitalist economy that was the focus of attention of Adam Smith, David Ricardo, Karl Marx, John Stuart Mill, and Alfred Marshall was quite different from the corporate capitalist economy of post-1900 America and Great Britain which was the focus of attention of Gardiner Means, Andrews, Kalecki, and Steindl. Means, in particular, did not find the ideas and arguments of Smith through Marshall very helpful in developing the administered price doctrine.[7] A second reason is that the dominant body of theory which Means, Andrews, and others reacted against was neoclassical price theory, as articulated and developed from 1920 onwards. The post-1940

---

[6] There have been attempts by Alfred Eichner (1991) and Mark Lavoie (1992b) to establish a core set of ideas, but they have not been successful.

[7] Means reiterated this point many times in his writings. Moreover, there were relatively few references to pre-1930 in the books, articles, and unpublished material that were seminal in the development of the doctrines.

developments in the doctrines were often carried out in opposition to the rise to dominance of marginalism in the 1930s.[8] Another reason is that although some of the ideas and arguments found in the doctrines have ancient roots, they were actually derived from contemporary publications – the multi-industry pricing model of Alfred Eichner derived from Sraffa (1960) who, in turn, drew upon the surplus models found in Ricardo and Marx is a well-known example. Finally, many of the developments in the doctrines were derived from contemporary research. Consequently, the doctrines which make up the theoretical milieu will be considered as something which emerged in the 1930s and developed from then onwards.

To establish that each of the doctrines developed over time towards the same sort of non-neoclassical theory of prices, the grounded theory (or "grounded hagiography," to use Warren Young's (1987) phrase) approach will be used. A hagiographer is one who deals with "ancient" and "sacred" personalities, documents and texts; thus in the context of this book, the grounded hagiography approach will involve the use of the ancient and sacred personalities, documents, and texts as a way to reveal a coherent body of ideas that forms the theoretical core of the three doctrines and the evolution of the doctrines towards a common non-neoclassical theory of prices. In particular, this means that in addition to published works, recourse will be made to biographical data, to un-published personal letters, lectures, and papers, to oral histories and interviews, and to notes, memoranda, and letters located in the files of private and public institutions. Biographical data, for example, contri-butes to understanding the circumstances that led an economist to initiate work on a particular idea (or theory) and the process by which he or she developed, elaborated, and refined it; while unpublished personal letters and lectures, and oral histories provide a personalized view of the development of the doctrines, especially with regard to what degree the economists saw their work as opposed to and different from neoclassical economics.

Each of the three doctrines will consequently be discussed in terms of the "ancient and sacred economist(s)" whose work forms their core, the historical developments which lead to the sacred economist's work on the core, and the subsequent theoretical developments which deepened and expanded the core. Identifying the origins and core

---

[8] The oppositional nature of developments in the price doctrines to marginalism or more general neoclassical price theory is evident in the marginalist controversy of the 1940s and early 1950s and in the administered price controversy of the 1930s and the 1960s and 1970s (Lee, 1984b; Lee and Irving-Lessmann, 1992).

economists for the administered prices and normal cost prices doctrines is unproblematical – Gardiner Means and his work on the modern corporation and the inflexibility of industrial prices for the former, and Philip Andrews, the Oxford Economists' Research Group, and full cost pricing for the latter. However, the origin of and the core economist for the mark up prices doctrine is more problematical because of its close links with marginalism. To clarify this, let us first consider the issue of theoretical development. For the purpose of this book, "theoretical development" is defined as those developments which remove marginalist concepts and ideas from the doctrine, develop the doctrine's non-marginalist ideas and concepts, and introduce into the doctrine novel non-marginalist ideas and concepts. Thus, over time the core doctrines, which already have significant non-neoclassical content and thus in various degrees lie outside of marginalism, will be shown to have grown and moved further down the path away from marginalism and towards a non-neoclassical theory of prices. A result of this definition of theoretical development is that the marginalist–neoclassically-based "contributions" to the doctrines are completely ignored. But this definition creates problems when used as a way to identify the origins and the core economist of the mark up prices doctrine.

By most accounts, Michal Kalecki's microanalysis constitutes the theoretical core of the mark up prices doctrine. Yet, all those economists who have studied Kalecki's 1936–43 writings agree that the price-theoretic foundation on which he rested many of his arguments was marginalist in content (see, for example, Basile and Salvadori, 1984–5; Kriesler, 1987; Carson, 1990, 1993m; Osiatynski, 1991, p. 498). There has also been considerable debate over whether Kalecki toned down or eliminated the marginalist content in his later writings. Thus, it would appear quite problematical to associate Kalecki and his marginalist microanalysis with the non-neoclassical mark up prices doctrine. However, there is a way around this problem. The microanalysis which Kalecki developed from 1929 to 1945, although saddled with a marginalist pricing core, can be considered as the origin of the doctrine largely because it directly influenced subsequent economists whose writings contributed significantly to its development. By the early 1940s, Kalecki had developed his microanalysis to the point where other economists could draw upon it for their own work and thereby extend and develop it. Consequently over the next 35 years, various economists made contributions to the doctrine, with the result that by the early 1980s it had lost most of its marginalist attributes.

Organization of the book

As noted above, each of the three doctrines will be discussed in terms of the "ancient and sacred economist(s)" whose work forms the core of the doctrine, the historical developments which lead to the sacred economist's work on the core, and the subsequent theoretical developments which deepened and expanded the core. This means that when dealing with the doctrine of administered prices (part I), the sacred and ancient economist is Gardiner Means and his work on administered prices constitutes the doctrine's core, while his work on the modern corporation and price inflexibility forms the historical development leading up to his work on administered prices and the work of Rufus Tucker, Edwin Nourse, Abraham Kaplan, and Alfred Chandler both deepened and expanded the core. Similarly, the sacred and ancient economist for the doctrine of normal cost prices (part II) is Philip Andrews and his theory of competitive oligopoly constitutes the doctrine's core, while Robert Hall's and Charles Hitch's work on full cost pricing forms the historical development leading up to Andrews' theory and the work of Harry Edwards, Paolo Sylos-Labini, Wilford Eiteman, John Williams, Jack Downie, Romney Robinson, and George Richardson expanded and developed his theory. On the other hand, there is no single sacred and ancient economist whose work constitutes the core of the mark up doctrine (part III). The origin of the doctrine is found in the microanalysis Kalecki developed from 1929 to 1945. During the war years, economists linked with Oxford and Cambridge, such as Fritz Burchardt, Steindl, Kaldor, and Tibor Barna, further developed the microanalysis. The post-war developments by various economists, including Kalecki, Piero Sraffa, Geoffrey Harcourt, Peter Riach, Kaldor, Joan Robinson, Adrian Wood, Alfred Eichner, Steindl, and Paul Baran and Paul Sweezy, concentrated on the representation of production, pricing and the degree of monopoly, investment decisions, and economic stagnation and monopoly capitalism.[9]

Although I have distinguished between the three doctrines and will be treating them separately and in spite of the different terminology associated with each doctrine especially with regard to costs, they are in fact quite similar. For example, Sylos-Labini made contributions to both the normal cost and mark up prices doctrines, while Eichner drew heavily on

---

[9] Absence from my discussion of the mark up prices doctrine are references to Abba Lerner's degree of monopoly power, Roy Harrod's discussion of the variations in the price elasticity of demand over the trade cycle, and Keynes' notion of the constant degree of competition, because they did not contribute to the doctrine's development.

the administered prices doctrine when making his contribution to the mark up prices doctrine. More significantly, many aspects of Andrews' theory of competitive oligopoly and Steindl's analysis of the business enterprise and economic stagnation are similar, especially regarding enterprise growth, prices, and profits over time. In fact, the common elements of both doctrines were widely known to British economists for the first post-war decade, as evident in Jack Downie's largely independent work on the competitive process. Finally, Romney Robinson's work on non-market clearing prices was assisted by his acquaintance with administered prices (R. Robinson, 1989p). Thus, the reader should not be surprised that similar arguments reappear frequently throughout the discussion of the three doctrines. It is precisely the tediously familiar arguments of the three doctrines which enable them to be brought together and form the theoretical milieu from which the pricing foundation for a Post Keynesian theory of prices can be developed.

The three price doctrines contain numerous theoretical arguments, insights, and empirical data that would be useful for developing a Post Keynesian theory of prices and even a Post Keynesian analysis of the business enterprise. However, to attempt to draw from the doctrines a coherent, empirically grounded non-neoclassical theory of prices would ultimately be unsuccessful as it would require theoretical arguments that are not part of the doctrines and an empirical grounding of theory which is beyond the scope of this book. Instead, drawing upon the data, arguments, formal modeling, and insights offered by the doctrines, the purpose of part IV is to put together an empirically grounded pricing foundation on which to develop a Post Keynesian theory of prices. This more limited but foundation-building endeavor is intended to illustrate the importance of each of the doctrines to Post Keynesians, to show the process by which a theory is empirically grounded, and to demonstrate the importance of having a grounded theory. Chapter 11 will examine and empirically ground the analytical costing, pricing, and price components of the pricing foundation. Over 100 empirical studies on costing, pricing, and prices will be used to establish the appropriate analytical delineation of the costing and pricing procedures and price policies of the business enterprise and price-setting market institutions and to delineate the properties of the prices based on the pricing procedures. Then drawing on the formal and mathematical methods associated with the mark up prices doctrine, the enterprise and market pricing equation which can be derived from the pricing procedures will be formalized and mathematized. Chapter 12 continues the development of the pricing foundation by first considering the characterization and representation of the production schema underlying the pricing model and its corresponding quantity model.[10] Following this, the pricing model will be set out and its features and properties delineated. Drawing on the production schema and the pricing model, the third section of the chapter will outline and discuss the pricing foundation, and the last section will discuss the implications of the pricing foundation for the development of a well grounded Post Keynesian theory of prices.

Before starting, it is necessary to define some terms in order to facilitate the subsequent discussion. "Costing" refers to the procedures a business enterprise employs to determine the costs that will be used in setting the selling price of a good before actual production takes place and hence the actual costs of production are known. The procedures are based on normal or standard volume of output or capacity utilization and can range from determining average direct costs to determining the normal or standard average total costs. "Pricing" refers to the procedures the business enterprise uses to set the price of a good before it is produced and placed on the market. That is, starting with the costs determined by its costing procedures, the business enterprise then adds a costing margin to costs or marks up the costs to set the price. Finally, the "price" is the enterprise's actual selling price which is determined via its pricing procedures and therefore is set before production and exchange takes place.

The pricing procedures that will be the focal point of this book include mark up, normal cost, and target rate of return pricing. "Mark up" pricing procedures consist of marking up average direct costs based on normal output to set the price, with the mark up being sufficient to cover overhead costs and produce a profit. "Normal cost" pricing procedures consist of marking up average direct costs based on normal output to cover overhead costs, which gives normal average total costs, and then marking up normal average total costs to set the price, with the mark up producing a desired margin for profit. Finally "target rate of return" pricing procedures consist of marking up normal or standard average total costs by a certain percentage that will generate a volume of profits at normal or standard capacity utilization which will produce a specific rate of return with respect to the value of the enterprise's capital assets determined at historical costs.

---

[10] A production schema depicts the principal flows of produced goods in the technically required sequence. On the other hand, a quantity model refers to a precise system of production equations where the level of final demand determines the level of output, intermediate inputs, and labor inputs. A pricing model refers to a precise system of pricing equations where the level of wage rates and profit mark ups determine prices. Linked together, the production schema and the two models form the price–quantity monetary production model of the economy as a whole (Leontief, 1951; Lowe, 1976; Pasinetti, 1977).

Appendix

Table IA.1 *Surveys of Post Keynesian economics, 1975–96*

Author(s)	Attention given to price issues[a]	Types of price-theoretic foundations discussed			Other price issues discussed		
		Classical/Sraffa	Kalecki	Other	Mark-up[c]	Firm	Pricing
Eichner/Kregel (1975)	Much		×		×		×
Shapiro (1977)	Much		×		×	×	
Davidson (1980)	None						
Crotty (1980)	Some		×		×		
Tarshis (1980)	Much			Marginalism	×		
Yellen (1980)	Some		×				
Harcourt (1982)	Much		×		×		
Dow (1985)	Some	×	×	Keynes			
Groenewegen (1986)	Much	×	×				
Hamouda/Harcourt (1988)	Much	×	×	Kaldor	×		
Dow (1988)	Some		×	Behavioral approach			
Sawyer (1990, 1992a, 1993)	Much		×	H–H[b] Means	×	×	×
Ludlow-Wiechers (1990u)	Much	×					
Arestis (1990)	Little			Eichner	×	×	×
Dow (1991)	Some	×	×	Eichner	×		
Lavoie (1992a)	Some	×				×	×
Arestis (1992, 1996)	Some	×	×	Eichner Wood	×	×	×
Arestis/Sawyer (1993)	Some	×	×	H–H[b] Eichner	×	×	×
Henry (1993)	Little	×					

Notes: [a] Comments in this column are relative to the length of the survey. [b] H–H refers to Hall and Hitch. [c] Entries in this column means that the surveys dealt with the determination of the mark up.

Table IA.2 *Pricing procedures and production models utilized by Post Keynesians, 1971–96*

Author(s)	MUP	NCP	TRRP	LBP	LMBP	Shape of ADC/AVC	Production models APM	BPM	CPM	Economists referred to
Eichner (1973, 1976, 1983, 1991)			×			AVC constant			×	Kalecki Andrews Sylos-Labini Weintraub
Kregel (1973)	×				×	ADC constant		×		Kalecki
Harris (1974)	×	×		×		ADLC^a constant		×		Kalecki Weintraub Harcourt
Asimakopulos/Burbidge (1974)	×			×		ADLC constant		×		Kalecki
Asimakopulos (1975a, 1975b, 1977)	×			×		ADLC constant		×		Kalecki
Harcourt/Kenyon (1976)	×				×	ADC increases due to vintage capital				
Rowthorn (1977, 1981)	×	×		×		ADLC constant		×		Kalecki
Weintraub (1978, 1979, 1981)	×			×			×			Kalecki

Study	(1)	(2)	(3)	Mark-up	(4)	(5)	(6)	(7)	(8)	Influences
Sylos-Labini (1979, 1983–4)				ADC constant	×	×			×	Kalecki; Weintraub
Grant (1979)			×	ADC constant	×	×			×	Kalecki
Dixon (1979-80, 1981)		×				×			×	Kalecki
Ros (1980)					×			×		Hall–Hitch; Andrews
Mitchell (1981)						×			×	Weintraub
Jarsulic (1981)			×	ADLC constant		×			×	Kalecki
Levine (1981)	×			ADC constant	×				×	
Ong (1981)					×				×	Steindl
Watanabe (1982–3)		×				×	×			Weintraub
Lianos (1983–4)			×	ADLC constant		×			×	Weintraub
Minsky/Ferri (1984)			×			×			×	Kalecki; Weintraub
Seccareccia (1984)		×				×			×	Kalecki; Steindl; Weintraub; Eichner

Table IA.2 (*cont.*)

								Theorists
Dutt (1984, 1987, 1988, 1990, 1992)	×		×	ADLC constant	×		×	Kalecki Steindl
Goldstein (1985)	×							
Frantzen (1985)	×		×				×	Kalecki
Taylor (1985)	×			ADLC constant	×			
Tarling/Wilkinson (1985)	×				×			
Bhaduri (1985)	×		×	ADLC ADC constant	×		×	Kalecki
Myatt (1986)	×							Kalecki
Lavoie (1986–7, 1992b; Lavoie and Ramirez-Gaston (1996)	×	×		ADLC constant	×		×	Weintraub Kalecki Eichner Wood Andrews Hall–Hitch
Auerbach/Skott (1988)	×			ADLC constant	×			
Skott (1988u)	×			ADLC constant				

Study				Cost assumption			Theorists
Agliardi (1988)	×			ADC/AVC constant			Kalecki; Eichner
Deprez (1990*u*)	×	×		ADLC constant	×		Kalecki
Sawyer (1990, 1990*u*, 1995)	×	×		AVC constant	×		Kalecki; Eichner; Harcourt; Wood; Hall–Hitch
Dalziel (1990)	×		×				Kalecki
Bloch (1990)	×		×				
Toporowski (1990*u*, 1993*u*)	×	×		AVC constant			Kalecki; Steindl
Thompson (1992)	×	×		ADC constant		×	Kalecki; Hall–Hitch; Eichner; Steindl
Canterberry (1992)	×		×				Eichner; Levine; Marris; Penrose; Ong, Wood; Shapiro

Table IA.2 (*cont.*)

Author		Cost basis		Theorist / Influence
Glick/Ochoa (1992)			×	Eichner
Bober (1992)	×	AVC constant	×	Kalecki, Eichner
Slattery/Slattery (1993*u*)	×	ADLC constant	×	Kalecki
Park (1993*u*, 1995)	×	ADLC constant	×	Kalecki, Steindl, Eichner, Harcourt
Mott/Slattery (1994)	×	ADLC constant	×	Kalecki, Eichner
Acharyya (1994)	×	ADLC constant	×	Kalecki
Amadeo (1994)	×	ADC constant		Kalecki
King/Rimmer (1994*u*)	×	ADLC constant	×	Kalecki, Steindl
Sen/Vaidya (1995)	×			Eichner, Weintraub

Notes:

ADC	Average direct costs.	BPM	Burchardt production model.	MUP	Mark up pricing.
ADLC	Average direct labor costs.	CPM	Circular production model.	NCP	Normal cost pricing.
APM	Austrian production model.	LBP	Labor-based pricing.	TRRP	Target rate of return pricing.
AVC	Average variable costs.	LMBP	Labor and material-based pricing.		

Part I

The doctrine of administered prices

1 The origin of the doctrine of administered prices: from the modern corporation to industrial prices

Gardiner Means was born on June 8, 1896 in Windham, Connecticut, and spent his pre-college days growing up in Massachusetts and Maine. He entered Harvard in 1914 and majored in chemistry, and with the outbreak of war in 1917 he enlisted in the army. In 1919 he joined the Near East Relief, and after completing his stint, Means entered Lowell Textile School in September 1920, a decision prompted by his experience of hand-weaving in Turkey. After two years of studying wool manufacturing, he left in March 1922 to set up a textile enterprise making a high-quality (and high-priced) woven blanket of his own design that was quite different to any made by other blanket manufacturers. Through the running of his business enterprise, Means became well acquainted with the Boston wool market and the textile machinery market, and quickly came to the conclusion that American industrial life was very different than what he had experienced in the oriental bazaar in Harput. In particular, Means found that while the prices of cotton and wool varied continuously as in a bazaar, the prices of cotton and wool yarns did not. He thus deduced that the pricing process for the yarns was significantly different from the pricing process for cotton and wool. Means also found himself setting his price prior to any transaction in the market and then engaging in many sequential transactions at this price.[1] For one five-year period in the 1920s, he maintained the same price, even though his costs and sales varied, and sold many thousands of blankets. When Means did change his price in 1929, he did so more in response to a fall in the price of wool than to a decline in sales and the subsequent price was also administered to the market. In any event, Means felt that he was acting

---

[1] This kind of entrepreneurial acumen was not new to Means, for his uncles had introduced administered prices to the shoe business before 1900 and made a small fortune by advertising "The Means' $4.00 Shoe" with administered wholesale prices (Means, 1964m).

rationally in adopting such a price policy (Means, 1933, 1975d, 1983, 1986*i*; University of Lowell, n.d.*u*; Carter, 1934; Ware, 1988*m*; and Lee and Samuels, 1992a).

While still maintaining his textile enterprise, Means became interested in the causes of business depressions and unemployment and therefore decided to take some economic courses in the Harvard Graduate School to find out how the American economy operated. In February 1924, he entered Harvard as a graduate student in economics. The course he took from William Ripley on the corporation and industry undoubtedly met this goal. Between 1924 and 1927 Ripley's course dealt with railroads, trusts, and corporations. Moreover, he argued, both in his classes and, subsequently, in his best seller, *Main Street and Wall Street* (1927), that the dispersion of stock-ownership was permitting the senior level management and directors of the corporation to enrich themselves at the expense of the stockholders. In addition to Ripley's course, Means took a course titled "Valuation" and thus spent the 1926 Spring semester listening to James Bonbright, who commuted from Columbia University, lecture on public utility regulation. As for economic theory, Means took courses from Frank Taussig and Allyn Young. He was introduced to the writings of Smith, Ricardo, Mill, the Austrians, Marshall, and Edgeworth. In addition, he was also probably introduced to Walrasian general equilibrium at this time, as presented by Gustav Cassel in his book *The Theory of Social Economy* which first appeared in English in 1923. In spite of his excellent introduction to neoclassical economic theory, Means found it hard to take it seriously as a theory which could explain the operations of the American economy of the twentieth century (Blitch, 1983; Weintraub, 1983; Mason, 1982; Carlson, 1968; Means, 1960*m*, 1975d; Green, 1986*p*; Hon. 1987*p*; Law, 1986*p*; Lee, 1990b; Lee and Samuels, 1992a).

When Means went up to Harvard in 1924, Alfred Marshall's *Principles* (1920) formed the background theoretical core which all graduate students were supposed to know, and it remained so well into the 1930s, even after Edward Chamberlin's book *The Theory of Monopolistic Competition* (1st edn, 1933) was published. Moreover, it was common practice among the Harvard economists (as well as among nearly all economists influenced by Marshall) to teach that the economics of Smith, Ricardo, and Mill were substantially the same as the economics of Marshall, Edgeworth, and even Walras. This espousal of the "continuity thesis" (or the "non-marginal revolution thesis") bred the feeling among economists that they were following in the footsteps of the great figures in the field and that Marxian and Institutional economists were outside the fold. Students such as Means, came out of Harvard espousing the "continuity thesis" and continued to do so for the rest of their professional careers. However, unlike the majority of his fellow students, Means used the "continuity thesis" to entirely reject neoclassical economic theory as being completely irrelevant to the US economy of the twentieth century. By the time he received his MA in 1927, Means had become quite disappointed with orthodox theory (Lee and Samuels, 1992a).

The modern corporation and private property

Soon after completing his MA, Means was approached by Adolf Berle to assist him on his research project on the modern corporation. He accepted the offer and was hired as a statistical and research assistant. Means collected the statistical evidence and provided the economic analysis while Berle provided the legal analysis, and the result of this collaborative effort was their book *The Modern Corporation and Private Property* (1932) (see Lee, 1990b).

Berle viewed the research project as a vehicle through which he could show the changes in property rights brought about by the existence of the corporate enterprise. In particular, he sought, through statistical, economic, and legal analysis, to verify his thesis that corporate management was moving towards a corporate oligarchy through encroaching upon the property rights of the stockholders and to advance his fiduciary theory of corporations (Berle, 1929*m*). Berle restricted the project (and hence *The Modern Corporation*) to

the relations between the corporation as managed by the group in control, and those who hold participation in it – its stockholders, bondholders, and, to some extent, its other creditors. (Berle and Means, 1932, p. 8)

Thus while he carried out the legal analysis, Berle directed Means to determine the relative importance of large corporations in the American economy and the dispersion of stock ownership, since the former would determine the extent of the system of corporation finance in the economy while the latter would indicate the extent "that a small, dominant management group [could] control the business operations of any corporation of reasonable size" (Berle, 1928, p. 190).

Believing that Berle's distinction between management and ownership lacked economic significance, Means worried that his statistical work on the corporation would not be effectively utilized. Thus, he convinced Berle that instead of thinking in terms of ownership and management, it would be more useful to employ three distinct concepts – ownership, control, and management. Separating ownership from control and management, Means defined "ownership" as solely owning the shares of the corporation. In distinguishing the latter two concepts, Means defined "management" as those individuals who actively ran the day-to-day affairs of the corporation and were responsible for its technical and financial health. For Means, management of the corporation consisted primarily of both the senior and junior officers and the board of directors. On the other hand, he defined "control" as power to direct the corporation's activities and determine the distribution of corporate profits. Since the legal control of the corporation resided in the board of directors and senior management, Means located the controllers of the corporation in any individual, or group of individuals, who had the power to select the directors. This threefold distinction, however, did not affect Berle's legal investigations because he was concerned only with the activities of the directors and the senior officers of the corporation with regard to the stockholders, and not with the economic problems that emerged with the separation of control. On the other hand, it did permit Means to analyze the theoretical implications the separation of owner-ship and control had for neoclassical economics (Berle and Means, 1932; Eichner, 1980; and Means, 1931c).

Means' statistical research showed, for the first time, how large the modern non-financial corporations were, the extent to which they controlled aggregate non-financial assets and net income and dominated the economic landscape, and the extent of the separation of ownership from control among them. He then proceeded to argue that with the separation of ownership from control, it was possible that the interests of those who controlled the corporation could diverge from its owners – as, for example, by pursuing a policy of personal enrichment to the detriment of the owners.

In assessing the legal implications of the separation of ownership from control, Berle first noted that historically the rise of the corporation had been accompanied by a shift in power from the shareholders to the controllers of the corporation. He then discussed the legal mechanisms and devices through which the board of directors and senior management had obtained the power to determine the stock participation rights of stockholders, to determine the routing of earnings as between shares of stock, and to alter the original contract rights of security holders. Thirdly, as a prelude to delineating his fiduciary theory of corporations, he argued that common law had both the board of directors and senior management and the controllers standing in a fiduciary capacity towards the corporation. Since the shareholders owned the corporation, Berle felt justified in concluding that corporate powers were powers in trust to be used in the interest of all shareholders, thus *repairing legally the possible breach between owners and controllers that Means suggested came with the separation of ownership from control.* The final aspect of Berle's legal investigations concerned the problem shareholders faced in the stock market due to the power the directors and senior management have in manipulating share prices.

Ownership, control, and neoclassical economics

In addition to his statistical work, Means also contributed all the economic arguments found in *The Modern Corporation*. Prior to 1932 Berle was not terribly interested in economic arguments *per se*. Thus it is highly likely that he let Means draft Book IV (which he then rewrote to reflect upon his particular style). In this book, Means drew out the implications that the separation of ownership from control had for traditional theoretical roles of private property, wealth, and the profit motive in directing economic activity and increasing social welfare. He also elaborated on these themes in a subsequent theoretical manuscript written after *The Modern Corporation* was completed. In the manuscript, which was submitted as part of his dissertation but rejected, Means assessed the implications of the separation of ownership from control and of corporate "bigness" for neoclassical economics (Means, 1933).[2]

With the separation of ownership from control, Means argued, the concept of private property split into two distinct categories – passive and active property. The former consisted of shares of stocks and bonds, each representing a claim on industrial wealth and a stream of income, while the latter consisted of the tangible property and goodwill that made up the corporation. One result of this is that the traditional concept of wealth found in neoclassical theory changes and divides. For the holder of passive property, wealth becomes "a bundle of expectations which have a market value and which, if held, may bring him income and, if sold in the market, may give him power to obtain some other form of wealth," while for the possessor of active property, wealth "means a great enterprise which he dominates, an enterprise whose value is for the most part composed of the organized relationship of tangible properties, the existence of a functioning organization of workers and the existence

---

[2] Absent from the manuscript is any discussion about profit maximization and its applicability to the modern corporation. In spite of the claims made by many economists, Means never considered this question to be one of the book's arguments, for two reasons. First, he accepted Berle's fiduciary theory of corporations which was designed to repair the theoretical breach between the owners and the controllers. Secondly, up until the late 1940s, Means believed that the managers and controllers strove to maximize the profits of the corporation.

of a functioning body of consumers" (Berle and Means, 1932, pp. 305–6).

The emergence of passive and active property mirrored another development, Means argued, that of splitting the traditional theoretical picture of the saving–investment process into two independent stages under the control of separate groups of individuals. One group included those individuals in the economy who save through buying corporate securities and the second included the controllers of the corporations who decide to add to the corporations' capital stock and thus issue new securities with which to obtain the funds for this expansion. With two independent processes occurring, Means did not expect that the market for securities would operate in the same fashion as the market for capital goods. To illustrate the first claim, he constructed an example in which individuals continued to save at the same rate while the corporate enterprises decided to cease buying capital goods and issuing new securities. In such a situation the economy would be in disequilibrium which would, if possible, be corrected by the movement of prices in opposite directions in the capital goods and the securities markets. Similarly, he argued that if individuals wanted to reduce their savings rate in an effort to increase their level of consumption while corporate enterprises' issuance of new securities remained unchanged, the net result would be the destruction of the passive wealth of the individuals without any increase in the amount of goods which individuals could consume. To illustrate the second claim, Means briefly argued that prices in the securities market were extremely flexible and thus operated according to the laws of supply and demand, while prices in the capital goods market were in comparison relatively stable and moved quite independently of each other, thus resulting in the value of capital goods being different from the value of securities representing them. In short, Means concluded, the splitting of the savings–investment process due to the separation of ownership from control ultimately resulted in the rise of separate and dissimilar capital markets which need not always be in consonance, thus undermining the smooth and harmonious coordination of economic activity pictured by traditional economic theory (Means, 1933, pp. 18–21).

With regard to the profit motive, Means argued that in neoclassical economic theory, surplus profits (i.e. the profits which remain after interest on capital and wages of management have been deducted) acted as a return for the performance of two separate functions – the taking of risk and the directing of the enterprise so as to maximize its profits. However with the emergence of the modern corporation and the separation of ownership from control, the two functions were now performed by two different groups of people, with the owners risking wealth and the controllers directing the corporation. Consequently, Means argued that the allocation of profits must be such that, if the profit motive was to be the guiding force in directing the corporation's economic activity so as to promote the community's welfare, the owners should get only the amount needed to compensate them for their risk (i.e. provide them with a satisfactory return), and the rest should go to the controllers as an inducement to the most efficient management and direction of the corporation.

Means noted that the legal system prevented such a division of profits, thus preventing the profit motive from having its maximum impact on social welfare. Moreover, because of diminishing managerial motivation with regard to increasing income, Means was not sure that the huge amount of surplus profits that could be diverted to the controllers would in fact spur them on to significantly better management and hence to significant increases in social welfare. In addition, he questioned the effectiveness of the profit motive to direct economic activity so as to increase social welfare because of the decline of the effectiveness of competition to regulate economic activity due to the rise of the modern corporation. Finally, Means wondered if the community's welfare would suffer if the rest of the surplus profits were given to the controllers since, it would undoubtedly increase the immense amount of economic power they already had in the economy. Thus he concluded it was simply not possible to blindly believe that, in an economy where the large corporation and the separation of ownership from control predominated, the profit motive as neoclassical theory pictured it was a socially benefitting and effective motivating force with regard to the directing of economic activity (Berle and Means, 1932; Means, 1933).

Corporate size and neoclassical economics

Means' statistical research relating to the size and economic dominance of the modern corporation led him in a series of articles and *The Modern Corporation* to question the adequacy and relevance of many theoretical concepts found in neoclassical price theory. First of all Means, armed with his facts, argued that Marshall's concept of the representative firm or the small owner–worker enterprise had ceased to be a relevant tool for economic analysis since the "representative" enterprise in twentieth-century America was the large corporation with many thousands of owners and employees and which dominated one industry after another. Individual initiative had consequently largely been replaced by group activity and co-operation. Moreover the nature of competition had also altered; the principles of duopoly were now more important than those of free competition. In particular, the large corporation, simply by virtue of its size, could affect market prices even though it was not a monopoly. Secondly, Means argued that the size of the corporate enterprise was neither limited by the wealth of the individual owners nor by technological inefficiency. Its size was rather limited only by the controllers' ability to administer the corporation's activities successfully; however, there was no reason why the controllers, given their ability, could not devise an appropriate administrative form necessary for successful management. Hence the notion of the "optimum-size enterprise" found in neoclassical price theory was simply irrelevant for the study of the modern corporate enterprise. Thirdly, Means noted that the corporation's costs of production were indeterminate. Finally he argued that administration and co-ordination of economic activities by management had largely replaced the co-ordination of economic activities by the forces of supply and demand in the market place. That is, the large corporation had internalized production activities that were once found in the market and subjected them to administrative co-ordination, while also entering directly into the market to co-ordinate activities on its own behalf (Means, 1931a, 1931b, 1983c; Berle and Means, 1932).[3]

Because the main theoretical focus of *The Modern Corporation* was on the implications of the separation of ownership from control, Means did not follow up these other theoretical implications until he turned to writing his dissertation. In the manuscript, he presented a more developed argument of how the existence of the large corporation called into question the "scientific" validity of neoclassical price theory. Restricting himself to what he considered the most fundamental postulates of the theory – the principle of supply and demand in determining prices, and the determinacy of costs – Means argued that they could not be sustained in their traditional form once the large corporation became a dominant feature of the economy. In particular, he argued that the demise of the principle of supply and demand in determining prices rested primarily upon the mere size of the corporate enterprise, as opposed to the separation of ownership from control. Means consequently devoted a part of the manuscript to the concept of administered prices and its destructive implications for the supply and demand determination of

---

[3] Means' rejection of neoclassical price theory as a tool for examining the US economy of the 1930s comes out quite strongly in a letter to Walker D. Hines of the Cotton Textile Institute written in December 1931. In the letter, Means objected to Isaiah Sharfman's critique of Hines' plan for regulating the cotton textile industry because it was based on neoclassical economic theory which was at complete variance with market realities, even in such a competitive industry as cotton textiles (Galambos, 1966).

prices. He also devoted a part of the manuscript to the indeterminacy of costs of the large corporation.

When discussing the management of a business enterprise, Marshall, in his *Principles of Economics*, had argued that the businessman undertook two distinct but specific activities – that of taking risks and that of organizing and supervising production. The first activity he equated with speculating or the buying and selling of existing goods by middlemen; the second he viewed as administrative or engineering activities (Marshall, 1920, p. 293). Means accepted this distinction, and went on to note that, for the large modern corporation, its primary economic activities were administrative. Internally the corporation administered its productive activities while externally it administered its prices to the market. Consequently, in an economy dominated by the large modern corporation, the character of the market altered in that the market price became a matter of administration rather than a matter of trading. Thus Means became concerned with the theoretical questions of how an administered price market operated and how its operation differed from the operation of a trading market assumed in neoclassical price theory. He answered both questions by arguing that in an administered price market prices were fixed by administrative fiat before transactions occurred and held constant for periods of time and hence for sequential series of transactions, and that supply and demand never equated except by coincidence.

To illustrate the concept of administered prices and their impact on the operations of the market, Means developed an elaborate example, based on a department store, in which he argued that variations in demand (or sales) would not affect the administered price, but rather affected the rate at which goods were sold; that variations in supply (or quantities of a good available for sale) would not affect the administered price; and that the administered price could be maintained for a series of transactions at which supply and demand were not equated. In addition, Means varied the time period covered by the supply and demand curves to show just how fortuitous the equation of supply and demand would be in an administered price market. As a result, he concluded that administered prices were neither long- nor short-period prices and, as a consequence, that administered price markets could not be described by the traditional tools and concepts employed by economists:

We are dealing with a phenomenon which conforms neither with the economist's short run nor with his long run supply and demand curves. Whereas there may be a tendency for the proportionate discrepancy between supply and demand to decrease in the long run, there is *no* tendency for the absolute amount of the discrepancy to decrease. One must, therefore, say that the supply and demand curves which so neatly cross in the economist's traditional description of the market cannot be employed to describe this market. (Means, 1933, p. 14)

In an effort to fully flesh out the nature of administered prices and their impact on the workings of the market, Means ended this part of the manuscript by delineating three additional features. First, with respect to price changes, he stated that administered prices changed in discontinuous jumps. He also stated that administered prices could either be sensitive or insensitive to variations in sales or inventories. Sensitive administered prices could be identified as those which remained constant for days at a time but having upwards of 50 or more discontinuous price changes per year, such as the administered price for standard cotton yarn; while insensitive administered prices, on the other hand, could be identified as those which remained constant for months or years at a time, such as the administered prices for automobiles, *The Saturday Evening Post*, or the New York subway. In either case, Means argued, after the price changes had been made, there would be no more justification to suppose that supply and demand had been equated than before under the initial administered price. Lastly, Means dealt with the employment of the factors of production in markets dominated by relatively insensitive administered prices in comparison to markets dominated by highly flexible prices. He noted that in administered price markets, variations in demand – and hence production (and sales) – resulted in variations in the employment of labor and capital, in part because their respective prices, wage rate, and interest rate were also *administratively determined*. However, in markets dominated by highly flexible prices, variations in demand would be entirely played out through changes in the market price, leaving both the level of production (and sales) and the employment levels of the factor inputs unaffected. This asymmetrical response to demand, Means concluded, was perhaps the explanation for the differing impact the Great Depression had on the agricultural (trading) and industrial (engineering) sectors in the economy – in the former prices declined while production and employment remained relatively stable, in the latter prices remained stable while production and employment declined (Means, 1933).

In the chapter on costs, Means provided additional support for his position that the traditional neoclassical tools and concepts could not be used to describe administered price markets. In this case, Means argued that in the modern corporation the costs of producing a specific good were completely indeterminate from the perspective of neoclassical cost theory because of the prevalence of joint costs and joint utility. While joint costs could arise from a variety of sources, such as from carrying a full line of goods to promote the sales of any particular one, he argued that the most significant source of joint costs came from the large size of the modern corporation itself. That is, as the business enterprise increased in size, production of a specific good became increasingly an inter-related and vertically integrated process so that a specific input became used in the production of more than one good. Hence it became increasingly important for the accountant to accurately allocate the costs of the multi-use inputs if the precise costs of a specific good was to be known. However, with the emergence of the large corporation and the resulting increased complexity of production, it became impossible for management and its accountants to ascertain the specific costs incurred in the production of a particular product. As for joint utility, Means argued that since the large corporation had a high degree of vertical integration, the cost of any product was dependent on two or more inputs, thus greatly increasing the confusion in trying to determine its specific costs. Means thus found it impossible to escape from the conclusion that the costs of goods produced by the modern corporation were completely indeterminate from the perspective of neoclassical cost theory. Consequently, it was not possible to utilize neoclassical cost theory – and, by extension, enterprise and market supply curves – to describe and analyze administered price markets (Means, 1933).

Advisor to Wallace, 1933–1935

On March 4, 1933 Roosevelt appointed Henry Wallace as Secretary of Agriculture. Faced with the crisis in agriculture and the need to develop recovery programs and legislation, Wallace realized that he would have to expand the staff associated with the Office of Secretary both to cope with the increased workload and to acquire information that neither the traditional staff nor his bureau chiefs could provide. On March 6, he established the position of Economic Advisor to the Secretary and selected Mordecai Ezekiel to fill it. Drawn together by their strong interest in statistics, their concern for bettering the economic and social lot of the farmer, and their views favoring production controls, Ezekiel proved to be an indispensable aid to Wallace. In particular, Ezekiel helped draw up the Agricultural Adjustment Act which established the Agricultural Adjustment Administration (AAA) and select the personnel to carry it out. Wallace also turned to Ezekiel for advice about agricultural policy. At this same time Rexford Tugwell, who was also concerned about the economic plight of the farmer and thought that production control was the way out of the agricultural crisis, was appointed as Wallace's Assistant

Secretary (Kirkendall, 1966; Saloutos, 1982; Macmahon and Millett, 1939; Baker et al., 1963).

Even though the AAA was just two months old, it had become obvious to Tugwell and Wallace that its success depended to a large degree on the recovery of the industrial sector, and hence on the recovery policies of the National Recovery Administration (NRA). Thus to obtain the kind of specialized information they needed, Wallace established, under Tugwell's prodding, another advisory position to be filled with an individual who would busy himself in seeing the staff aides of other federal agencies in order to learn what recovery policies were in hand that would have an impact on the recovery of the farm sector. The individual would then draw up reports of his findings and submit them to Wallace. In this manner, the individual would be able to aid both Tugwell and Wallace in thinking through their points of view regarding the place of agriculture in the whole economy.

As a result of Charles Beard's review of *The Modern Corporation and Private Property* which appeared in the *New York Herald Tribune* in February, Tugwell and Wallace were quite aware of Means and his knowledge of industry. Calling on him at Columbia University where he was teaching an economics course in the Law School's summer session, Tugwell asked Means whether he would consider joining Roosevelt's war on the farm crisis. Means went to Washington to talk with Tugwell and Wallace and the outcome was that Wallace immediately appointed him to the advisory position and gave him the informal title of Economic Advisor on Finance. So instead of pursuing the quiet academic life, Means joined the war effort in June on a part-time basis until he had completed his summer school teaching and then on a full-time basis (Macmahon and Millett, 1939; Baker et al., 1963; Ware, 1982m; Means, 1953dm, 1986i).

Working out of the same office, which was adjacent to Tugwell's, as did Ezekiel and Louis Bean, Wallace's Economic Advisor to the AAA, Means quickly became a member of committees in the NRA and a participant in the growing controversy over the NRA's price policy. Following the signing of the first code of fair competition in July 1933, the code approval process adopted by the NRA permitted or even encouraged inclusion in the codes of many price-fixing and price-stabilizing provisions, such as minimum cost provisions, uniform methods of cost finding, and open price provisions. Members of the Consumers' Advisory Board (CAB) viewed these developments with dismay since they seemed to favor capital over the consumer; in addition, Tugwell and the US Department of Agriculture (USDA) saw the provisions as fostering higher industrial prices and thus canceling out the gains to the farmers brought by the AAA. The concern over the codes was further fueled by the rise in industrial prices that was taking place as they were being approved. In an effort to deal with these concerns, Alexander Sachs, the head of the Research and Planning Division of the NRA, established a number of policy committees, one of which was the Price Policy Committee. The Committee's first meeting was held on September 16, 1933 and the participants included Sachs, John Dickerson, the Assistant Secretary of Commerce, and Means. Soon thereafter Stephen M. DuBrul of the Code Analysis Section in the Research and Planning Division also became a member. Over the next few months the committee concerned themselves with problems of costs, cost formulas, loss leaders, and sales below costs; but, in spite of the memoranda they sent out, the Committee's work had little impact on the ongoing debate over the NRA price policy (Hawley, 1966; Minutes of Committee on Prices, 1933*m*; Carter, 1934; Roos, 1937; Means, 1953d*m*; and Ohl, 1985).

In taking the job with Wallace, Means took it for granted that he would be trying to develop policies and instruments that would make the economy work more effectively. Because he strongly believed that economic matters did not take care of themselves but were subject to a high degree of administrative decision-making, he saw consumer partici-pation in the decision-making process necessary if truly equitable and effective economic policies were to emerge. Since the existence of the CAB was quite consistent with his views, the well publicized resignation of William F. Ogburn, the CAB's first director, in August caught Means' attention. He went to the CAB to talk with its chairperson, Mary Rumsey. She received him graciously into her office, but when she learned that Means was an economic advisor to Wallace, she grabbed his arm and said

"Young man, come with me." Called her chauffeur, they got in a car and she said to the chauffeur, "Now you just drive around. I don't want to answer any telephones. I want to talk to this young man." (Ware, 1982*m*, p. 44)

For the next few hours Means and Rumsey talked about the consumer's role in the New Deal and found that they were very much in agreement. By the time the ride had ended, Means had agreed to help her find a successor to Ogburn, and on September 26 Rumsey made him a member of the CAB. Although not involved with its day-to-day running, Means did become involved in the CAB's struggle with the NRA's price policy. Many staff members came to adopt his arguments concerning admin-istered prices, concentration, and price control when presenting their critique of the price provisions in the codes at various public price hearings and code-making sessions (e.g. see Ayres and Baird, 1935, pp. 875–9). However, Means' greatest contribution to the CAB was his articulate defense of their position that consumer interest was different from public interest. Basing his argument on the thesis that in an economy dominated by administered prices and where administrative decision-making was the primary form of "market coordination," Means contended that consumer interest was distinct from the public interest, which also included the interests of labor, business, farmers, and others. Hence it was necessary for separate consumer representation in the administrative decision-making process to exist if appropriate economic policies were to be forthcoming that would put the economy back on its feet (Ware *et al.*, 1982; Ware, 1982*m*; *The New York Times*, 1933; Means, 1934; Minutes of Consumer Advisory Board, 1933*m*; Campbell, 1940).

Concerned about the mounting criticism towards the NRA's price policy, the Brookings Institution publication *Price-Control Devices in NRA Codes*, by George Terborgh, spurred Roosevelt to appoint, in May 1934, a Cabinet Committee on Prices, consisting of the Secretaries of Labor, Commerce, and Agriculture, and the Attorney General, to look into the price situation and effects of various code provisions on the price structure. At the Committee's first meeting, a Sub-Committee was established to investigate the price structure of various industries with a view to making recommendations as to the policy that should be pursued in the formulation and revision of the codes. Members of the Sub-Committee included Isador Lubin of the Bureau of Labor Statistics, Leon Henderson of the NRA, Dickerson and Means, who represented Wallace. Prior to the Sub-Committee's first meeting at which its investigative directives would be given a more concrete orientation, Means circulated a short note among the members outlining what he thought they should be. Playing down the significance of the developments toward price control under the NRA, he argued that they were simply an outgrowth

of the changing characters of the pricing process which has taken place throughout the industrialized parts of the world and has brought price controls of various sorts into operation in other countries ... [and] ... of the basic pressure on business men growing out of the changed character of the market ... (Means, 1934a*m*)

He therefore suggested that the objectives of the investigation should include the testing of "the hypothesis that there has been a radical change in the character of the pricing process," the analyzing and developing of a generalized description of the new pricing process if the hypothesis is sustained, and exploring "the possibilities of pricing processes where the economic machine can be made to function effectively." Means also advocated specific investigations dealing with:

1 The character of modern pricing processes, particularly with reference to price-fixing over periods of time–price rigidity-administered prices
2 Relation of prevalence of administered prices to industrial concentration
3 Relation of fluctuations in price to fluctuations in volume
4 Relation of fluctuations in price to man hours worked
5 Relation of administered prices to wage rates
6 Relation of administered prices to overhead costs
7 Relative adaptability of administered prices
8 Relation of prices, production and profits by industries with particular reference to price rigidity. (Means, 1934a*m*)

However, Means' suggestions did not become the basis of the Sub-Committee's investigation. Rather, with the hiring of Walton Hamilton as the Director of Research in June, the investigations became primarily concerned with "prices as pecuniary manifestations of industries at work" (Henderson, 1934*m*; Minutes of Cabinet Committee on Prices, 1934*m*; Means, 1934a*m*; Hamilton, 1934*m*; Lubin, 1935*m*).

NRA and AAA and the reorganization of industrial policy-making

Washington in the summer of 1933 was overflowing with energy usually only found in proverbial towns on the make; but instead of being directed towards making money, the energy was directed towards making the economy and society healthy again. Politicians and bureaucrats were open to any plans for recovery; explanations for the depression by the Right and the Left were eagerly discussed even if they offended conventional economic dogma; and the pervading atmosphere was that something, anything, had to be done – even if it was wrong! Therefore, it is not surprising that Means' explanation of the Great Depression and plan for recovery received attention in Washington; on the other hand, it is surprising, given the number of competitors, that his analysis of depression and recovery became so influential, especially with members of Roosevelt's administration. When Means began working for Wallace, one of the many explanations for the depression floating around Washington was the purchasing power thesis. The explanation, a favorite of the Liberal-Left, ascribed the cause of the depression to the lack of purchasing power which resulted from the maldistribution of income. In turn, it was argued that the maldistribution of income was caused by the rise of big business and monopoly price-fixing. Yet even at this level of articulation, the thesis was not tightly delineated; consequently, Tugwell could (and, in fact, did) adopt it to explain the "unbalancing" of agricultural and industrial prices and the subsequent depression of the farm sector (Rosenof, 1975, 1983).

Although agreeing in principle with the purchasing power thesis and its application to the farm sector, Means found Tugwell's specific analysis of the depression and the farm crisis, and his plans for recovery ill-formed because he did not adequately take into account the existence of inflexible or administered prices or the impact of business control over the making of industrial policy on the overall balance of the economy. Means attributed the Great Depression to the interaction of specific long-term developments in the US economy:

> those which necessitated great and rapid economic readjustments if the economy was to be kept in balance; those which decreased the flexibility of the economic structure and tended to impede automatic readjustment; and those which transformed the usual economic drives from forces working toward economic readjustment into forces tending to produce further maladjustment and greater unbalance in the economy. (Means, 1935c, p. 74)

With respect to the first developments, Means divided them into two groups, those which were secular developments – such as the disappearance of the frontier; the increase in the production and use of the automobile, bus, truck, and tractor; the development of electricity; technological improvement in industry resulting in greater output per worker; and the shift from a debtor to a creditor nation – and those developments which emerged as a result of the First World War – such as the post-war construction boom; instability of international monetary relationships and the emergence of large international imbalance of trade; the changing status of war debts and reparations; the post-war expansion in American loans; the development of economic nationalism; and the farm debt.

If these developments were not to cause significant dislocation in the economy, it would be necessary, Means argued, for important economic readjustments to take place and this in turn required that the economic system be highly flexible, especially with respect to prices. However, developments had taken place which greatly reduced the flexibility of the American economy and impeded the making of the necessary economic readjustment, the most important of which was the increasing concentration of economic activity resulting in inflexible administered prices. Other developments which also reduced the flexibility of the economy included the building up of internal debt and the inability of governmental institutions to deal with the economic problems growing out of the new conditions established by the rise of economic concentration. In conjunction with these, Means continued, a third set of developments had emerged which had subverted forces which in a flexible economic system would have promoted the required economic adjustment, into those that now aggravated any significant maladjustments once they had developed. The most significant of these developments was the making of industrial policy by individual business enterprises. Instead of industrial policy being made by the impersonal forces of the market place, it was being made in accordance with the enterprise's desire to maximize profits, which generally meant, in face of declining demand, holding prices constant and reducing production. Thus, in place of market forces working to maintain the full use of the nation's resources, the business policies of big business aggravated any initial decline in demand by maintaining prices and throwing workers out of work, thereby doubly reducing the purchasing power of the community. Other positively disrupting factors included the increasing mechanization of production, the increasing importance of consumer capital goods, and the increasing inadequacy of the banking system in the presence of inflexible administered prices (Means, 1935c).

When presenting his analysis to Tugwell and others in the Department of Agriculture, Means found that it was well received and quickly absorbed. His arguments on the relationship of concentration and inflexible administered prices and the relative inflexibility of industrial prices compared to agricultural prices were already familiar to members of the group. Moreover, his analysis of the relationship between inflexible prices and production fitted in quite well with Tugwell's and Wallace's view of the basis of the farm crisis. Thus Means' arguments quickly became employed by his USDA colleagues to critically analyze the negative impact the NRA codes had on the recovery of the farm sector. However, in spite of the attention that his colleagues in the USDA, CAB, and Price Policy Committee gave to his views, Means' arguments did not have any significant effect on the thinking of the policy-makers in the USDA or in the Roosevelt Administration in general. This was, in part, due to the reluctance of many to accept his argument that the rise of industrial concentration, by permitting manufacturing businesses to set inflexible administered prices and flexible production policies, had irrevocably disrupted the automatic price and output adjustment mechanism found in a competitive market economy. It was also in part due to a belief among many that the problem with the NRA and AAA lay in the particular form the codes of fair competition or marketing agreements took. Means' claim that the codes simply reflected the radical changes which had occurred in the making of prices and industrial policy, and that the real problem with the NRA and AAA lay in developing the right kind of techniques that would regulate and co-ordinate all economic activity so as to bring about the full utilization of the nation's resources thus fell on deaf and unconvinced ears (Carter, 1934; Bean, 1952m; Kirkendall, 1966; Means, 1934fm, 1934gm; Frank, 1935m).

Believing that the policy-makers would not take his arguments seriously unless they were accompanied by dramatic empirical evidence, Means on his own initiative undertook, starting in late Spring, 1935 a

statistical analysis of wholesale prices to bring out the basic difference in behavior between farm commodity prices and the administered prices of industry and to help clarify the thinking of the policy leaders in the [USDA] and in the rest of the administration. (Means, 1953dm)

Upon the completion of the investigation, he found the results "much more startling and in conflict with the classical analysis than even [he] had expected" (Means, 1953dm). Drawing upon his previous analysis of administered prices and a study of the California cling peach marketing agreement made at the request of Wallace, Means used the statistical evidence as a stimulation to writing a paper delineating the reasons for the failure of the NRA and AAA with regard to the making of industrial policy and possible techniques that both the NRA and AAA could use for making better industrial policies. Although the paper was entirely analytical, trying to indicate what the characteristics of the problem were, Means expected it to be used by the makers of industrial policy (Means, 1938am, 1938bm, 1952bm, 1953dm; Frank, 1935m; Lee, 1988).

Statistical evidence

To properly determine the extent to which administered prices occurred among the entire population of prices in the American economy, Means would have had to obtain transaction price data from each business enterprise in the economy. Moreover the data itself would have had to be commodity-specific and consist of the transaction price for each transaction of a long series of sequential transactions. In addition he would also have had to obtain information as to how each enterprise in the economy set its selling price, the degree of market concentration held by each business enterprise for each good it sold, and the degree to which market forces influenced the enterprise when setting its prices. Means had neither the time or the resources to carry out such a research project; assuming frequency of price change as a rough indicator of whether a price was administratively determined or determined in the market, he turned to the monthly wholesale price date collected by the Bureau of Labor Statistics (BLS) to carry out his investigation. In 1934, the BLS collected monthly price data on 784 commodities grouped into 10 product categories, with numerous sub-group categories. Even though some of the 784 commodities were composite commodities and thus not suitable for Means' purposes, most of them, being highly specific, were. Each commodity had at least one if not more price reporters from which the BLS obtained their price data. Thus, with permission from the BLS, Means looked at the confidential price reports and gathered both monthly price quotations and frequency of price change on 750 specific commodities.[4] For those commodities which had two or three reporters, he took the average of the number of price changes reported by each of the reporters or, where the number of reporters was more than three, the number of changes by a single reporter which appeared to be typical of the group was taken. The time period covered by the study was 1926–1933, broken down into two four-year periods, one consisting of the pre-Depression years 1926–9 and the other consisting of the Depression years 1930–3. This was done to see if there was any significant change in the frequency of price change or any important shifting of items as a result of the onset of the Depression, such as commodities with relatively infrequent price changes in the pre-Depression years experiencing relatively frequent price changes with the onset of the Depression. The number of possible price changes for each commodity for each four-year period was 47 and hence the total number of possible price changes over the entire eight-year period was 94 (instead of 95 as would normally be the case for an eight-year period) (Means, 1935a*m*, 1935b*m*, 1964*m*; Blair, 1964, 1972).

Upon inspecting the price data collected with regard to a frequency of price change, Means discovered a U-shaped distribution indicating that the economy consisted of two different kinds of prices – administered prices and market prices – and market adjustment mechanisms – market prices adjusting in the market to conditions of supply and demand and administered prices remaining relatively unchanged while economic adjustments were chiefly made by changing the volume of production. Next he related the frequency of price change to magnitude of price change and found that prices with infrequent price changes tended to drop little in the Depression and vice versa. Finally, drawing on production data culled from the *Survey of Current Business* and on agricultural and related data supplied by the USDA Bureau of Agricultural Economics, Means demonstrated the existence of an inverse relationship

---

[4] In the study, Means left out railroad rates, utility rates, some corporate items, and composite commodities (such as automobiles, harnesses, suit cases, coal, plows, wagons, bricks, cement, gravel, sand, fertilizer, furniture, and tires and tubes). However in those cases where the composite commodities contained two or three items, Means used the separate items as though they were separate and independent commodities (Means, 1935a*m*, 1935b*m*).

between magnitude of price change and production change for the agricultural implements industry and various product groups and sub-groups in the BLS wholesale price series (Means, 1934*u*). Thus, through a series of analytical and empirical steps, Means demonstrated that the existence of inflexible administered prices undermined the traditional market adjustment mechanism and thus brought to the forefront the problem of making industrial policy (Means, 1934*u*; Lee, 1988).

Administered prices and industrial policy

To explain how administered prices impaired or destroyed the market adjustment mechanism that was relied upon to maintain the full use of the nation's resources, Means distinguished between industrial policy determined by the impersonal market mechanism and that determined by individual business enterprises. With the rise of concentration of economic activity, he argued, the enterprise now had the power to make a business policy with regard to prices and production that would maximize its profits, with the policy most generally adopted being one in which prices were administered to the market for a period of time and series of transactions and production was allowed to vary in accordance with demand. Consequently, when a decline in demand did occur, these enterprises maintained their prices and let production decline, with the overall result being a multiple decline of production for all of them. In this manner, Means concluded, the making of business policy was also the making of industrial policy. On the other hand, when concentration of economic activity was non-existent, the making of industrial policy was done by impersonal market forces. In this case, the business enterprise was unable to control either its prices or production, with the result that prices changed with nearly every transaction and declines in demand were met by price declines significant enough to maintain production at its original level.

As long as a significant segment of the economy was dominated by business-based industrial policy, the result would be a poorly functioning economy. To correct the situation, it might be thought that business enterprises should be broken up to the point where they would have no power to affect market prices or that government ownership of business enterprises was the solution. However, Means rejected the former because of the technical inefficiencies that would accompany it, and the latter because the problem of a poorly functioning economy was one of a distribution of control not a locus of ownership. Rather, in his view, what was needed was to develop ways to let a wider range of economic groups have a say in the making of industrial policy.

To devise an industrial policy that would balance the economic interests of the various groups in the American economy and would produce the full use of the nation's resources was, in Means' view, the primary purpose of the NRA and AAA. To do this, he argued, they must first identify the

key decisions for each industry which, if made right, would so condition the other elements of industrial policy that the latter could be left to the actions of individuals and the operations of the market. (Means, 1934*u*, p. 5)

and, secondly, set up a mechanism that would distribute control among the various economic groups in a manner which would get key decisions made correctly. In this context, Means discussed four possible mechanisms which could be adopted by the NRA and AAA, ranging from a code authority made up solely of business persons to a committee consisting of several economic groups, through which the key decisions could be made. Although not advocating any one of the mechanisms, he did suggest that whatever was adopted must be congruous with the existing situation and American traditions if it was to work at all adequately. In closing his discussion, Means noted that any method for determining industrial policy must be supplemented by techniques for dealing with the volume of money, directing the flow of investment, and providing social security (Means, 1934*u*; Lee, 1988).

Reception of Means' conclusions

Thinking the paper important, Means gave it the title "NRA and AAA and the Reorganization of Industrial Policy Making," had it typed up (by August 29) and widely distributed with the following note attached, briefly indicating to the reader its important features:

I am enclosing a series of four charts which show the very wide extent of *rigid prices* in our economy. They clearly indicate the existence of *two* quite different types of market mechanisms, one of the type described by traditional economists, and the other quite different, yet the dominant influence in our present economy. The character of this second market is of *vital importance to the policies* of the Administration. It is a major element in bringing about the present conditions and indicate clearly the function in our economy which AAA and NRA must perform. The character and implications of this market with respect to NRA and AAA are set forth in the accompanying ten-page memorandum [and appendices]. (Means, 1934b*m*)

The paper quickly generated a great deal of response with regard to Means' statistical and economic analysis and his discussion of industrial policy-making (Means, 1934*u*). Accepting the evidence that the magnitude of many prices did not decline during the downswing in economic activity, the conservative economists and business leaders sought to deflect what they saw as a possible criticism of business practices employed by the large industrial corporations. They argued that the lack of decline in industrial prices was due primarily to forces beyond the control of the individual enterprise or corporation, such as the role of unions in the determination of wage rates, the rigidity of transportation costs and taxes, and the fact that industrial demand was quite unresponsive to price changes in the short term. They felt that by not giving enough stress to these factors, Means had, perhaps unintentionally, laid too much of the blame for the Depression at the feet of the large corporation (Harriman, 1934m; Whitney, 1934m; DuBrul, 1934am, 1934bm). A second response to Means' paper came from economists who disputed the empirical evidence he presented and his criticism of neoclassical price theory. The most negative response in this regard came from Charles F. Roos, an economist in the Research and Planning division of the NRA, who argued that the empirical evidence was nonsense and that

traditional theory need not be cast aside. It is necessary, however, to add to theory a discussion of supply and demand for labor and its relation to inventories of labor saving devices. This does not require discarding *modern* economic theory. It does require considerable revamping of Adam Smith's doctrines, but it is incorrect to assume that changes have not already been made. (Roos, 1934m)

However Roos retained his most truculent criticism for Means himself, apparently because Means had had the audacity of not only questioning the relevance of neoclassical price theory, but also advancing an explanation for the Depression and plan for restoring business that went far beyond the confidence thesis that he accepted (Lee, 1988).

Although not with the same air of vindictiveness as Roos, other economists also questioned Means' empirical evidence and explanations. Some argued that the quoted prices of the BLS tended to overstate price magnitude rigidity because they did not reflect secret rebates or special discounts, while others argued that his explanation of frequency of price change was incomplete because it did not take into account the product's characteristics or the nature and character of the market in which the product was sold. The overall feeling of these economists has been captured by Willard Thorp (who was one of them) 50 years later:

I know that I was skeptical of the statistics of that time, believing that actual prices were more flexible than those quoted because of changes in product, discounts, sales assistance, credit extension, etc. I never liked the word "administered" because it implied a fairly free choice whereas the nature of supply and demand, the character of the product, and the market structure all affect the freedom of choice. (Thorp, 1987t)

In spite of the criticisms, some economists found the paper quite interesting and suggestive, while other offered constructive suggestions, such that there existed pricing systems other than administrative pricing which also needed to be studied, that the forms of administrative pricing could be discussed only in terms of their peculiar characteristics, and that price magnitude might easily become rigid downward but not upward (Clague, 1934m; Whitney, 1934m; Thorp, 1934u; Homan, 1934m; Hamilton, 1934m; Stocking, 1934m; Means, 1934dm; Lee, 1988).

In regard to his discussion on the making of industrial policy, Means received numerous comments concerning the mechanisms he put forth and the intra-industry approach he took towards the problem itself. In spite of his disclaimers, it was evident to many readers that Means favored an administrative committee approach to the making of industrial policy which consisted of various economic groups, including labor and consumers, with the government presiding over the decision-making process to ensure that the groups produced a policy in the public interest. Although not disputing the need for government intervention in matters of the making of industrial policy, some commentators did question the adequacy of the approach, while others were concerned with the manner in which the government representatives were chosen. However, the most prevalent feeling was that a mutually agreeable industrial policy was nearly impossible to devise, short of a government edict, because the economic interests of the various groups were incompatible and economic power was unevenly distributed between them. As for the latter criticism, Frank (1938am) argued that by not recognizing the need for inter-industry co-ordination when dealing with the making of industrial policy, it would not be possible for Means' administrative committees to reach the right key decisions. Hence, instead of making the situation better, the industrial policies promulgated by the committees would make matters worse (DuBrul, 1934bm; Whitney, 1934m; Harriman, 1934m; Roos, 1934m; Lee, 1988).

Industrial prices and their relative inflexibility

In the four months following the initial distribution of "NRA and AAA" Means was largely tied up with his work for Wallace and, beginning in November, for the National Resources Board (NRB). In addition, he spent some of his free time speaking on the paper's core ideas at The Brookings Institution and responding to a *New York Times* editorial on AAA production controls. However, he did manage, in October, to revise the paper through adding two additional charts dealing with prices and production for agricultural and consumer and producer goods, and providing a more complete description of the data contained in the charts. Moreover, having agreed to give a paper on price inflexibility and monetary policy to a session jointly sponsored by the Econometric Society and the American Statistical Society at their December meetings, Means decided to base it on his "NRA and AAA" paper. He deleted nearly all the reference to the making of industrial policy, summarized the empirical evidence and the discussion about administered prices, responded to various criticisms made about the paper, added new empirical material on relative price dispersion, made sharper statements as to the relationship between administered prices and concentration, and expanded his thoughts on monetary policy. The resulting paper was titled "Price Inflexibility and the Requirements of a Stabilizing Monetary Policy"[5] (Means, 1934b, 1934d*m*, 1934e*m*, 1935b; Homan, 1934*m*).

Erroneously suspecting that Means' paper was being suppressed, the long-time foe of monopoly and bitter enemy of the NRA Senator Borah of Idaho had the Senate pass a resolution on January 3, 1935, titled "Monopolistic Influence Upon Industrial Prices," demanding that Wallace submit the paper to the Senate. In light of the resolution, Means had virtually no time to revise the paper beyond reorganizing it, including the charts on relative price dispersion from "Price Inflexibility," and better clarifying the concept of administered prices. Missing from this revised version were responses to earlier criticism and the statements on administered prices and concentration found in "Price Inflexibility." Wallace submitted Means' revised paper to the Senate on January 15 under the (nearly) original title "N.R.A., A.A.A., and the Making of Industrial Policy"; however, when published two days later as Senate Document no. 13, it bore the title of *Industrial Prices and Their Relative Inflexibility*, with the original title appearing on the first page (Eichner, 1980; Means, 1935a; and US Congress, 1935).

The publication of *Industrial Prices* occurred with much fanfare and caught the attention of economists and politicians alike. *The New York Times*, *Washington Post*, and *Washington Herald* all noted Borah's resolution and gave a quick summary or flavor of the paper under the headings of "Wallace to Urge Monopoly Curbs," "Monopoly Hit in Borah Move," and "NRA Launches Hearing Today on Price Fixing." At this time, the NRA was holding public hearings on the price

---

[5] Means presented his paper "Price Inflexibility" at a session on "Monetary Policy and Price Changes During Recovery: A Survey of Relevant Evidence." The session was chaired by Irving Fisher and contained papers by Willford King and Frank Graham. The discussants included George Warren, Harry Gideonse, and Roos. The extent of the audience is unknown, but it did include Rufus Tucker, who later wrote on big business and administered prices (see pp. 70–3 below).

provisions of the codes of fair competition. With CAB's presence at the hearings, combined with the testimony by Bean and Henderson, Means' view on prices received additional publicity. Consequently *Industrial Prices* received much play in the popular press and journals. More importantly, Means received many requests for the document from economists and institutions. By the end of February, over 7,000 copies of *Industrial Prices* had been distributed (Bean, 1935*m*; Hawley, 1966; *The New York Times*, 1935; *Washington Post*, 1935; *Washington Herald*, 1935*m*; Campbell, 1940).

The publication of *Industrial Prices* concluded the first stage in the development of the doctrine of administered prices. After 1935, while working for the National Resources Committee (NRC), Means turned his attention towards developing a theoretical picture of what would constitute a balanced, fully employed economy which was dominated by large corporate enterprises and administered prices. This initially led him to delineate the structure, organization, and co-ordination of economic activity of the American economy. Later in the 1950s–1970s he dealt with pricing and the corporate enterprise and with administrative inflation. Throughout this 40-year period when Means developed his doctrine of administered prices, he continually drew upon his initial analysis of administered prices made between 1930 and 1935 (Lee, 1990a; Lee and Samuels, 1992a).

2 Gardiner Means' doctrine of administered prices

As a graduate student, Means was taught that the economy was a self-regulating machine which ensured that, in the short term, all national resources were fully utilized, international trade was always in balance, and the general price level varied directly with the money supply; and, in the long term, economic waste was eliminated, income distributed according to the marginal productivity principle, and the effective use of resources realized. He was also taught that these macro results were predicated on the economy being inhabited by small competitive owner–worker enterprises which employed little fixed capital, made a single good, and produced a negligible share of market output; and on the profit motive which, by compensating the owners for risking their capital and managing their enterprise, was the guiding force in directing the enterprises' economic activity. Most importantly, it was impressed upon Means that for the economy to be self-regulating, the coordination of all economic activities – and, thus, the making of industrial policy – had to occur in the market and was predicated on all prices and wage rates being perfectly flexible.

While he thought neoclassical economic theory was clearly relevant to the British economy of Smith and Ricardo's time, to the American economy prior to 1840, and to the economic activities of the oriental bazaars, Means found it completely irrelevant to the American economy of the twentieth century where the large corporate enterprise was the "representative firm," the ownership and control of the corporate enterprise rested with different individuals, thus undermining the effectiveness of the profit motive to increase social welfare, and the corporate enterprises had the market power to administer both their wage rates and market prices. He concluded that the coordination of economic activity as pictured in neoclassical economics had ceased to occur, and with it the ending of the economy as a self-regulating machine which ensured the full, efficient, and effective use of resources, the balance of international trade, and a stable price level. The clearest evidence of the collapse of the "traditional" coordination of economic activity for Means was the Great Depression. Thus, he set out to determine the manner in which economic activity was actually coordinated in a corporate-enterprise, administered price-dominated economy and the manner through which economic policy was actually made so as to achieve non-market-determined levels of economic activity. In recasting economic theory in a more realistic vein, Means centered his attention on the role administered prices played in the coordination of economic activity. His doctrine of administered prices was thus primarily concerned with the fundamental problem of setting out the forces, such as administered prices, which affected the coordination of economic activity and determined the actual manner in which the modern corporate economy operated.

The structure, organization, and coordination of economic activity

Means developed his doctrine of administered prices within the context of a specific conception of the American economy. Utilizing the methodological approach advocated by Frederick Mills (1935) – that of studying a functioning working economic system as a whole – he was concerned with identifying the relatively permanent features of the archetype corporate economy which gave it its salient characteristics. In this light, Means considered the US economy the best and most relevant example of a corporate economy and thus used it as a proxy. Since he observed that in the US economy most economic activity was repetitive or continuous over short periods of time and changed relatively slowly over longer periods, Means concluded that one salient characteristic of a functioning economy was that of economic continuity, meaning that consumers and business enterprises generally repeated their economic activities over time. Consequently, in a functioning economy character-ized by economic continuity, consumers buy various consumer goods on a regular and systematic basis, while business enterprises, employing the same methods of production, produce the same goods repeatedly in response to the consumer demand for them. With this concept in hand, Means then identified those characteristics of the US economy which structured its economic activity.

The first characteristic that Means identified was the structure of consumer wants. Adopting a lexicographic approach, he argued that the consumer ranked his or her wants according to biological and social needs. Then assuming that the general biological and social needs, and hence the ordering of wants, were broadly the same for all consumers, Means aggregated the individual orderings and denoted the new synthetic ordering as the structure of wants for the economy. Given the basis of its construction, Means noted that the structure was unaffected over short periods of time by changes in economic forces short of a complete upheaval in the economic system and society. However, he acknowledged that the structure did change over long periods of time and that changes in specific wants within a particular broad category of wants could occur within short periods of time. Consequently, over any specific time period, consumers would allocate their income in a manner that would satisfy their primary wants first and secondary wants last, thus generating repeating buying patterns for broad – and, perhaps, specific – categories of consumer goods.

The second characteristic that Means identified was the structure of resources and production. With respect to resources, Means identified six categories – three (natural resources, productive plant, and labor power) which were consumed in the process of satisfying wants, and three (physical environment, technology, and social institutions) which conditioned production without being consumed in the process. As for production, Means delineated its geographical structure, which consisted of showing the location of specific types of economic activity in relation to resources and consumers, its structure of the physical flow of produced goods, and its structure of money flows. Means argued that the physical flow of produced goods consisted of one-way and circular flows, with the one-way flows being specific to consumption goods, while the circular flows were found in agricultural and manufacturing industries. Consequently, as long as the consumed but not reproducible resources remained in abundance, the structure of production automatically ensured that the material inputs and capital goods needed for the production of consumer goods were continuously reproduced (Means, 1938a, 1939a).

Overlaying but integral to the structure of the physical flow of produced goods of a corporate economy, Means argued, was a continuous flow of money and series of money transactions. This included a circular flow between producers and consumers in the form of producers dispersing money for labor services and its return to them through the purchase of their goods by the consumers. It also included a circular money flow between producers reflecting inter-industry transactions, and a quasi-circular flow between producers and consumers with respect to savings and the return on savings. The importance of the various money flows was that they created a single integrated monetary economy, i.e. an economy in which both production and consumption were continuous and repetitive and that monetary market transactions were always taking place, that could not be decomposed into a "real" and "monetary" sector. In particular, in a monetary economy the series of money transactions allowed a wide variety of monetary prices to act as mechanisms for the coordination of market activity between producers and consumers. Consequently, Means noted, factors which affected money flows, such as changes in the total supply of money, changes in the money balances held by particular economic groups, shifts in the relative flow of funds into current consumption and capital formation, and changes in price relationships, would have a pronounced effect on both the volume and direction of the physical flow of produced goods.

Since both production and consumption were continuous and repetitive in a functioning monetary economy, Means noted that market transactions were always taking place, and taking place in historical time. Business enterprises were consequently continually producing goods for demand which they know, in general, would exist, and buyers were always entering the market to buy goods which they know were being produced for them to buy. Thus each specific market in the economy was clogged with sequential transactions in historical time and each business enterprise which entered it was also engaged in sequential production and transactions in historical time. To facilitate the continual rush of economic activity within the business enterprise, Means argued, canalizing rules and goals became established.[1] In the case of the corporate enterprise, many of the formal rules which would affect the internal coordination and direction of its economic activity were established in its articles of incorporation, especially with respect to the powers possessed by the board of directors and senior officers regarding the distribution of profits and the lines of activity the corporation was allowed to pursue. In addition, informal rules or customs, such as the use of double-entry bookkeeping or the place of work on the shop-floor, helped facilitate and coordinate production and commercial activities of the business enterprise. As for goals, Means noted that the acceptance of profit-making as the primary goal of the enterprise acted as an "invisible guiding hand" directing members of the enterprise to a common coordi-

---

[1] For Means, the coordination and organization of economic activity through canalizing rules occurred when the actions of individuals were limited to those which support it without being subject to administrative control. In this context, legal rules and regulations, accepted procedures, and customs constitute canalizing influences which narrow down the scope of individual action without determining it. As for the organizing and coordinating economic activity through the acceptance of common goals, Means argued that

a number of people, having accepted a common goal, may be able to act independently and without communication, yet their activities may be to a greater or less extent coordinated by the logic of their accepted goal. (Means, 1939a, p. 98)

nated ending without the intervention of specific instructions (Means, 1939a; Commons, 1924).

Similarly for Means, rules and goals also facilitated the coordination of market transactions between business enterprises and buyers in the market. Informal rules, such as the widely accepted "one-price" rule or the custom of accepting money in exchange for goods, or formal rules, such as the prohibition of deceitful selling practices, helped facilitate the coordination and flow of market transactions. However, of the mechanisms for the coordination of market activity which he identified, Means placed most of his emphasis on the market mechanism and administrative coordination. He referred to the market mechanism as the organization and coordination of the economic activities of many separate producers and consumers through price and buying and selling. "Administrative coordination" referred to situations where a common authority, such as an owner or manager of a business enterprise or government bureau, organized economic resources under its control and coordinated the resulting economic activity. For Means, the clearest example of administrative coordination was found in the internal operations of the large modern corporation.

Although he discussed the four organizing and coordinating mechanisms separately, Means realized that they operated in combination in a functioning economy. In particular, he realized that even large administrative units used the market in coordinating their activities, especially with respect to the prices and wage rates they set for goods they sell and labor they hire. Means noted that in a functioning monetary economy, market coordination of economic activity took place through a continuous series of money transactions:

[the] circuit [of money] flows are made up of a series of money transactions which facilitate the organized use of resources. Through these money transactions, manpower and capital funds are made available to producers; raw materials, semifinished products, and capital goods are transferred from one producer to another, and finished products or services are made available to consumers. These money transactions also provide a system of prices which are stated in terms of a common money medium and which act as a guide to the use of resources, stimulating some uses and repressing others. (Means, 1939a, p. 108)

By providing the context in which the system of prices operated, the flow of money transactions permitted the organization and coordination of economic activity via prices regardless of whether the prices were flexible and determined within the market or inflexible and administered to it. Thus the flow of money transactions permitted administrative units to use prices to coordinate and organize economic activities between themselves and with small business enterprises who did not have the market power to determine their own prices. However, Means noted, the "adequacy" with which the flow of money transactions was coordinated in the market depended on the extent to which flexible market prices dominated market transactions.

In considering this question, Means noted that the specific organization and coordination of economic activity in a market economy depended upon the relative dominance of each of the four mechanisms and of the specific canalizing rules and common goals in existence. Not being interested in analyzing traditional, feudal, or centralized economies, he directed his attention to dealing with a market economy and the particular rules and goals associated with it. However, he realized that even a market economy could have many forms – depending, for example, on whether the market mechanism was dominant or not, and on the specific goals and canalized rules in existence. Using the degree of aggregate and market concentration of economic activity as a basis, Means identified three basic types of market economies – atomistic economy, factory system, and corporate economy. He defined an atomistic economy as one with virtually no aggregate or market concentration. In such an economy, the form of production was owner–worker enterprises producing a single good to sell on the market to equally small buyers, and the mode of transaction was haggling and bargaining through which an agreed-upon price and quantity was determined. He equated the atomistic economy with the competitive economy described by Marshall and subsequent neoclassical economists, but thought its historical existence in the United States was limited to the period prior to 1840. The factory system emerged in the United States around 1840 as a result of a significant increase in the degree of aggregate and market concentration, with the latter increasing more than the former, as a result of the increased scale of production of the individual enterprise. Consequently, large numbers of workers became employed in the enterprise and thus subject to managerial administration as to the hours and the manner they worked. Aside from administering economic activities within the enterprise, the owner could also administer wage rates and the price at which he sold his goods. In fact as the size of the business enterprise grew, the owners realized that administrative price-setting reduced the cost of making transactions. So as the size of the business enterprise grew, so did the pervasiveness of administered prices and wages. As a result, the mode of transaction changed from haggling and bargaining to the "one-price–no bargaining" approach.

Finally, Means defined a corporate economy, which he felt began to emerge in the United States in the 1890s, as one in which both the degree of aggregate and market concentration had increased, with the former increasing to a much greater extent. The corporate form of enterprise consequently controlled a significant portion of the economy's economic activity. As in the factory system, the corporation administered its internal economic activities, and the prices at which it sold its goods. Moreover, the mode of transaction of "one-price–no bargaining" was maintained and extended. On the other hand, unlike in the factory system, the owners of the corporation did not necessarily control or manage it, thus undermining the role of profit in the organizing and coordinating of economic activity. In addition, while the corporation could administer its wage rates, it also might have to bargain with unions over them. Finally, in the corporate economy, the interest rate and the price of new security issues were also administratively determined (Means, 1933, 1939a, 1962).

In delineating these three types of economies, Means realized that the American economy of the twentieth century did not match any one precisely. Rather, it was a hybrid in which some markets were unconcentrated and thus behaved as if in an atomistic economy, while others were relatively concentrated and behaved as if in a factory system or corporate economy. However, he felt that as an analytical device, the US economy could be divided into two sectors – the administered sector in which internal and market coordination was the dominant mechanism coordinating economic activity, and the market sector in which the market mechanism was the dominant coordinating mechanism.[2] Thus, before examining the role prices play in the coordination of economic activity

[2] In categorizing the two sectors according to market concentration, Means defined an unconcentrated market as, using Marshall's well known phrase, one of "trees in the forest." The market for cotton was unconcentrated in Means' view because, of the 4,850,000 farms producing cotton in 1935, the four largest produced 0.14 percent of the output. In contrast, in 1935 there existed less than 170,000 separate manufacturing enterprises and in the least concentrated manufacturing industry (women's, misses' and children's apparel n.e.c.) there existed about 10,000 manufacturing establishments with the four largest enterprises producing 1.4 percent of the total output (or ten times the amount of the four largest cotton farms). Thus for Means all manufacturing markets were relatively concentrated and therefore belonged in the administered sector since it was not possible to have a forest of competing enterprises in each market as in the case of the cotton market. More generally, Means felt that retail distribution and consumer services' markets and various natural resources and securities' markets were relatively concentrated and belonged in the administered sector, while agricultural markets, construction markets, and some natural resources and security markets were relatively unconcentrated and belonged in the market sector. It is also of interest to note that because of the scale of production of an efficient manufacturing establishment was large in comparison to the market, Means felt that it was not possible in general to "atomize" a manufacturing market, even if each establishment was made a manufacturing enterprise (Means, 1933a, 1939a, 1962, 1964m).

within and between the two sectors, it is first necessary to delineate the price-setting behavior of the archetypical business enterprise in each sector.

Pricing and the business enterprise

For Means, the structure of production and costs of the business enterprise, and the pricing procedures it adopted, were determined by its time horizon and business strategy which, in turn, were determined by its scale of production and the degree to which enterprise could assert its presence in the market. These latter two factors were ultimately determined by the interaction of technology and the managerial and organizational structure of the enterprise. Thus, for example, if the interaction of technology and organization created a small-sized enterprise with virtually no market power, then, as Means argued, the enterprise would adopt a very restricted time horizon and devise an appropriate business strategy in light of it which would manifest itself in the structure of production and costs and pricing procedures adopted by the enterprise. Inherent in this argument was that varying degrees of enterprise size were correlated with relative degrees of market concentration, implying that pricing, prices, and the enterprise itself differed between the market and administered sectors. Therefore to adequately delineate the role of prices in the coordination of economic activity, it is necessary to do so in the context of (1) the atomistic enterprise found in the market sector and (2) the corporate enterprise found in the administered sector.

Atomistic enterprise

The atomistic enterprise, which Means considered to be the archetype neoclassical competitive enterprise, was an owner–worker enterprise, i.e. an enterprise in which ownership, control, and management resided in the same individual or a group of individuals. Consequently, the owners assumed both the risks and the responsibilities of the enterprise and, thus, received not only the wages of "management" and interest on capital, but also the pure profits. Since it was the glitter of profits which induced the owners to undertake these responsibilities, they devised business strategies designed to maximize their profits. Moreover, the owners–controllers also made the decisions of how much to save and when to acquire new capital equipment. Thus both the owner's wealth and the size of their enterprise were determined by their own actions and limited, in part, by their preexisting wealth. Finally, because the owners were also the workers, there was virtually no administration of work in the workplace by a central management and the enterprise's scale of production was ultimately limited by the amount of work the owners were willing or could do. With respect to the technological foundation of the atomistic enterprise, Means argued that the technology employed by the enterprise did not require the use of much fixed capital or material inputs produced elsewhere. Rather, the production processes based on the technology were labor-intensive, did not have a significant division of labor, were not vertically integrated to any extent, generally utilized a single type of material input, and produced a single good (or line of goods). Correspondingly, the costs of the enterprise were determinable and divided into pay-out costs (that included wages of management and some material input costs), and capital costs (that included both depreciation and the competitive rate of profit). Inherent in such technology and production processes was that the enterprise's scale of production was extremely small and limited to the declining physical and mental exertion of the owners which, in turn, produced a gently upward-sloping marginal cost curve. The interaction between technology and the organizational and managerial structure of the atomistic enterprise conspired to severely limit its scale of production.

Because of its small scale of production, the owners of the atomistic enterprise faced a very large market in which its contributions to market output are extremely small. Consequently, their enterprise was just one in a forest of enterprises competing in the market while another forest of enterprises was waiting in the wings for the first sign of high profits. As a result, they did not possess any market power to determine their fate, such as determining the price for their goods based on their specific market situation. In devising their business strategy, the owners of the enterprise were therefore forced to limit their time horizon in regard to making profits to the immediate transaction under consideration. In particular, the owners had to approach each market transaction as an isolated event in which their objectives were to get the best price for their goods and leave the market empty handed. Then using the market price of the previous transaction as a proxy for the next transaction, they would produce the amount of goods that would maximize their profits (or at least produce an acceptable level of income) for the upcoming transaction, which meant producing the amount that equated the enterprise's upward-sloping marginal cost curve to the expected market price. As a result, production took place in discrete batches which were taken to the market to be sold. Finally, in selling their goods on the market, the owners essentially engaged in an act of trading or haggling and bargaining over the price with prospective buyers in an effort to reach the best price possible that it would also clear the market of their goods.

The importance for Means of the trading/haggling and bargaining pricing process for reaching a transaction price was that the price was determined in the pricing process itself. Hence it reflected the particular and largely episodic economic forces operating in the market at that time rather than the needs of the atomistic enterprise. Moreover, because of this, the transaction price for a series of transactions was extremely sensitive to variations in these economic forces, especially those from the side of demand, since the amount of goods supplied to the market was largely fixed for any particular transaction. Transaction prices would consequently vary with nearly every transaction, increasing or decreasing in response to increases and decreases in demand. However, as long as the transaction prices remained above the enterprise's average pay-out or variable costs, the owners could and would continue to engage in subsequent acts of production and exchange, at least for a limited period of time; but if the transaction prices persistently failed to cover the enterprise's capital costs, they would leave the market. Thus while the pricing procedures of the atomistic enterprise produced profit-maximizing and market clearing prices, they also produced extremely flexible prices which did not reflect the owners' desire to maintain their enterprise over time (Means, 1933, 1939a, 1962).

Corporate enterprise

Within the administered sector, the business enterprise, Means argued, had two logical forms – that of a small single establishment, non-corporate enterprise and that of a large single or multi-establishment corporate enterprise. While both engaged in administering prices and other aspects of administrative competition, the non-corporate enterprise primarily existed in those markets especially characterized by easy entry, competitive rate of profit, competitive waste, and focused on profits in the current pricing period. However, Means viewed such an administrative enterprise and its market situation as a logical construct more than as an operational piece of economic reality, and as economically insignificant in a sector which was dominated by large corporate enterprises. Thus, when developing his doctrine of administered prices, he virtually ignored the non-corporate enterprise (Means, 1962).[3]

---

[3] Means' analysis of the non-corporate enterprise was undertaken as a response to the Chamberlin–Robinson theories of monopolistic or imperfect competition. That is, stung by comments from economists that *"you failed to utilize Chamberlain's [sic] description and analysis of what he calls monopolistic competition"* (Frank, 1938b*m*; also see Means, 1938c*m*), Means attempted to fashion an explanation of administered prices based on traditional monopoly analysis but without utilizing the marginalist apparatus associated

In the administered sector, Means argued, the corporate enterprise took the form of a single plant – or, more commonly, a multi-plant operation. In the former case, ownership and control were generally vested in the same person, while management of the plant's operations was carried out by a supervisory staff. The management structure was centralized, and the supervision of the workers in the workplace, while immediately in the hands of the staff, was closely watched by the owner himself. However, the most prevalent form of the corporate enterprise, he argued, was the multi-plant industrial corporation, in which ownership and control were separated, while control and management were closely linked. As a consequence, the controllers and high-level management, as opposed to the owners, were the center of policy formation and directed the coordination of economic activity. As a result, they controlled the destiny of the corporate enterprise. Moreover, because management could continuously reorganize itself so as to make itself efficient at any scale of production, Means argued, the size (or number of operating plants) of the corporation had no limit (Bonbright and Means, 1932). Consequently, management, in its drive to have the corporation grow larger, could internalize many former market activities while taking on new ones by employing a bureaucracy to coordinate them (Means, 1939a).

Because of the large size of the corporate enterprise, Means argued that there existed barriers to entry to the markets in which it operated. Consequently, management did not have to be primarily concerned with making the maximum amount of profits on each transaction or for the current pricing period (which covered a number of sequential transactions). Moreover, because the managers had no legal claim over corporate profits, they had no reason to try to maximize the corpor-

---

with the Chamberlin–Robinson theories (see Means, 1944m, 1947, 1948m, 1953bm, 1953cm, 1957). However, this project which took place over a ten-year period from 1943 to 1953, was undertaken against Means's better judgment since his own experience as a monopolistic competitor had led him to reject the relevance of Chamberlin's theory as early as 1934 (Means, 1983) and, moreover, since he completely rejected marginalism:

My own hunch is that the current marginalist theory of business behavior as applied to conditions of imperfect competition will ultimately be put in a museum along with the dodo and the theory of consumer surplus. (Means, 1953am; see also Means, 1946m, 1980m, and Amihud, 1980m)

Consequently, when Abraham Kaplan's and Robert Lanzillotti's work on target rate of return pricing appeared (see pp. 78–9), Means re-fashioned his explanation of administered prices, while consigning his monopoly analysis to the non-corporate enterprise that inhabited markets where entry was easy. But such enterprises and markets, he noted, were unimportant in a corporate economy (Means, 1959a, 1962; Lanzillotti, 1960m).

ation's profits in the "long period." Rather, as a result, they had the freedom to adopt a policy of obtaining profits over time which would not induce entry or otherwise inhibit the growth of corporate profits or the corporation itself. Given this latitude, management could and did in fact engage in a multitude of competitive activities aimed at maintaining the corporate enterprise as a going concern while meeting dividend and other obligations.[4]

To carry out their growth strategy for the corporation, management adopted, Means argued, an administered price policy. That is, within the current pricing period, management set its price and administered it to the market for a series of transactions.[5] Thus rather than having the price determined in the process of the transaction itself, as it was for the atomistic enterprise, management determined its price prior to the transaction itself. As a result, it had the freedom to alter its administered price frequently in response to changes in sales or inventories or maintain it for a long period of time covering many sequential transactions. At the same time, corporate management also adopted a production policy, which Means called the "flow principle of production," that let the level of market activity regulate the rate of production at the given administered price (Means, 1962).[6]

By uniting administered prices with the flow principle of production, corporate management was explicitly stating that the variations in the cost of producing a unit of output brought about by changes in demand did not affect the administered price at which the output was sold during the pricing period. That is, when producing its output, Means noted that

---

[4] In the 1940s, Means had begun dismissing the notion that management tried to maximize current profits (see Means, 1974, 1949*m*). He subsequently reached the more revolutionary position that corporate management seeks neither short- or long-period maximum profits nor frames its business strategies in terms of long or short periods as theoretically defined in neoclassical economics or classical political economy.

[5] Means defined the "pricing period" as a period of calendar time which covered a series of sequential transactions. Depending on the aims of management and the nature of the market in which the corporate enterprise competed, the pricing period could be as short as a week or as long as three months or a year. The number of transactions within the pricing period could vary greatly as well. Defined in this manner, the pricing period is neither the same as the short period found in neoclassical economics or congruent with the analytical units of time utilized by economists in general. Although the pricing period is a necessary element in Means' definition of administered prices, his first reference to the concept comes in 1947 (see Means, 1947a*m*) and he does not fully integrate it into his definition until 1962.

[6] The flow principle of production is also a necessary feature of Means' definition of administered prices, but which was not articulated until after S. DuBrul (1957*m*) sent him a copy of Wilford Eiteman's monograph, *Price Determination: Business Practice versus Economic Theory*, in late August 1957 (see pp. 124–9).

the corporate enterprise incurred both pay-out or variable costs (which consisted of such items as raw materials and operating labor costs), and fixed costs (which consisted of supervisory labor, depreciation, interest, and property taxes). Moreover, he noted that average variable costs were constant while average fixed costs were declining with respect to increases in the flow rate of output, with the consequence that average total costs declined with an increase in the flow rate of output. Thus, for management to set a cost-based price which did not reflect the cost changes resulting from every variation in the flow rate of output, Means argued that they had to utilize the standard flow rate of output approach to eliminate the problem of cost variability. In utilizing the standard flow rate of output, management was able to calculate its standard average total cost (SATC) – a cost that, by virtue of the manner in which it was determined, was independent of the actual costs of producing any specific unit of output. Thus, Means argued, any price based on SATC would not reflect the costs of producing a specific unit of output (Means, 1962).

The uniting of administered prices and the flow principle of production also implied that the actual events surrounding any specific transaction or the variation in conditions prevailing during the current pricing period did not affect the mark up for profit. To do this, Means stated that management selected a target rate of return on equity capital invested in producing the output to determine a total amount of profit needed to be raised during the current pricing period for growth purposes. In deciding upon the specific rate of return, Means argued that management took into account the degree of market competition and the prices of competitors, and thus arrived at a rate of return that would not undermine the corporation's position in the market.[7] Hence the rate of return decided upon by management was designed to maintain a healthy financial condition for the corporate enterprise and to generate enough funds to permit a continued expansion of capacity so as to maintain its desired growth rate. In this manner, Means argued, management would maximize the corporation's value as a going concern. With the rate of return (and, hence, the total expected profits) for the current pricing period determined, management would then calculate the mark up for profit which, when attached to SATC, would yield the administered price.[8] Because the target rate of return was expected and based on the

[7] Means had begun articulating this position by the mid-1940s. Means also recognized that a single rate of return would not be generally applied to all products (Means, 1947, 1949m, 1962).

[8] In a short note, Means (1938b) once argued that corporate enterprise capital expenditure was a function of the current and the preceding years' level of production. Thus, since the corporation desires to generate its investment funds internally, it is possible to argue that

long-term prospects of the corporation's growth, Means noted that it was not readily altered over time and certainly not altered during the current pricing period. By setting the administered price in this manner – i.e. before production and the current pricing period starts and based on SATC and a long-term growth-determined target rate of return – it was, Means concluded, inflexible with respect to sequences of market transactions and variations in the flow rate of output over the current pricing period.[9]

Means viewed competition among corporate enterprises as consisting of a series of strategic moves and counter-moves. Thus the intensity of competition could be measured by the frequency and number of moves made over a specific time period. In this context, he argued that the potential for severe competition existed among corporate enterprises because of the continuous and sequential nature of market activity combined with the desire by corporations to increase their share of market transactions and volume of market sales. Since simple price competition to obtain such an objective would not work because all competitive price declines would quickly be met and thus would threaten the corporation's financial health, corporate managers would be driven to adopt competitive tactics that would not be easily matched by strategic counter-moves or would directly threaten the corporation's financial integrity. Means therefore argued that sales promotion designed to create, maintain, or alter goodwill among the buyers but which did not disturb prices in the market fitted the bill quite nicely. Thus competition among corporate enterprises emerged as an extension of their internal administrative activities as embodied in the administered prices in the market and the administered sales campaigns designed to alter customer goodwill, and hence market share and growth rate. Since the competitive pressure of the sales campaign was felt with each passing transaction in the market, Means concluded that constant and severe competitive pressures confronted all corporate enterprises (Means, 1962; Clifton, 1977, 1987).

the target rate of return (and, hence, the mark up for profit) is largely a function of the desire for investment funds. However, when faced with the argument Means demurred, arguing that while the need for investment funds could play a role in pricing, it was only one of several factors (Means, 1978b*m*; Eichner, 1978c*m*).

[9] In those industries where material inputs make up a large part of the value of the product and whose prices frequently change, resulting in frequently changing output prices, Means noted that the administered mark up for profits remained relatively stable for many sequential transactions. Thus, in such industries, corporate managers frequently revise their administered prices to match any changes in cost while infrequently revising their administered margin for profits they add to their costs (Means, 1939a, 1939b).

Administered prices and production, employment, and inflation

Adopting John Commons' terminology, Means denoted a continuous and functioning monetary economy in which the continuous flow of economic activity was coordinated by market and administered prices, administrative coordination, rules, and goals, and all market transactions had a social basis as a going concern. However, because the mechanisms that coordinate and organize economic activity within the market and administered sectors differ in degree and emphasis, Means realized that a good overall coordination of activity between the two sectors could not be assumed. In particular, the clash of market and administered prices, of maximizing profits on each transaction and the desire for long-term unmaximized profits, and of market and non-market controls would affect the overall coordination of economic activity and with it the full use of the economy's resources. To explore the impact of the clash of market and administered prices on the operation of the economy, Means utilized the twin concepts of balanced economy and balanced price structure. He defined the former as a going concern in which the utilization rate of productive plant and natural resources and rate of employment remained stable over time; while the latter was defined as a specific set of market and administered prices associated with a given balanced economy, and hence with a given rate of employment and of plant and resource utilization. Thus in a balanced economy with a balanced price structure, there would be no variations in the economy's growth rate or large continuous variations in production and employment in specific industries. However, if the price structure became unbalanced due to a change in the level of aggregate demand, or to administrative action then, as Means argued, the resulting clash of market and administered prices would directly affect the utilization of all economic resources, including labor, productive plant, and natural resources.

Administered prices and business fluctuations

Means noted that in the market sector, market prices behaved pro-cyclically over the fluctuation of business activity, while production remained relatively unchanged. Specifically, he argued that during the decline in business activity, market prices declined significantly (as measured by percentage change in magnitude) and relative to declines in production, while during the upswing of business activity, they advanced significantly and relative to production. Such behavior, he felt, could be explained by reference to the economic behavior of the owners of the atomistic enterprise. As noted above, the owners limited their profit-making activities to the immediate transaction at hand. Thus, using the market price of the previous transaction as a proxy, the owners would produce the amount of output that would maximize their profits at the proxy price. But, when they actually entered the market, they had to obtain the best price possible that was consistent with selling all their output. Hence, over a series of transactions, given the fortuitous nature of demand, the owners would face a sequence of changing market prices and, as a consequence, would constantly be altering the amount produced.

Now in the context of a decline in business activity, Means argued that the owners would discover that the market price in each successive transaction was lower than the preceding market (proxy) price. Because the marginal cost curve of the atomistic enterprise increased slowly, the incremental decline in the market price with each successive transaction would be matched with a much greater incremental decline in production. However, as the downturn lengthened and the market price declined, the owners would reluctantly accept a reduction in their standard of living, and hence in their wages of management, thus shifting the enterprise's marginal cost curve downward and therefore limiting the extent to which production had to be reduced. The net result of all this, Means concluded, was that over the length of the downturn, the owners of the atomistic enterprise would reduce their production relatively little in comparison to the reduction of the market price. Conversely, and for the same reasons, the owners would increase their production relatively slightly in comparison to the increase in the market price during the upswing of business activity. Thus in aggregate, the market price of a good would vary frequently and incrementally but significantly and pro-cyclically over the cycle of business fluctuations, while its market production would vary frequently and pro-cyclically but relatively little.

With regard to the behavior of prices and production in the administered sector, Means argued that administered prices were relatively insensitive to changes in aggregate demand over the cycle of business fluctuations, while production was sensitive and reacted in a pro-cyclical manner. Specifically, he argued that during the decline of business activity, administered prices either declined relatively little in comparison to declines in production, declined not at all, or behaved perversely and increased, while during the upswing, they increased relatively little, increased not at all, or behaved perversely and declined. Such behavior, he felt, could also be explained by reference to the economic behavior of the corporate enterprise. The managers of the corporate enterprise administered the price for the length of the pricing period, even though many transactions occurred and the volume of sales associated with each transaction varied greatly. Since both the downturn and the upturn of business activity covered a number of pricing periods, they had the option of altering their prices at discrete points over the cycle of business activity in the light of existing and future economic conditions, as noted above. Assuming that management decided to maintain its current target rate of return and standard flow rate of output over the fluctuation of business activity, for example, the administered prices of the corporate enterprise would alter from one pricing period to the next depending on the change in input costs. Thus, if non-labor input costs declined during the downswing, the corporation would reduce its price accordingly. If management administratively reduced wage rates, it would also reduce its prices at the same time. Finally, if a new union wage contract resulted in higher standard labor costs per unit of output, then the corporate enterprise would increase its prices accordingly, in spite of the decline in production – i.e. perverse pricing would occur. With particular regard to perverse pricing, Means argued that it would be more likely to occur if management, adopting a short-term pricing policy, altered the standard flow rate of output from one pricing period to the next in order to reduce the difference between the actual and the predetermined target rate of return for each pricing period as opposed to over the whole cycle of business activity.[10] In contrast to their administered price policy which kept the magnitude of price change small, both absolutely and relative to changes in production, management's production policy permitted the flow rate of output to vary directly and sharply with every variation in aggregate demand (Means, 1933, 1934cm, 1935a, 1939a, 1947a, 1952am).

If the market sector dominated the economy, then variations in aggregate demand over the cycle of business activity would work themselves out primarily through price adjustments and secondarily through output adjustments, hence through variations in the level of employment. On the other hand, if the administered sector dominated the economy, the coordination of economic activity would not be worked out through price adjustments so as to ensure full employment. Rather, it would be largely in the hands of the managers of the corporate enterprises whose business policy consisted of administering their prices

---

[10] Means, following John M. Blair, referred to this pricing policy as "full cost pricing;" however, both were mistaken in this regard (see chapter 4). Means also attributed perverse pricing to other causes, such as the risk of entry, expectations of inflation, or the costs of maintaining idle capacity. Although he always recognized the existence of perverse prices since they always appeared in the price data he worked with, it was Blair's work that made Means realize their theoretical and practical importance (see p. 67) (Means, 1939a, 1939b, 1983, 1988u).

to the market while letting production, and hence employment, adjust accordingly. Thus, as noted above, while administered prices do assist in organizing economic activity, they cannot coordinate it to maintain full employment in the face of variations in aggregate demand. However, in the modern corporate economy both the market and administered sectors exist and are interdependent, thus preventing the coordination of economic activity solely through price adjustments. If a balanced (although not necessarily a fully employed) economy with a balanced structure of market and administered prices suffered a decline in aggregate demand, the immediate result would be an unbalancing of both the economy and the price structure. On the one hand, prices in the market sector would decline or deflate, thus maintaining production and employment, while production and employment in the administered sector would decline in the face of relatively stable administered prices. Because of this asymmetrical response, the level of economic activity would decline further due to the decline in demand caused by the existence of unemployed workers combined with relatively stable administered prices, resulting in a still further deflation in market prices and hence unbalancing of the price structure, and decline in production in the administered sector. An increase in aggregate demand at this point would, conversely, reflate market prices, thus bringing the price structure back into balance, and increase production in the administered sector. Thus with the existence of administered prices, the coordination of economic activity so as to maintain a fully employed, balanced economy with a balanced price structure was completely undermined. Instead of business fluctuations being solely the "dance-of-prices," administered prices made it both a price and a production and employment phenomenon (Means, 1935a, 1939b, 1939–40, 1947, 1964, 1972m, 1978am).

Administered prices and inflation

Means identified three types of inflation involving administered prices – monetary inflation with administered prices, reflation, and administrative inflation. The first type, he argued, was similar to the classical inflation analyzed by neoclassical economists. That is, in a fully employed, balanced economy with its associated balanced structure of market and administered prices, an increase in aggregate demand brought about through increasing the money supply would result in a rise in prices comparable to the end result of a classical monetary inflation. However, instead of all prices increasing simultaneously and proportionately, Means argued that the immediate result of an increase in aggregate demand was an unbalanced rise in prices in which market prices increased relative to administered prices. The unbalanced rise in prices would continue until the average of market and administered prices was high enough to raise the demand for money to the level of the increased supply. At this point a readjustment between market and administered prices would take place, with the former declining and the latter increasing until the price structure was in balance again. On the other hand, reflation, as noted previously, pertains to the rise of market prices during the upswing of business activity, in spite of the existence of idle labor and other economic resources, so as to restore the initial balance of the structure of market and administered prices (Means, 1962, 1974, 1975a).

In testimony before the Senate Subcommittee on Antitrust and Monopoly, Means argued that most of the rise in the general level of prices of the past two years (1955–7) was due to the rise in prices in the administered sector of the economy. Since he attributed the unplanned increase in these prices to the power of the corporate managers to administer their prices to the market and not to any expansionary forces in the market, Means denoted this decidedly non-traditional "spontaneous" inflation as administrative inflation:

the area of discretion implicit in administered prices could lead to creeping inflation without an initial impetus from fiscal and monetary expansion while fiscal and monetary expansion might serve to maintain employment only at successively higher price levels. I suggest that we could properly call this type of inflation administrative inflation, in contrast to the traditional monetary inflation which arises from too much money chasing too few goods. (Means, 1957, p. 84)

Thus, for Means, administrative inflation occurred when price increases in the administered sector took place even though no change in demand occurred or was expected, and hence dominated the general rise in the price level since the prices in the market sector remained relatively stable because of the absence of demand pressures. Because he attributed administrative inflation to corporate pricing power, Means sought to explain it primarily in terms of administrative actions by corporate management.[11]

---

[11] Means differentiated his notion of administrative inflation from the hypothesis that most economists have substituted in its place – namely that the higher the degree of concentration, the greater the price rise:

The two hypotheses are not at all the same. If the second hypothesis were valid, the first would necessarily follow. But the second could be far from true when the first was true. For example, if prices rose little in the two or three *most* concentrated groups but went up in the next most concentrated groups and not at all in the less concentrated groups, the first thesis would be supported, the second would not. Or, stating it another way, to say, "The bulk of the rise in the wholesale price index came where there was substantial

Means recognized that if labor increased wage rates faster than productivity gains the result would be higher administered prices since the use of target rate of return pricing procedures enabled corporate management to pass along the higher costs in the form of price increases. However, he felt that the historical record showed that labor's contribution to administrative inflation was relatively small in that their quest for higher wage rates was largely a belated attempt to catch up with the increases in the cost of living brought about by management's unilateral action to raise prices. Means argued that administrative inflation was thus primarily due to corporate management increasing its mark up for profit and adopting perverse, or current period, pricing procedures. Since the management of the corporate enterprise finances much of its capital investment internally – i.e. through the retention of profits – any increase in the cost of investment goods or in the taxes on corporate revenue or profits would necessitate increasing the mark up for profit and an increase in the target rate of return. In addition, management might also use its pricing power to increase the mark up for profit to reduce the rate of capacity utilization at which the corporate enterprise would just break even. Both of these administrative actions would result in management increasing its prices even if demand was not increasing or expected to increase.[12] As noted in the section on business fluctuations (pp. 59–60), perverse pricing occurred during the downturn of business activity when management adopted the pricing practice of revising its standard flow rate of output from one pricing period to the next. Because management was not as quick to make downward price adjustments as in making upward ones, Means concluded that perverse pricing would lead to a relatively permanent increase in administered prices and hence in the general price level over the cycle of business activity (Means, 1959b, 1962, 1971m, 1974, 1975b, 1975c).

Because administrative inflation caused the structure of market and administered prices to become unbalanced, Means argued that it would probably push the economy into a recession or a prolonged stagnation if not counteracted by an expansion of the money supply. That is, assuming a balanced economy with its associated balanced price structure, an increase in administered prices brought about by, for example, corporate management increasing their mark up for profit would unbalance the

pricing power" is not the same as saying, "Where there was substantial pricing power, prices went up most" (Means, 1963m).

[12] Means also argued that management's misuse of the target rate of return pricing procedures, such as using labor costs or capital costs per man-hour instead of per unit of output, resulted in creeping inflation because it effectively increased the mark up for profit and increased the target rate of return (Means, 1975b, 1975c, 1988u).

price structure and increase the general price level. As a result, Means argued, the real purchasing power of the money stock held by consumers and business enterprises would decline, hence reducing the real level of aggregate demand below the level required for the economy to remain in balance. Consequently, if the money supply was not increased so as to restore the real purchasing power of the money stock held and to raise market prices and restore the price balance, a decline in economic activity and employment would result, although somewhat mediated by the subsequent fall in market prices (Means, 1962, 1975c).[13]

The doctrine of administered prices and the visible hand of coordination

In conceiving of the corporate economy as a continuous monetary flow of economic activity that was coordinated by market and administered prices, by administrative coordination, and by rules and goals, Means sought to dispel the notion that the American economy operated as a cybernetic mechanism which automatically tended to eliminate under-utilization of all economic resources, including labor, productive plant, and natural resources. Given the existence of administered prices combined with the investment behavior of business enterprises and the distribution of consumer income and savings, he argued that "a serious deficiency of buying is unlikely to be corrected by any of the economic forces inherent in the modern [corporate] economy in such a way as to bring about and maintain reasonably full use of resources" (Means, 1939m, p. 23). He also felt that if unused resources did exist, it was not due to the lack of consumer wants to be filled. Thus he concluded that the under-utilization of economic resources was a problem of social organization which could be corrected only through social or government making of industrial policy (Means, 1939a, 1939b).

In a going concern corporate economy without the benefit of govern-

---

[13] As a result of his work on the modern corporation, Means began questioning whether the striving for industrial profits could any longer be treated as a satisfactory incentive to action in the conduct of industry (Means, 1933). Thus it was not surprising to him that management's administrative adjustment of the mark up for profit or the target rate of return resulted in administrative inflation and upset the balance of the economy. In fact, in a pre-administrative inflation 1947 study of inflation, Means all but stated that management's administrative adjustment of the mark up for profit would have serious inflationary consequences:

if serious increases in sensitive prices begin to occur before or as soon as full employment is reached either as a result of *arbitrary price action by management* or as a *result of arbitrary wage increases forced by labor*, the inflationary problem is a serious one. (Means, 1947, p. 6, emphasis added)

ment involvement in the coordination of economic activity, Means noted, industrial policy was not made in the market but rather was primarily the result of the interaction of corporate enterprises' administered activities in the market with institutions outside the market who could directly or indirectly affect those activities. One such institution was the corporate community. That is, through interlocking directorates, inter-corporate minority stockholders, the activities of the larger financial corporations in the use which they make of their investment funds at their disposal, and the interrelationships resulting from the servicing of the large corporations, there existed, he argued, a corporate community in which corporate managers resided. Moreover, within the corporate community there also existed corporate interest groupings which consisted of a core corporate institution(s) and a number of satellite corporate enterprises. As a result of these community relationships, Means felt that "the controls exercised by this corporate community among the larger corporations are of major importance" (Means, 1939a, p. 163). He also felt that the influence of these controls extended beyond to the corporate community and affected the whole corporate economy, including the economic activities in the market sector. Means also noted that private economic interest groups, such as business associations, labor unions, farmer organizations, and consumer organizations affected the economic activities of all business enterprises, either through direct contact with the enterprises or through influencing government policy, public thinking, and legislation; while Federal, State and local government units affected the coordination and organization of economic activity by sanctioning (or not) particular rules and goals that governed market behavior and by direct participation in the development of industrial policies in regulated industries.

In this context, Means argued that the government could devise an industrial policy which relied solely on the market mechanism to create the full use of resources or one which relied on modifying the existing system of administrative policies and activities of the corporate enterprise in a way that, when combined with the market mechanism, their ensuing interaction would result in full employment. The first policy would require major structural changes, such as the breaking up of corporate enterprises and the consequent elimination of the corporate community, the elimination of any large-size private interest groups and governmental units, and the reintroduction of perfectly flexible prices, which he felt were politically unfeasible, economically impossible, and economically inefficient. Consequently, Means advocated the second policy approach because it was in the realm of possibility and sought to make the already highly efficient corporate economy work better. He believed that the government policy-makers could develop a variety of coherent industrial policies, depending on the techniques they used, to affect financial flows, the rate of capital formation, and the operating policies of industry, especially with regard to the flow of production and the administering of prices. For example, he argued that if the government was to devise an industrial policy in which the key decisions regarding the operating policies of industry were cooperatively determined, as was the case with the codes of fair competition under the NRA, then it was necessary to establish a mechanism or technique that would distribute economic power among the various economic interest groups in a manner which would ensure that the policies were made correctly. Or the government, through the use of experts, could develop a series of national economic plans whose implementation would be left in the hands of elected officials. Similarly, when considering the problem of administrative inflation, he argued that the government should take an active role in affecting the administered price policies of corporate enterprises, such as by establishing price guidelines and a price advisory board, creating an index of administrative inflation, and urging corporate enterprises to adopt a longer-term horizon when administering their prices (Means, 1935a, 1940, 1975b; Lee, 1990a).

In 1932, Means argued that the rise of the modern corporation required economists to forge new concepts and create a new picture of economic relationships. His doctrine of administered prices was his attempt to do just that. In articulating the picture of economic relationships embodied in the doctrine, such as the target rate of return pricing, administered prices, administrative inflation, market power, and non-market control of economic activity, Means emphasized their human and institutional nature and hence their amenability to social action. Thus, since the corporate economy did not automatically tend to full employment, the implication of the doctrine of administered prices was that non-market government involvement in guiding economic activity was both necessary and desirable if the quality of human life was to be enhanced. Since the visible hand of coordination, whether it be advisory, in the form of codes of fair competition or creating regulatory boards, is both a necessary component as well as a necessary outcome of the doctrine, Means clearly developed a novel and non-neoclassical analysis of the modern corporate economy.

3　Developments in the doctrine of administered prices

Means worked on his doctrine of administered prices for 50 years. This, combined with the intense controversy over administered prices, meant that many of the non-Means' contributions to the doctrine occurred simultaneously with his own work. One contribution, perverse prices, was developed by John M. Blair. Blair had, since 1938, been interested in Means' doctrine of administered prices. One aspect of the doctrine in which he had particular interest was the movement of prices and production over the cycle of business activity. In 1958 he "discovered" the phenomenon that "in periods of moderate underutilization of capacity, prices in oligopolistic industries will not decline, will not remain inflexible, but will tend to rise" (Blair, 1959, p. 435). Blair initially couched an explanation of these "perverse prices'" movements in terms of cost-push inflation, shift from price to non-price competition, and business enterprises increasing their target rate of return; by 1972 he associated them with a short-term variant of target rate of return pricing. He argued that perverse price movements occurred when a business enterprise using target rate of return pricing procedures attempted to attain its target rate of return in the short term instead of over the cycle of business activity by adjusting the standard volume flow rate of output variable. Once the explanation for perverse prices was articulated, Means quickly absorbed it into his doctrine (see p. 60 and n. 10) (Blair, 1959, 1972, 1974).

A second contribution concerned the elaboration and development of the concept of power embedded within the doctrine of administered prices. As noted above, the modern corporate economy in Means' view operated through the visible hand of co-ordination – or, in other words, through the exercise of power which he defined as "the ability of one individual or group to influence the policies in respect to the use of resources which are adopted by another individual or group" (Means, 1939a, p. 153). Although Means largely restricted the concept to the administering of prices and the organizing and coordinating economic resources, he was quite well aware that the existence of power meant that politics and industry merged together to the extent that economic decisions were political decisions as well, as in the case when the making of industrial policy was done by the management of a business enterprise, the corporate community, economic interest groups, and/or the government. The role of power in affecting market activities was elaborated on and extended by John K. Galbraith through his concepts of "countervailing power" and "technostructure." Regarding the former, Galbraith argued that the exercise of power in a corporate economy begets its own neutralizer, with the result that the setting of prices and the co-ordination of economic activity was conducted through the medium of power instead of competition.[1] The role of government, laws, and courts in fostering the formation of countervailing power was particularly emphasized. As for the latter, Galbraith argued that the modern corporation was being directed by a technical and managerial technostructure whose chief goals were wealth and power for themselves through the aggrandizement of their enterprises. To achieve the goals, the technostructure attempted to mold consumer buying patterns and use public policy for its own benefit.[2]

Adolf Berle, on the other hand, expounded on corporate power and the politicization of the corporation's internal and external economic activities. He also noted that the evolution of corporate capitalism over time was played out in terms of changes in the distribution of power between the corporation and the state. Finally, he pointed out that the "free market" in the modern corporate economy where business enterprises compete was a political artifact, maintained by laws, regulations, and state-sponsored sanctions. A third contributor to the theme of power was Walton Hamilton and his analysis of corporations as political entities and private governments, cartels and other such institutional arrangements as systems of private governments, and the coming together of state politics and corporations for the making of industrial policy. The thesis emerging from these contributions was that the

---

[1] Galbraith's arguments outlining the benefits of creating countervailing power for those who face economic coercion from the powerful echoed Means' own statements regarding economic coercion and economic freedom – see Means (1944*m*, 1949*m*).

[2] In acknowledging his debt to Means, Galbraith has stated:

THE NEW INDUSTRIAL STATE is built on the notion not of monopoly prices but broadly speaking of administered prices. It is administration which provides the certainty which the modern, very large technocratic organization requires. I have gone on from administration of prices to the management of the other economic parameters including that of consumer demand. (Galbraith, 1970*m*)

modern corporate economy of the United States was a system of power and that the doctrine of administered prices illuminated one important part of it. Means made no substantial attempt to articulate such a system; however it has become a central concern of Institutional economists (Means, 1939a; Galbraith, 1952, 1967; Berle, 1954, 1959, 1963; Latham, 1957; Burrowes, 1966t; Hamilton, 1957; Dugger, 1992; Klein, 1987).

The third contribution to the doctrine, and the focus of this section, made over a period of 40 years by related group of economists, Rufus Tucker, Edwin Nourse, Abraham Kaplan, and Alfred Chandler, is the area of big business, business leadership, and administered prices. After the First World War, economists, business leaders, and directors of philanthropic foundations began to believe that it was possible through the gathering and interpreting of economic data to arrive at technocratic solutions for stabilizing the American economy. Central to this vision was the presumption that once they were given this data, the makers of microeconomic decisions – that is, the businessmen – would appropriately alter their course of action without coercion. Inherent in this presumption, although not often stated, was that big business was a permanent feature of the economy and its existence did not, by itself, undermine the economy's competitive nature or its ability to operate smoothly. That this view was widely accepted by the philanthropic foundations is not unexpected since most of them were dependent on big business for their funds. Thus throughout the 1920s, philanthropic foundations funded many studies whose primary purpose was to generate economic data which could be used for the microeconomic management of an economy in which big business was a permanent feature.

With the coming of the Crash in 1929, American capitalism faced a popular uprising. While the masses, politicians, and academic economists generally complained about the monopolistic tendencies of many business enterprises, a few politicians and economists specifically argued that big business charged monopoly prices and made monopoly profits, was inefficient and less innovative when compared to small business, and was destroying the democratic nature of the economy and replacing it with a financial oligarchy. Some economists also argued that big business weakened the flexibility needed by the economic system to ensure full employment by setting rigid prices, which meant that demand variations played themselves out in output and employment variations rather than in variations of the price level. Thus the picture that emerged from these attacks was that big business *per se* and its pricing policies were a major cause of the Depression; the solution was to exorcise big business from the economy, heavily regulate its activities, or engage in some sort of national economic planning.

Such solutions violated some foundations' view that solutions to economic problems should be compatible with the existing social and economic systems. Foundation monies were directed to research institutes and universities or allocated directly to study groups to look at the question of the role of big business in the American economy. In some cases, the purpose of the funding was to produce studies that would mold public and government opinion regarding the efficacy of big business and to alter the critical opinions many economists had towards it. An example of such foundation-sponsored studies were the corporation study funded by The Twentieth Century Fund in the 1930s, The Brookings Institution studies of industrial pricing and big business which were funded by the Maurice and Laura Falk Foundation and the Alfred P. Sloan Foundation from the 1930s to the 1950s, and the rise of big business studies funded by the Sloan Foundation in the 1960s–1970s. These studies were important in shaping economists' and public opinion about big business; however, for the purpose of this book, their importance lies in their unwitting contribution to the development of the doctrine of administered prices (Lee, 1997).

In response to Berle and Means' *Modern Corporation and Private Property* (1932), Harry Laidler's *Concentration of Control in American Industry* (1931), and the consequent widespread belief of the enormous degree of concentration of control in American industry, the Twentieth Century Fund in May 1934 approved funding for a study on the domination of industry by large units and its effect upon the nation's life, and appointed Rufus Tucker as its research director. He carried out the study by collecting statistics on the size of individual plants in various industries and statistics showing the differences between corporations of various sizes with reference to the proportion of their capital which took the form of long-term debts. In addition, Tucker directed a statistical investigation on the relative standing of big business in the American economy and on the profitability of big business. The research, which was published in 1937, showed that big business played a large role in the economy, but was unevenly spread, with some sectors completely dominated by large business enterprises while others were completely devoid of them. These results corrected the Berle and Means' impression that big business was pervasive and dominated the economy. The research also indicated that the rates of return for big business were smaller but more stable than those for small business; that there was no determinant relationship between size and profit, size and change in costs, and costs and change in gross income; and that big business paid out more dividends than small businesses. The conclusion drawn from the research was that it was not possible to say whether big business was, on the whole, good or bad, and conversely, whether small business was better or worse than big business (The Twentieth Century Fund, 1934*m*, 1934–5*m*; Tucker, 1934–5*m*; Bernheim, 1937a, 1937b; Lee, 1997).

Tucker took advantage of the study to collect statistics showing the extent to which large corporations controlled the markets of various industries. These statistics, he felt, were relevant to understanding

the distinction recently made between administrative and market prices … and … the differences in price fluctuation shown by the products of different industries. In some cases, prices have hardly fallen at all during this depression and in some of those cases it is reasonable to suppose that prices have been controlled by a monopoly or a semi-monopolistic understanding. In other cases there are good reasons to explain why prices have not fallen and why perhaps it was better for the country that they should not fall. (Tucker, 1934–5*m*)

Consequently, and in conjunction with collecting the statistics on corporate control of markets, Tucker also collected statistics on sensitive and insensitive (or administered) prices. Although not published with the other findings of the study, Tucker used his collected statistics to argue, in a series of papers and an unpublished monograph, that insensitive or administered prices were an historical and permanent feature of the American economy and hence not tied to the existence of big business. More importantly, he articulated a micro explanation for the existence of administered prices which was not yet present in Means' writings.

Using the statistics he had collected, Tucker established that prices which changed frequently and those which changed infrequently had both existed in the American economy since the 1830s. The explanation for the frequency of price change could not therefore be attributed solely to the size of the business enterprise setting the price, since "big business" had not yet emerged in the 1830s. Tucker therefore sought the explanation in the cost, demand, and product characteristics which impinged on the pricing of a product. With regard to farm products, he noted that they were perishable, their demand was non-postponable, and their costs were largely fixed and hence deferrable; on the other hand, industrial products were durable or non-durable but not perishable, their demand could be postponed, and their costs consisted largely of items (such as direct labor and material costs and variable overhead costs) which required regular and timely pay-outs.[3] So, if demand declined for farm

---

[3] Tucker provided statistics which showed that fixed overhead costs constituted a much smaller proportion of their prices for industrial products than for farm products – the

products, it was possible for the farmer to have lower prices and still carry on farming. However, for industrial enterprises, a fall in demand for their products could not be countered with a significant reduction in price because of the high proportion of pay-out cost in the price; moreover, Tucker argued, reductions in price would not increase sales appreciably in any case. Thus, a reduction in the price of an industrial product would not increase sales sufficiently so as to reduce costs and maintain the current mark up for profit.[4] Therefore variations in demand unaccompanied by changes in wage rates and in material input prices would produce frequent changes in farm prices with actual production and employment being affected little, whereas it would produce virtually no changes in industrial prices with industrial production and employment being directly affected.

The importance of the argument to Tucker was that he was able to explain the infrequency of changes in industrial prices without invoking the phases "monopoly," "semi-monopolistic," and "concentrated industries." Rather, industrial enterprises which engaged in an administered price policy of infrequent price changes, he argued, must be viewed as engaged in *competitive* pricing since each time a decision was reached regarding a change in prices, the reactions of competitors were taken into account. Consequently, in Tucker's view, price changes were generally based on changes in input costs; if such costs did not change, then prices would not change, but if input costs declined, as many did from 1929 to 1933, then the competitive industrial environment would generate price reductions.[5]

Because labor costs was the principal item in pay-out costs, the rigidity of wage rates, in Tucker's view, was the chief explanation for the facts

ratios being 25 percent for industrial products and 75 percent for farm products (Tucker, 1938b*m*).

[4] Tucker explicitly argued that the price elasticity of demand was extremely small if not non-existent for industrial products; rather it was variations in market demand which determined the level of production of industrial products. Moreover, he noted that any attempts to measure the price elasticity of demand by studying prices and sales over a period of time was very problematical given the essentially static nature of the concept (Tucker, 1938a*m*, 1938b*m*).

[5] Tucker also attributed the infrequency with which industrial prices changed to the fact that manufacturing and retailing enterprises were compelled to announce prices in advance, which sales people used to drum up business and retailers used to plan purchases. Such price announcements were accompanied by price lists and advertisements which usually stayed in effect for three months or longer. Because administered prices were calculated to cover costs and make a profit and were maintained for long periods of time, Tucker argued that "they probably conform more closely at any given time to what classical economists called 'natural prices' than do the prices of farm products" (Tucker, 1938a*m*, pp. 101–2).

that industrial prices changed infrequently and fell relatively little compared to output from 1929 to 1933.[6] In arguing that administered prices were compatible with competitive conditions, Tucker rejected the concept of perfect competition and adopted the view that active competition existed when two or more industrial enterprises were trying to make sales to the same group of buyers.[7] Thus the degree of competition was not measured by numbers or size of competitors, but primarily by the variability of market shares and profit rates among the competing enterprises over time. Since statistics were readily available showing variability of market shares and profit rates among big enterprises in the same industry, Tucker concluded that big businesses were extremely competitive even though they were members of concentrated industries and administered their prices to the market (Tucker, 1938a, 1938b, 1938a*m*, 1938b*m*, and 1940).

In the 1930s, The Brookings Institution undertook a project on the distribution of wealth and income in relation to economic progress which was financed by the Falk Foundation. The conclusion of the project was that the fundamental reason for the lack of economic progress in the American economy was the inadequate purchasing power among the masses of people and the greatest problem at hand was to determine how

the flow of the income stream to the various groups in society can be modified as to expand progressively the effective demand for goods and thus evoke an ever greater volume of production – which would mean a steadily augmenting aggregate income to be divided. (Moulton, 1935, p. 87)

After dismissing several possible remedies for this problem, such as wage increases and taxation, it was concluded that the low-price policy was the only method that could distribute income so as to increase consumer purchasing power and maximize economic progress. However, it was also noted by the Brookings economists that for the low-price policy to work, the economy had to be freely or classically competitive; whereas in the current economic situation the existence of industrial combinations, cartels, and trade associations ensured that the economy was much less than freely competitive. Moreover, industrial combinations, cartels, and trade associations quite frequently adopted price stabilization policies, thus destroying any chance that economic progress based on expanding

---

[6] Tucker produced statistics which showed a close correlation between the reduction in industrial prices of goods from 1929 to 1933 and the reduction in hourly wage rates in the industry producing those goods (Tucker, 1938a*m*, 1938b*m*).

[7] Tucker viewed the economists' concepts of perfect competition and monopoly as virtual nonsense and "the product of the itching imaginations of uninformed and inexperienced arm-chair theorizers" (Tucker, 1938b*m*, p. 3; see also Tucker, 1940).

consumer purchasing power through price reductions would occur (Critchlow, 1985; Knapp, 1979; Moulton, 1935; Lee, 1997).

This striking but ambiguous conclusion was not lost on the economists at The Brookings Institution. Moreover, some businessmen claimed that a low-price policy for economic prosperity was impossible to carry out, while others claimed that it was in fact being actively carried on. Therefore the Brookings economists decided that a follow-up study was needed. The study, funded by the Falk Foundation and carried out by Edwin Nourse (and Horace Drury), focused on the practicability of price administrators in carrying out a low-price policy. As a result, Nourse became quite interested in the concept of price policy *vis-à-vis* the business enterprise and in the role of business leadership in devising price policies. The outcome of this research were two books on price policy, *Industrial Price Policies and Economic Progress* (Nourse and Drury, 1938) and a follow-up, also funded by the Falk Foundation, *Price Making in a Democracy* (Nourse, 1944). In addition, Nourse had become aware of Robert Gordon's research on business leadership in the large corporation. Finding it an empirical complement to his own work on price policies, he brought Gordon to Brookings where he completed the manuscript which was then published by the Institution as *Business Leadership in the Large Corporation* (1945). The importance of Nourse's work, as supplemented by Gordon's, to the administered price doctrine was his discussion of the business enterprise, business leadership, and the business leadership's administration of price policies and prices within the context of a competitive corporative economy (Lee, 1997; Nourse, 1945).[8]

Nourse's objective in his two books was to put forth Brookings' low-price policy as a practical economic policy that would, if adopted by business enterprises, restore the economic health of the American economy. This required him to realistically delineate the large business enterprise and its price policy, since it was the business leadership of such enterprises that he hoped would spearhead the adoption of the low-price policy. Adopting the same assumption as Means, Nourse divided the economy into a market sector where prices were determined in the process of the sale and an administered sector where prices were determined in the office of the business executive and then administered to the market. Ignoring the market sector, he concentrated on delineating

---

[8] Nourse rejected perfect competition and "automatic price-setting" because the former had no basis in the real world and the latter was not consistent with active business leadership, especially with regard to price policy. Rather, he believed that the only real expression of business enterprise was imperfect competition and price administration (Nourse, 1944).

the business enterprise and the factors which affected business leaders when formulating price policy and setting prices in the administered sector:[9]

All the prices that we are considering are "administered" prices. That is, they are prices established by the decision of executives who have power to decide in advance the price at which goods shall be sold and to back up that decision by expanding or contracting operations in volume large enough to have a significant effect on the market ... But "administered price" is not a term of reproach. It is merely a convenient way of describing the facts of economic life as lived in the modern industrial world. (Nourse and Drury, 1938, p. 9)

The large business enterprise, in Nourse's view, was a multi-product and a large-scale producer. These attributes, he argued, were based on technological advantages and economies of scale, on management and managerial resources such as management, science, and engineering personnel, and on vertical integration. Of the three factors, Nourse considered the contribution of management the most important, and therefore concentrated on it. For Nourse, management in the large business enterprise was an administrative network through which the business leaders (i.e. the senior managers) ran the enterprise.[10] The administrative network was organized in a hierarchical form – senior managers and middle and lower managers. The senior managers, through various committees, initiated, approved, and co-ordinated policy decisions with regard to prices, marketing, output, research and development, labor, capital investment and research and development, dividends and reinvestment policy, and external finance with little interference from other interest groups, such as directors, stockholders, and bankers; the actual implementation and continuation of the policies

---

[9] Nourse held the view that the American economy went through three stages of development – mercantile capitalism, factory system, and corporate economy. He associated administered prices (including administered wage rates) with the last two stages, and in the corporate stage they dominated the economy. Areas of the economy where administered prices dominated included, Nourse argued, the manufacturing of locomotives, rails, trucks, pipe, machine tools, boilers, generators, and other industrial sectors. Market prices, on the other hand, were found in exchange markets for highly standardized agricultural and raw material commodities and in auction and small haggling markets for perishable or personalized goods (Nourse and Drury, 1938; Nourse, 1944).

[10] Although Nourse defined control as the power to select or change senior managers, he did not equate the controllers with the active business leaders of the business enterprise. In his view, such leaders did not have to own or control the enterprise to have the power to direct its economic activities and apportion its revenues among its demanding constituencies. Thus, for Nourse, active business leadership in the modern large business enterprise could be summarized as power without property (see Gordon, 1945; Berle, 1959).

was carried out by the middle and lower managers.[11] Senior managers, for example, established the policies for setting and changing prices, although they rarely actually set or change a specific price. This more concrete aspect of pricing and changing prices was carried out by lower level managers, either through committees or by individuals. Thus, the establishment of a price policy and the setting and changing of prices was an administrative activity which was conducted through the administrative network of the enterprise (Nourse and Drury, 1938; Nourse, 1941, 1944; Gordon, 1945).

The business leaders of the large business enterprise, Nourse argued, viewed their enterprise as a going concern – i.e. an enterprise without a finite lifespan. Thus the goals which they had for it and for themselves extended over a long period of time and changing complex situations. Hence, he felt that the view that business leaders adopted the goal of simply maximizing their enterprise's short-period or long-period profits could not be sustained. Rather, while the business leaders did pursue a profit-making goal for the enterprise, the goal, Nourse argued, was not solely an end in itself; instead it was in part an intermediate goal which permitted the achievement of other desired goals, such as growth, expanding market share, increasing current volume of market sales, and entering or creating new markets. The profit goal that the business leaders had for their enterprise was thus a complex mixture of various specific goals which together ensured that the enterprise remained a profitable going concern (Nourse, 1941, 1944; Gordon, 1945).[12]

To achieve these goals, Nourse noted that the senior managers of the enterprise established a price policy covering the methods to be used for pricing and the objectives of the prices set.[13] The pricing methods used were derived from the cost accounting procedures utilized by the enterprise and involved using a normal capacity utilization figure to determine the normal average total costs which were then marked up to set the price.[14] Nourse then noted that the senior managers had many

[11] Nourse also noted that unions conducted a scheme of administered prices, that is wage rates, and thus were price administrators as well (Nourse, 1944).

[12] Since business leaders were not owners of the enterprise, they did not receive the profits they created; thus the question emerges as to why they should strive to generate what they could not receive. Nourse and Gordon had various answers for this: business leaders were becoming more professional and thus carried out their activities efficiently; business leaders were imbued with the instinct of workmanship; performance-based salaries; and the urge for power and prestige (Nourse, 1944; Gordon, 1945).

[13] Nourse noted that to achieve the goals, business leaders would also have to make resource allocation decisions and decisions regarding wage rates and the allocation of profits to dividends (Nourse and Drury, 1938).

[14] Nourse noted that management, in conjunction with their cost accounting procedures,

objectives for their prices, such as opening a new market, exploiting new products and processes, and generating greater sales and market share, and that these objectives were "embodied" in the profit mark up selected for setting the price.[15] While the managers had the freedom to set and administer their prices to the market, they did face various constraints in carrying out their administrative activity. Two significant constraints, Nourse noted, were the unresponsiveness of market sales of industrial and consumer goods to different prices and the possible reaction of competitors to the prices set.[16] Business leaders reacted to the latter constraint and its possibilities of destructive price wars by building market institutions such as trade associations and basing-point pricing systems, to facilitate co-operative and co-ordinated fixing of the market price, and establishing acceptable customs and codes of competitive behavior, such as codes of fair competition. In this context, competition between enterprises took on, in Nourse's view, an administrative nature, in that, within an administratively maintained market context, business leaders utilized their administrative networks to set and administer competitive prices and engage in other competitive activities in order to achieve specific objectives.[17] Nourse concluded his analysis of business leadership with the argument that it was the visible hand of the business leaders and their administrative networks which set and administered the prices in the market and determined the direction of the business enterprise and with it the economy at large (Nourse and Drury, 1938; Nourse, 1941, 1944).[18]

determined the allocation of overhead costs among their product lines and that the use of normal capacity utilization ensured that variations in actual utilization, and hence costs, would not affect prices (Nourse and Drury, 1938).

[15] In some cases where financial institutions controlled the enterprise, Nourse noted that the financial controllers selected high profit mark ups to set high prices simply to generate high profits for the benefit of their institutions as opposed to engendering the dynamic expansion of the enterprise (Nourse and Drury, 1938; Nourse, 1941).

[16] Nourse did not employ the concept of price elasticity of demand in his work because he found it of little use owing to its *ceteris paribus* assumption. Moreover, he found that market sales were not continuous with price, but had significant breaks, thus rendering the concept nugatory (Nourse, 1944).

[17] Nourse argued that the large business enterprise did not have unlimited market power, in that there was always potential competition, government intervention, and continual technical change which limited their market power (Nourse and Drury, 1938).

[18] As Nourse stated:

[I]t is in the office of the industrial executive that we find the birthplace of prices for an increasing number of industrial products ... An essential feature of industrial price-making lies in the fact that, instead of passively accepting the market's pricing of a supply subject to no central control, it sets a price objective and directs a controlled productive mechanism toward attainment of that price level. With this charge the price-

Although Nourse and Gordon based their arguments on interviews and discussions with senior management and staff specialists of many business enterprises, supplemented by published material, the manner in which they were presented did not highlight these sources of support sufficiently, with the result that their arguments did not appear well grounded empirically or historically. However, this was rectified by the empirical and historical works of Abraham Kaplan and Alfred Chandler on pricing and the visible hand of management. The post-1945 political environment was not, to some business leaders, supportive of big business. Thus, in March 1947, some General Motors employees thought that it would be desirable to have an authentic unbiased study made of the effect of big business on the economy, not only its economic implications but also from the social and political side. The senior managers liked the idea and approached Harold Moulton about whether Brookings would like to undertake the study. After consulting with Kaplan, who had just come on the Brookings staff and wished to follow up his earlier study on small business with an excursion into the behavior of big business, Moulton agreed to undertake the study if big businesses co-operated through revealing their records and accounts of actual business practices. Funding for the study was obtained from the Alfred P. Sloan Foundation and the Falk Foundation. Kaplan headed the research team which interviewed the senior managers of 28 corporations on a number of topics, including pricing, pricing policies, and the administering of prices. The price information derived from the interviews was published in *Pricing in Big Business* (Kaplan *et al.*, 1958; Lee, 1997).

What emerged from the material collected was that normal cost and target rate of return pricing procedures were used by nearly all of the enterprises interviewed; in addition, the procedures were shown to be based on costing procedures used by cost accountants; and, finally, the interviews revealed that profit mark ups and target rates of return varied among the several product lines of an enterprise and were partially based on generating internal funds for investment and research and development, on custom, on market strategies, and on competition. The material collected also revealed that large business enterprises employed at any

---

making executive takes over from the 'Unseen Hand' as guide and regulator of the economic process in a considerable part of our business world. He takes upon himself the responsibility for the standard of living for an ever larger proportion of our people. Much as he generally hates the phrase, he becomes in fact the economic planner of our society rather than merely the adapter of his personal affairs as best he can to a largely automatic price mechanism. (Nourse and Drury, 1938, pp. 253–4; see also Nourse, 1944, pp. 17–21, 449)

point in time a range of pricing policies, including pricing to achieve a target rate of return on investment, pricing to maintain or improve market position, pricing to meet or follow competition, pricing subordinated to product differentiation, and stabilization of price and profit margins, although one would be considered dominant. However, over time the dominant pricing policy could change due to court antitrust rulings and changes in the competitive market environment. Thus, the enterprises interviewed could not be characterized by a single all-encompassing behavioral motive. Finally, the material collected showed that in all the enterprises pricing was an administrative activity carried out by a group or committee of managers drawn from different departments and levels of management, and that the price administrators used their pricing procedures as a way to administer the prices they determined to the market. The interview evidence collected by Kaplan supported rather conclusively many of Nourse's and Gordon's statements on pricing, price administration, price policy, and goals of the business enterprise; in doing so, it contributed to the empirical grounding of the doctrine of administered prices. Moreover, the evidence directly influenced Means (see pp. 53–4, n. 3), with target rate of return pricing becoming a permanent feature in his post-1958 work (Kaplan *et al.*, 1958; Lanzillotti, 1958, 1960*m*).

Following the completion of Kaplan's study of big business, the Sloan Foundation decided to sponsor a study on the historical evolution of big business in the United States under the direction of Alfred Chandler. The purpose of study was to strengthen many of Kaplan's results by providing them an historical grounding; and the end result was Chandler's well known volume *The Visible Hand: The Managerial Revolution in American Business* (Chandler, 1977). In the book, Chandler focused on the historical context of when, why, where, and how big business began to grow, and of where, how, and why it continued to grow and maintain its position of dominance. He felt that answers to these questions would emerge only if approached via policy-making by the business enterprise and the administrative networks necessary for its effectiveness. Thus *The Visible Hand* charted the rise of big business, based on the evolution of the necessary administrative networks from the railroads in the 1850s to the manufacturing and commercial enterprises of the 1920s. In carrying out the comparative historical survey of the rise of big business, Chandler provided abundant historical documentation for the role of cost accounting conventions in pricing decisions, of the emergence of administrative price determination and the existence of administered prices, that business enterprises utilized a range of pricing policies to achieve a mixture of goals, and that inter-enterprise price fixing was widespread.

He also made it quite clear through the marshalling of the historical evidence that the "visible hand" of management had replaced the "invisible hand" of market forces, although its actions were continually subject to the competitive forces that abound in the market place. Chandler thus provided historical grounding both for Kaplan's results and for many of Nourse's and Gordon's statements on pricing, price administration, price policy, goals of the business enterprise, and the visible hand. In doing so, he contributed to the historical grounding of the doctrine of administered prices (Lee, 1997).

Part II

The doctrine of normal cost prices

4 The origin of the doctrine of normal cost prices: the Oxford Economists' Research Group and full cost pricing

In May 1934, Hubert Henderson resigned his Civil Service position as economist for the Economic Advisory Council and accepted a senior research fellowship at Oxford's All Souls College. His arrival at Oxford coincided with the Fellows of the Sub-Faculty of Economics encouraging the University authorities to create a University laboratory in economic statistics. In addition, All Souls had just offered to contribute to a satisfactory plan for an Institute of Economic Statistics by providing the money for the establishment of a Readership in Statistics. The University authorities took All Souls' offer to be a good basis on which to approach the Rockefeller Foundation for funds for the development of social sciences at Oxford, including funds for such an Institute, since it was thought that the Foundation preferred supporting a comprehensive plan for the development of the social sciences instead of a more narrow plan which dealt only with a Statistics Institute. The University thus appointed a committee to advise it on how best to secure an orderly development of social studies at Oxford, and the committee in turn, went to the various Faculty Boards for information and suggestions. Within this context the younger Fellows of the Economics Sub-Faculty devised their own plan of action.

In July 1934, James Meade, in a short memorandum, outlined a request for statistical data that would be of use for specific theoretical issues in the area of the short-period demand for labor. Roy Harrod saw Meade's memorandum as a basis on which to develop a program of quantitative inquiries whose results would be of interest to theorists; he thus arranged a meeting with the "economic theorists" at Oxford – which basically meant the younger economic Fellows – and proposed that they draft a memorandum advocating the establishment of an Economics Institute that would support both theoretical and empirical research. Such a memo was drafted in November and sent to the University committee. The memo raised concerns among the older social scientists, since they were more interested in the Institute being a place solely for research in applied economics, as opposed to research in mathematical statistics and economic theory. What they had in mind for the Rockefeller grant was that it be used to fund a series of round table study groups that would deal with economic problems of immediate practical importance. The resolution of these conflicting views over the Institute was that once the Rockefeller grant was obtained in 1935, the Institute of Statistics was established, but its purpose was not defined – that was left to the standing committee who were to manage the Institute, and to Jacob Marschak who was appointed as Director (Young and Lee, 1993; Chester, 1986).

Upon his arrival in Oxford, Henderson became involved in the formation of the Institute of Statistics. His interest in the Institute was driven by his view of what he saw as deficiencies in current economic studies. When working with the Economic Advisory Council, he had become quite skeptical of economic theories which eschewed reliance on facts and become more insistent on empirical research. So when coming to Oxford he had his sights set on undertaking a realistic investigation of economic theory. However in light of the young Oxford economists' memorandum, combined with Harrod's membership of the Hebdomadal Council, Henderson became concerned that the Rockefeller grant, if obtained, would be used to establish an Institute that would emphasize research on mathematical statistics and economic theory. Consequently, he began searching for another method of undertaking empirical research directed at testing economic theory, and he found it in the establishment of a study group to deal with problems in economic theory which have immediate practical importance (Howson and Winch, 1977; Young and Lee, 1993; Henderson, 1931).

Because of his belief in the need for facts before constructing theory, Henderson felt that the young economic Fellows and their theories needed to be confronted with the experience of the businessman to show that their formal economic systems were much too simplistic for dealing with the complicated interdependence of the economic world. To this end, he sent a letter to Harrod on February 20, 1935, spelling out his idea of bringing businessmen to Oxford where the Fellows could ask them questions. In particular Henderson suggested that the Fellows, through their questions, might be able to elicit information from businessmen that would have some bearing on major economic controversies of the day. Harrod presented Henderson's proposal at a meeting of the Economics Sub-Faculty on February 25 and the Fellows responded enthusiastically, partially because the proposal permitted them to undertake interesting and novel research during term when their lecturing and tutoring load prevented them from doing little else, partially because it opened new sources of economic data, and partially because it would promote the wedding of economic theory to fact-finding so as possibly to lead to great advances in economics on lines that were not being much attempted elsewhere.

Henderson and the Fellows worked out the particulars of establishing a study group, called the Oxford Economists' Research Group (OERG), and by the beginning of the Hilary Term 1936 it was in operation. Initially members of the Group took minutes of the meetings and Harrod and Henderson took the responsibility of having them sent to the interviewees for their comments; these activities were then taken over by Marion Bowley who was recruited as the Group's secretary in June 1936. Late in 1937, Bowley left the Group for a teaching position in Scotland and her place was taken by Philip Andrews early in 1938. The Group was popular among the Oxford economists. Starting with nine Fellows as members, its membership grew to include most of the Oxford Fellows, Marschak, and some research assistants from the Institute. Although the total membership of the Group grew to 19, usually only eight or 12 showed up for any particular meeting (Hargreaves, 1973; Phelps Brown, 1980*i*; Roberthall, 1979*p*, 1980*i*; Young and Lee, 1993; Lee, 1991).

The Oxford Economists' Research Group

The Group was formed with the object of investigating the influences determining the trend of economic activity in Great Britain since 1924. More specifically, Henderson and the Oxford Fellows wanted to find out what factors affected businessmen when making their business decisions, and how businessmen made their decisions over the trade cycle. Two topics quickly emerged for the Group, one being the effect of changes in interest rates on business behavior over the trade cycle and the second the price policy of businessmen over the trade cycle. The Group's objective and topics obviously reflected the massive unemployment of the inter-war years and the arguments over how to eliminate it. The first topic reflected the prevailing interest in whether government action to control the trade cycle, such as instituting public works or reducing the interest rate, would ignite the appropriate response from the private sector to be successful. In particular, it not only reflected the interests the Fellows had in Keynes' and Hawtrey's arguments about the effects of the interest rate on investment, but also reflected Henderson's long-standing disagreement with Keynes over the causes and cures of unemployment and the National Government's claim that their cheap money policy had promoted the 1930s' housing boom. The second topic reflected interest in the arguments by members of the Macmillan Committee, Henderson, and numerous industrialists that a reduction in money wages would reduce costs and prices, making the export industries more competitive, and thus decreasing unemployment. To see if these arguments were sound, the Fellows needed to know if a fall in money wages would reduce prices or re-divide national income in favor of capitalists and rentiers; and this required knowledge of how enterprises actually set prices. Thus in a very real sense, the topics investigated were a microcosm of the contemporary interests and concerns of economists in general (Kittredge, 1936m, 1937m; Andrews, 1952b; Shackle, 1979p; Phelps Brown, 1980i; Harrod, 1972).

The primary method of investigation used by the OERG was to interview businessmen at Oxford and have field interviews with businessmen at their enterprises between terms. To bring the businessmen to Oxford, Henderson would send a letter to the prospective businessman, who was usually the chairman or chief executive of the enterprise and already personally known to him, outlining the nature of the OERG and its interest in having him come to talk. Some introductory letters included a list of questions on which information was desired; otherwise, a list of questions would be sent to the businessman once the invitation had been accepted, indicating the points on which information was desired. The questions, which were continually revised so as to help the businessman understand and focus on the particular concerns of the Group, served as an outline for the discussion that would then take place. The areas covered by the questions included those on the determination of direct and overhead costs, the determinants of price changes, the carrying of stock, and the role of the interest rate in making investment decisions. The businessman would then come to Oxford, usually on a Friday or Saturday night, and dine with Henderson at All Souls College, which meant a fine meal and wine. After the meal, some eight to 12 members of the Group would join them. Mellowed by the good food and wine and in an informal atmosphere (everyone sat in armchairs or equivalents and not around a table), it was hoped that the businessman would be willing to give real insights into his thoughts. The field interviews required that the member of the Group go to the particular enterprise and discuss with the chairman or chief executive topics such as the factors determining decisions on the timing of changes to greater mechanization, or about the policies of pricing, both for purchases and for retail sales. The interviews in both cases were then written up and circulated among the members of the OERG and sent to the businessmen for their comments (Roberthall, 1979p; Henderson, 1936m, 1937m, 1938bm; Andrews, 1939m; Phelps Brown, 1936am,

1936b*m*, 1937*m*, 1979*p*, 1980*i*; Shackle, 1979*p*; Bretherton, 1980*p*; Hargreaves, 1973; Harrod, 1936*m*).

The meetings at Oxford were a lively and open affair. The businessman would start with a brief summary of the business itself, such as the goods produced by his enterprise, the enterprise's size, and the degree of competition within the industry. Then he would proceed with how his enterprise set prices and finally end with a discussion of the factors which affected his enterprise's investment decisions. When the businessman talked about pricing policy, the members of the Group would interject with questions aimed at clarifying what he actually meant, thereby gaining a better understanding of how prices were set. The businessman might start by describing price-setting according to the simple formula of average direct costs plus overhead costs divided by expected output plus a profit margin:

$$ADC + OHC/EO + PM = p.$$

Then the question would be raised as to whether prices would be increased when sales declined. The businessman would think that the members were daft until the expected output variable was referred to, in that a lower expected output implies a higher price, all other things being equal. Then he would bring competition into the price-setting decision. In spite of this give and take atmosphere and the clear and consistent descriptions businessmen gave of their pricing procedures, there were still some misunderstandings by both the businessmen and the members of the OERG over the terms each used. Part of the problem, George Shackle noted over four decades late, was due to the assumption tacitly made in most economic theorizing that individuals possess all the data they need in order to act rationally, whereas businessmen were describing how they set their prices in face of constant and unforeknowable shifts in market conditions, changes in technological knowledge, financial conditions, and politics. Another aspect of the problem was that the businessman was not familiar with the theoretical points the members of the OERG were interested in. For example, when the businessman explained how prices were set, he always assumed some expected level of output on which to determine costs. Since the description of price-setting did not conform to the marginalist approach to pricing so familiar to the members of the OERG their reply would be: "How do you know that the predetermined level of output will sell at the price based on those costs?" However, because the businessman was in almost all cases unfamiliar with the theoretical basis of the question (i.e. the inter-relationship between price and output as implied by a demand curve), the ensuing discussion resulted in some frustration and bafflement on both sides. The final aspect of the problem was that businessmen were seeing common phenomena in a different light than the members of the OERG. The most important example of this, according to Robert Hall (later Sir Robert Roberthall), was that *businessmen saw prices as non-market-clearing and not even designed to clear the market, while the members saw prices a market-clearing* (Roberthall, 1980*i*). Thus the members of the Group had to "re-see" prices. Fortunately, Henderson was able to help bridge many of the misunderstandings, that arose between the participants because his involvement in both the academic and business world had enabled him to learn both languages (Phelps Brown, 1980*i*; Roberthall, 1980*i*; Shackle, 1979*p*, 1980*p*; Harrod, 1972, 1953; Kittredge, 1936*m*).[1]

The success of the OERG was immediate. Within two years, the members realized that, in spite of the diverse and sometimes confused replies to their queries, they had novel results with respect to pricing and to the effect of interest rates on investment. Shackle felt that the most interesting question raised by the Group concerned the non-influence of the interest rate on the businessmen's decision to invest because it revealed that uncertainty was the over-riding factor when they made their investment decisions. Moreover, Henry Phelps Brown noted in a 1937 letter to Wesley Mitchell that the Group had "found no manufacturer or distributor yet who had ever been influenced in his decisions by the rate of interest" (Phelps Brown, 1937*m*). Similarly, Henderson in a 1938 letter to Tracy Kittredge of The Rockefeller Foundation noted that

as a result of these interviews we [the OERG] are able to lay down certain propositions with regard to the effects of interest rates with a high degree of confidence. Broadly they amount to this[:] that the importance of the rate of interest does not lie mainly in its effects on the ordinary businessmen, whether industrialist or trader; but rather in its effects on Government finance and public utilities on the one hand and on the expenditure of private individuals through the medium of Stock Exchange values on the other. *These conclusions entail a considerable modification of what is commonly asserted without any evidence in abstract economic discussion. I do not think, however, that there can be any reasonable doubt as to the truth of our conclusions and I am in some hopes that they will be accepted a sufficiently conclusive and so give a new term to the shape of economic analysis in [the] future.* (Henderson, 1938a*m*, emphasis added)

However, in the same letter, Henderson noted that the Group's work on "how far trade fluctuations are affected by the method adopted in different industries in fixing the selling prices of their goods" would

[1] Given the above discussion, it is clear that the OERG was not involved in a game of "20 Questions" or that they left their "evidence" unchecked and unprobed. Those economists who dismissed the findings of the OERG on these ground were simply wrong to do so.

probably not produce any results worth publishing (Andrews, 1952a; Shackle, 1980*l*; Bretherton, 1980*l*; Young and Lee, 1993; Lee, 1991).

Hall and Hitch and price theory and business behavior

All of the members of the Group, except David MacGregor and Henderson, were confirmed marginalists and accepted the imperfect competition/monopolistic approaches to prices. On the other hand, the information they received from the businessmen clearly indicated that the latter thought of prices in terms of some relationship to average total costs and totally ignored the marginalist approach to pricing. In fact severe questioning by the Group failed to uncover any evidence that the businessmen paid any attention to marginal revenue or costs in the sense defined by economic theory, and that they had only the vaguest ideas about anything remotely resembling their price elasticities of demand. The Oxford economists were shocked, to say the least. But what caught their attention even more was the relative stability of prices over the trade cycle, and this became the phenomenon which really needed to be explained. Hall, in particular, brooded about this – why an enterprise's price based on a cost-plus formula could be stable if it faced a downward-sloping demand curve. This dilemma was resolved when he hit upon the idea of a kink in the demand curve. In November 1937 Hall read a paper to the Group, entitled "Notes on the Behaviour of Entrepreneurs During Trade Depression," in which he introduced the concepts of full cost pricing and the kinked demand curve. Only Charles Hitch saw at once that it was an idea which needed developing. So collaborating with Hitch, Hall prepared a revision of the paper which Harrod, as President of Section F of the British Association, found interesting enough to urge him to present it at the August 1938 meetings in Cambridge.[2] The paper was presented on August 23 under the title of "The Business View of the Relation Between Price and Cost." After the meetings, Hall further collaborated with Hitch to produce their well known article, "Price Theory and Business Behaviour" (Andrews, 1952b; Lee, 1989, 1991; Hall, 1937*m*, 1938*m*; Roberthall, 1979*p*, 1980*i*; Young, 1989).

Hall and Hitch opened the article by briefly delineating the essence of the marginalist theory of pricing as found in the writings of Harrod, Joan Robinson, and Edward Chamberlin. They felt that for the marginalist

---

[2] The paper was well received, but the Cambridge economists did not think it cast doubt on the general applicability of marginal analysis of prices and output (Roberthall, 1980*i*; E. A. G. Robinson, 1980*p*).

theory to explain the price setting behavior of businessmen, the businessmen

should in fact: (a) make some estimate (even if implicitly) of the elasticity and
position of their demand curves, and (b) attempt to equate estimated marginal
revenue and estimated marginal cost. (Hall and Hitch, 1939, p. 112)

However the evidence obtained from the businessmen did not indicate
that they used marginal revenue and marginal cost or the price elasticity
of demand to set their prices. Rather it indicated "that they are thinking
in altogether different terms," which Hall and Hitch collectively concep-
tualized as full cost pricing (Hall and Hitch, 1939, p. 113; Andrews,
1952a).

To gain a clear understanding of full cost pricing, it is best to start
by assuming away any competitive restraints facing a businessman. In
this situation, he would set his price by adding together direct material
and labor costs per unit output plus indirect costs determined at
expected or standard volume output plus a predetermined (conventional) profit margin. In addition, any selling and interest costs the
businessman incurred were generally included in the predetermined
profit margin. Hall and Hitch called the resulting price the full cost
price and the price-setting procedure full cost pricing.[3] However,
because the business enterprise lives in a competitive oligopolistic
industrial environment, the profit margin added to its average total
costs at the expected volume of output would generally be modified so
that a single market price would emerge. For example, in the industrial
situation of price leader–price followers, the price leader would set its
full cost price and the price followers would match it by adding a
modified profit margin to their costs. In a different industrial situation
where there is no overt co-operation among the competing enterprises,
a single market price would emerge when the enterprises used the same
"representative" standard per unit cost and profit margin. In the
former case, profit margins would differ among the enterprises in the

[3] It should be noted that Marshall and his students used the term "full cost prices"
frequently when describing long-period competitive prices. Therefore it is not surprising
that the term was employed by Harrod in his 1937 paper "Notes on Interviews with
Entrepreneurs" to identify the "moral" rule to which businessmen appealed when
challenged about the principles on which they fixed prices. In their 1937 papers both Hall
and Hitch took the term from Harrod because it encapsulated the objective of
businessmen to use pricing procedures which set prices that covered both direct and
overhead costs and produced a "normal" amount of profit at standard volume output.
Because of its descriptive accuracy, the term was used by Hall in his 1938 paper which was
the basis of the 1939 article (Hitch, 1937m; Hall, 1937m, 1938m; Harrod, 1937m;
Roberthall, 1979p; Andrews, 1966m).

industry as their expected average total costs differed, while in the latter case the profit margin of the enterprises would differ as their average total costs differed from the "representative" standard average total costs.[4] What must be noted is that in either industrial situation, the full cost pricing procedure is followed although competitive constraints dictate non-conventional profit margins (Hall and Hitch, 1939, pp. 113–14; Andrews, 1951m).[5]

Although the businessmen interviewed saw the prices set by full cost pricing as the "right price" or the price that ought to be set,[6] there were other substantial reasons, Hall and Hitch noted, for using the price-setting procedure as opposed to using the marginal approach:

1 Since the businessmen did not know consumers' preferences and since they were also oligopolists and thus uncertain of their competitors' reactions to a price change, they could not carry out the necessary experimentation to determine their marginal revenue and demand curves.

2 Although the businessmen did not know their competitors' responses to a price change, they feared that all price reductions would be followed while all price increases would generally be ignored.

3 Because of the view that market sales would respond rather poorly to market price reductions, price leaders or other co-operative industrial arrangements would not advocate price reductions.

4 Conversely, market prices would not be set where the profit margin would be above the conventional profit margin since, in the long period, it would invite entry and thus undermine the prevailing enterprises' existence – even though in the short period it would be a profitable maneuver.

5 Frequent price changes would be costly and unpopular with salesmen and customers.

While these reasons provide a good understanding of why businessmen used full cost pricing procedures for price-setting, they are also substan-

---

[4] At this point, Hall and Hitch mentioned that the profit margin applied to average total costs to set the price would not be the same for each good of a multi-product enterprise.

[5] In spite of claims made by many economists, Hall and Hitch never assumed that business enterprises always set their prices to cover their full costs irrespective of the level of output. Discussions with businessmen regarding the level of output over which average overhead costs were calculated figured prominently, especially with textile businessmen who faced depressed conditions and destructive price competition throughout the 1930s (Andrews, 1951m).

[6] When defending the price they would set as the "right one", the businessmen interviewed often resorted to "ethical" arguments. The members of the Group regarded these arguments as fundamentally lacking rationality, although Harrod (1939) cautioned the Group that, despite appearances, there might be a general rationality which eluded them.

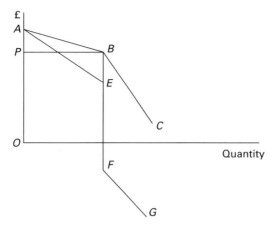

Figure 4.1 The kinked demand curve

tial reasons for why businessmen did not use the marginalist approach to price-setting as well as for the existence of stable prices. Reasons 1 and 5 eliminated the *possibility* and desirability of equating marginal cost to marginal revenue, while reasons 2, 3, 4, and 5 tended to establish a stable market price which included only a conventional profit margin (Hall and Hitch, 1939, pp. 114–16).

At this juncture Hall and Hitch decided to provide a marginalist explanation for the existence of stable prices. To this end they introduced a kinked demand curve for an oligopolist enterprise in which the kink occurred at the predetermined full cost price (*OP*) (see figure 4.1). The upper portion of the curve (*AB*) reflected the fear that competitors would not follow price increases (i.e. it was elastic), and the lower part of the curve (*BC*) reflected the fear that competitors would follow price decreases with market sales responding poorly to decreases in the market price (i.e. it was much less elastic). Consequently, the marginal revenue curve (*AE*, *FG*) would be discontinuous, with the *FG* segment being negative.

Given the position and shape of the kinked demand curve and the average total cost curve excluding profits, there would exist a limited but definite range of temporary shifts in demand (i.e. an acceptable range of levels of output) which would leave the full cost price unaffected. This is due on the one hand to the nature of the full cost pricing procedure, and on the other to the nature of the kinked demand curve itself. In the former case, the costs used to set the full cost price are based on standard or expected output and therefore are predetermined before production

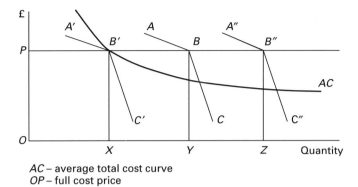

AC – average total cost curve
OP – full cost price

Figure 4.2 The Hall–Hitch marginalist explanation for the existence of stable prices

takes place. Thus the actual average total costs of producing a particular level of output has no bearing on the full cost price being charged.[7] In the latter case, the kinked demand curve represents the competitive pressures the business enterprise faces not to change its full cost price. Thus as demand, say, shifts to the right, the kinked demand curve would shift out, maintaining its kink at the full cost price (see figure 4.2). Consequently, by combining the full cost pricing procedure with the kinked demand curve, Hall and Hitch were able to give a marginalist explanation for stable prices based on full cost prices (Hall and Hitch, 1939, pp. 116–18).[8]

However it would be incorrect to assume that the full cost price would not change under any circumstances. If demand shifted far enough to the left so that the average total costs associated with the amount of output greatly exceeded the full cost price, the businessman might reduce his price in an effort to increase his output so as to avoid bankruptcy. On the other hand, if demand seemed to have permanently shifted to the right so that the average total costs associated with the amount of output resulted in a profit margin much greater than the conventional profit margin,

---

[7] Since the businessmen interviewed did not include normal profits in their calculations of average total costs, Hall and Hitch also did not include normal profits in their average total costs.

[8] Hall and Hitch also argued that:

If the demand curves shift, but the kink remains at the same price, there will still be a range between the two marginal revenue curves on the perpendicular below the actual position of P: and price will be stable for a wide range of marginal costs. (Hall and Hitch, 1939, p. 117)

then the businessman would re-evaluate his full cost price so as to reduce the profit margin to the conventional level and thus prevent long-period entry. If this re-evaluation did not occur then an unstable price situation would exist because of the entry of new enterprises. The rightward shift in demand could cause an unstable re-evaluation of the full cost price if the shift resulted in full capacity utilization, thus giving the businessman an idea of a profitable price which was markedly different from the full cost price. Considering costs, if wage rates and material prices common to all enterprises in the industry changed, then the full cost price would be re-evaluated to reflect this change. This re-evaluation of the full cost price would occur also if a new technique was widely adopted by the industry. The final example Hall and Hitch gave for a re-evaluation of the full cost price was a change in income tax, which businessmen treated as a cost (Hall and Hitch, 1939, pp. 118–22; Hall, 1938m; Roberthall, 1979p; Andrews, 1952a).

The temporary shifts in demand also illuminated another property of full cost pricing. Given the average total cost curve, temporary shifts in demand which did not disturb and full cost price would result in the conventional profit margin differing from the actual profit margin. For example, in figure 4.2 when demand shifts so that output was X, then the actual profit margin would be zero; on the other hand, when demand shifts so that output was Z, then the actual profit margin would be greater than the conventional profit margin (by virtue of the falling average total cost curve (Roberthall, 1979p; Andrews, 1951m, 1952a, 1952b, 1952d).

In closing the article, Hall and Hitch noted that nearly all enterprises irrespective of their size or market position used full cost pricing, thus preventing the use of marginal tools – such as marginal cost and revenue, price elasticity of demand, equilibrium, and marginal products – to analyze the normal price-setting behavior of businessmen in the short period. This was especially so since the long-period analysis of price, as given above, applied in the short period. Thus the full cost price was neither a purely long-period price not a short-period price, but rather it was a hybrid or, more significantly, a mutant (Hall and Hitch, 1939, pp. 122–4; Hall, 1938m; Robertson, 1949).

Full cost prices and marginalism

The significance of Hall and Hitch's article to the other members of the Group was its delineation of the businessmen's explanations for price stability and its introduction of the kinked demand curve. The virtue of the latter was that it appeared to reconcile the logic of marginalism with the empirical evidence of full cost pricing and price stability.[9] In focusing their attention on price stability and the kinked demand curve, Hall, Hitch, and the other Oxford economists did not pay significant attention to the full cost pricing procedures themselves. This not only contributed to obscuring the Group's findings with regard to price-fixing over the trade cycle, but also the extent to which full cost prices were incommensurate with marginalist prices. To establish this point, let us take a closer look at the concept of the full cost price (Brown, 1979*p*, 1988; Andrews, 1952a, 1952b, 1952d, 1952e).

One of the startling revelations Hall gained from the interviews was that businessmen did not view the prices they set as market-clearing or even having a tendency to clear the market. Moreover, the interviews clearly showed that manufacturers set their prices via full cost pricing procedures well in advance of production. This latter revelation, Hall felt, undermined the relevance of the marginalist tools for pricing since they required actual movements in output and prices to be applicable. Given these characteristics, it would be easy to conclude, as Hall did, that full cost pricing procedures are different from marginalist pricing procedures; that full cost prices are different from prices set by marginal revenue and marginal cost; and that full cost prices are stable. However, a deeper conceptual understanding of these last two conclusions is necessary if the novel and non-marginalist nature of full cost prices is to be completely understood (Roberthall, 1979*p*, 1980*i*).

For a price to be not intended to clear the market implies that the market itself is non-clearable. That is, in the marginalist framework, the market is defined as a locality where buyers and sellers meet and exchange a specific amount of a good at a specific price. In addition, these transactions occur at a point in economic time, denoted as either the market period, short period, or long period. Since the entire quantity

[9] Upon reflecting on the Group's view of the kinked demand curve, Andrews made the following comments:

We were more than content with Hall's and Hitch's kinked demand curve. Now since this led to the conclusion that business men would accept *any* level of prices once established, the curious thing is that it involved the abandonment of marginal analysis. But it did not look like that. The causes for the abandonment were expressed in marginal terms – the indeterminacy of marginal revenue – which was satisfactory in so far as we thought it explained why business men did not pay much attention to marginal revenue–elasticity calculations. In our teaching, therefore, it was possible to proceed quite smoothly through all the maze of pricing theory until we came to pricing in practice which was dealt with on a factual basis and with the quite abandonment of our tools – the marginal analysis explained why they should be blunted, and we and our pupils were satisfied with a denouement which left our marginal edifice untouched for examination purposes. (Andrews, 1952b, pp. 172–3)

of the good brought to the market is sold, we can say that the market is cleared and the market price is a market-clearing price. However, if, as Hall argued, the prices businessmen set are not designed to clear the market, then the markets in which these prices reign cannot be markets which clear, implying that the results indicated by marginalist theory are unlikely to be obtained. More specifically, such markets cannot be defined in terms of a specific set of buyers and sellers exchanging specific amounts of a good at a specific price and at a specific point in economic time. What is implied is rather that the market is an abstract concept which collectively denotes all the transactions of a specific good irrespective of the buyers and sellers or quantities involved, or the prices associated with particular transactions. This conception of the market can best be illustrated by referring to an economy in which all goods are produced means of production. For the economy to reproduce and grow through time, each of its goods must be produced and exchanged in a continuous and sequential manner. Moreover, because there is generally more than one manufacturer/seller and buyer of any good, the continuous and sequential transactions of a particular good will generally involve different buyers and sellers, different quantities, and possible different prices. Thus a market in such an economy is not definable in terms of specific buyers and sellers, quantities sold, or prices and, therefore, cannot be seen as something which is clearable. Hence it is this conception of the market which must be associated with prices that are designed not to clear it.

The implication of this conception of the market is that the market price need not be defined and simultaneously determined by a specific transaction of a particular amount of a good at a particular point in time.[10] A specific market price can now be common to many sequential transactions involving different buyers and sellers and quantities of the good being exchanged. However, to be common to many transactions, the market price cannot simply be nominally identical for each of the sequential transactions; in addition, its components must also be invariant with each of the many sequential transaction. That is, it is possible that nominally identical market prices can emerge with each sequential exchange if the peculiarities of the transaction result in the adjustment of its components so as to leave the nominal price unchanged. But not only is such a course of events unlikely, it also means that the nominally identical market price for each of the many sequential transactions is

---

[10] However, if market prices are affected by the peculiarities associated with each exchange in the market, then they take on a market-clearing attribute, even though the market itself is not designed to clear. Such a market price occurs in the course of price wars.

actually specific to each transaction and to the peculiarities of the exchange. Thus for a market price to be common to many sequential transactions, not only must its nominal value be unchanged with each transaction but its components must be unaffected by the peculiarities of the specific transaction. Hence, for such a market price to exist, it must be established prior to production and exchange – that is, prior to the specific events surrounding a specific transaction. Moreover, if such a market price is established, it acquires the property of not being designed to clear the market: if the market price is common to any exchange in the market and specific to none, it cannot be a price which clears the market. It is thus easy to conclude that this common market price is the non-market-clearing price that businessmen set – or, in Hall and Hitch's words, is the full cost price.

To conclude that, as a theoretical concept, the full cost price was different from marginalist prices, Hall and Hitch had only to point to its non-market-clearing property and to the fact that it was set before production commenced. However, there was another substantial yet subtle reason for the difference between full cost and marginalist prices of which Hall and Hitch were not fully aware. Because the full cost price is unaffected by any specific transaction, it is also unrelated to the actual average total costs associated with any specific transaction. That is, the actual per unit costs associated with the quantity of goods involved in a particular transaction will have not any effect on the full cost price or any of its components. Hence the indirect relationship between price, costs, and output in the marginalist framework cannot be found. It is in this respect that full cost prices are conceptually distinct from marginalist prices. In addition, it is this lack of an output–cost price relationship which give full cost prices their characteristic stability. Such a radical break from the existing *Weltanschauung* concerning price, costs, and output was not clearly perceived by Hall and Hitch. However, the absence of any analysis of actual per unit costs with respect to different flow rates of output and the explicit depiction of an invariant full cost price in the face of different output/average total costs indicates the extent to which they did perceive the break.

While full cost prices are a theoretical possibility, their actual existence requires that additional constraints be placed on the prices that can exist for sequential transactions within the market. Because many sequential transactions involving different buyers and sellers can occur in the market, the possibility exists that not only can every transaction have its own particular price but that a single seller's actions in a particular transaction at a particular point in time can affect all subsequent transactions even when the particular seller is not present. A most obvious example is a seller lowering his price for a particular transaction thus forcing all sellers involved in subsequent transactions to lower their prices. The key to the existence of stable, and hence full cost, prices, Hall and Hitch felt, lay in identifying the constraint which eliminated or reduced inter-enterprise price competition and thus prevented the prices from being associated with the quantities associated with a particular transaction. In referring to their interviews with businessmen, they identified the constraint by the well known phrase "businessmen follow price decreases but ignore price increases." In turn, they argued that the constraint was inherent to the market in that it was based on the enterprise's propensity for survival and growth and on the inherent unresponsiveness of market sales to market price changes. Given this constraint, business enterprises within the market will establish explicit or implicit rules which result in a single market price to be used in all transactions. Hall and Hitch concluded that consequently, not only do stable or full cost market prices exist, but that they are pervasive throughout the economy.

Implicit in the above analysis is that full cost market prices are neither short- or long-period prices nor profit-maximizing prices. Because full cost prices are common to many sequential transactions, they do not reflect the particularities of each transaction as would a short-period marginalist price. Therefore they cannot be considered a short-period price, even though they are based on a given set of plant and equipment. On the other hand, full cost prices are not long-period prices since the latter are based on unrestricted re-organization of the underlying plant and equipment. Rather it would appear that full cost prices require a new and possibly conceptually novel time category which captures the property of a common price to many sequential transactions in the context of given plant and equipment. Such a time period, denoted as a pricing period, not only displaces both the short- and long-period time categories of marginalist analysis but also ensures that full cost prices are not profit-maximizing prices. That is, because the pricing period is neither the short nor the long period, it is incorrect to say that full cost prices are short- or long-period marginalist prices and hence that full cost prices maximize short- or long-period profits. Moreover, because the full cost price is common to all the transactions in the pricing period and thus is not related directly or indirectly to the costs/output specific to each transaction, the possibility of maximizing profits in a marginalist-manner simply does not exist.

The above analysis indicates why Hall and Hitch's concept of full cost prices contained a more serious criticism of marginalism than they suspected or intended. Philip Andrews, on the other hand, eventually came to concentrate his attention on full cost pricing procedure and full cost prices themselves, as opposed to price stability and the kinked demand curve, and thus discovered their non-marginalist characteristics. He then proceeded to develop an alternative theory to the marginalist theory of prices and the enterprise – his theory of competitive oligopoly (Roberthall, 1982p; Andrews, 1952d).

5   Philip Andrews' theory of competitive oligopoly

In 1937, Philip Andrews arrived in Oxford as a postgraduate student and quickly became involved with the OERG, eventually assuming the position of the Group's secretary. In 1941 he became the chief statistician to the Nuffield College Social Reconstruction Survey, and later in 1943 he became involved in the Courtauld Inquiry on the relationship between the scale of enterprise and efficiency. Initially Andrews, with the help of Elizabeth Brunner, investigated Courtaulds and other rayon manufacturers, but later the Inquiry was extended to include the boot and shoe industry. Early on in the Courtauld Inquiry, Andrews realized that his work on the rayon industry could lead to a book which examined the chances of small enterprises in British industry. In particular, he saw the book as a general report surveying the problem of how far the efficiency of an individual business was affected by its size and considering how far large-scale business did or did not enjoy real advantages which would not be available to smaller-scale businesses even with appropriate changes in the organization of industry and in the economic environment of business. The book would also pay special attention to the reasons for the survival of relatively small businesses in industries where they were important and thus indicate contributions that smaller-scale businesses made both to its own industry and to the economy of Great Britain as a whole. Finally, Andrews felt that it would be possible to publish a report on the boot and shoe industry because it was possible to conceal the individual enterprises who were investigated, but not on the rayon industry because the clear dominance of Courtaulds made it impossible to conceal its data.

Work on the book progressed to the extent that in August 1946 Andrews had drawn up an outline which included chapter titles such as "The ownership of business," "The reckoning of business income," "Markets and prices – (a) selling, markets, and prices; (b) buying, technical factors and the efficiency of business," "The size of businesses," and "Business and the community." At this point he saw that the theme of the book had changed to a study of the effects of environment and organization on the running of manufacturing businesses. Andrews sent the chapter on the reckoning of business income along with the outline of the book to Harold Macmillan, who agreed to publish it. In November 1948 he completed the book and Macmillan published *Manufacturing Business* in June 1949 (Andrews, 1949a). As for the publication of the report on the boot and shoe industry which Andrews had originally planned to accompany the book, Margaret Cole in 1946 made a speech in Northampton, the home of the boot and shoe industry, in which she mentioned the possibility of nationalizing the industry based on Andrews' research. The business enterprises with whom Andrews was dealing asked that their data not be published, so the planned report was left uncompleted and unpublished.

The road to *Manufacturing Business* also included an intellectual revolution in Andrews' theoretical view of the business enterprise and neoclassical price theory. As a result of his research on manufacturing businesses, Andrews accumulated a great deal of data which, when viewed with an open mind, produced conclusions that were quite inconsistent with many of the theoretical propositions found in monopolistic competition and imperfect competition. His investigations of Courtaulds, where the production of rayon was a highly specified chemical process, and of the boot and shoe industry, where production was arranged in terms of teams of machines, led Andrews to view the organization of production in terms of plant segments which consisted of a specific combination of capital equipment and material and labor inputs needed to produce a specific flow rate of output. Consequently, if an enterprise constructed a plant that included many identical plant segments, then its short-period average direct cost curve would be horizontal, not upward-sloping as depicted in neoclassical cost theory. In addition, Andrews adopted David MacGregor's position that managerial organization was a technique which could be altered as the enterprise's scale of production increased. Thus not only would the enterprise's average managerial costs decline in the short period when the managerial technique was given, but also in the long period when it could be altered. Therefore Andrews concluded that the enterprise's short- and long-period average total cost curves declined instead of being U-shaped as in neoclassical cost theory, with one implication being that the neoclassical notions of the optimal size of the business enterprise and enterprise equilibrium had no theoretical (or empirical) validity.

Through his analysis of the data Andrews also became dissatisfied with the downward-sloping enterprise demand curve and its implication that manufacturing businesses could in some way control their sales through their price policy. In particular, he rejected downward-sloping marginal revenue curves (and with them downward-sloping enterprise demand curves) and denied the relevance of the concept of short-period price elasticity of demand for analyzing the price behavior of enterprises. Rather it appeared to Andrews, in the light of his data, that goodwill was the decisive factor which determined an enterprise's share of market sales, while the level of national income determined its level of sales. In addition, he became convinced by his analysis of the data that competitive markets need not be defined in terms of the competition of enterprises producing identical products, that oligopoly was the normal characterization of markets, and that oligopolistic markets were competitive irrespective of the number of enterprises in them. As a result of his investigations, Andrews finally came to believe that manufacturing businesses did not think it was a good policy to play about with their prices in the search for maximum profit and that they did believe their normal cost pricing policy gave them the correct prices subject to the emergence of actual competition. Thus when trying to analyze the rayon industry in terms of conventional oligopoly theories such as the kinked demand curve and Joan Robinson's theory of imperfect competition and the boot and shoe industry in terms of Chamberlin's theory of monopolistic competition, he found that they simply did not fit the facts. So Andrews began rejecting marginalism and replacing it with a more realistic analysis of costs and a new theory of the relation of businessmen to their markets.

Drawing in part from his experiences with the OERG and the Nuffield College Social Reconstruction Survey, from his research with the Courtauld Inquiry, and from MacGregor's work on the business enterprise, Andrews struggled to develop a new and different theory of the manufacturing business which included theories of normal cost pricing and prices, explanation for price stability, and a delineation of the enterprise's environment. In particular, his intellectual debt to Hall, Hitch, and the Group was their documentation of the widespread usage of cost-plus pricing systems by businessmen and of the "ethical" arguments espoused by businessmen to defend the price they set as the "right price." Andrews came to realize that both sets of data implied a range of theoretical ideas regarding price-fixing and prices which were incommensurable with marginalism. However, the data collected by the Group was not sufficient in itself to enable Andrews to develop his theory of manufacturing business. What he lacked was detailed knowledge of individual manufacturing businesses. This was put right through his work with the Survey and the Courtauld Inquiry.

During this period he became aware of the compatibility of his theory with Marshall's theory of prices as applied to industrial markets. This awareness was reinforced through his relationship with MacGregor. Andrews viewed MacGregor as a "true-blue" pupil of Marshall and hence a source of an interpretation of Marshall that was uncontaminated by Arthur Pigou's equilibrium firm and Joan Robinson's theory of imperfect competition (both of which he felt were a betrayal of Marshallian tradition). Moreover, MacGregor's own research on the business enterprise provided Andrews with an example of Marshall's method of analysis in action and with particular insights into the working of the enterprise which could not be found elsewhere. Thus Andrews considered his theory of the manufacturing business as the only legitimate descendent of Marshall's theory of prices as applied to industrial markets.

Andrews' first presentation of his theory of the manufacturing business appeared in an article in 1949 in *Oxford Economic Papers* (Andrews, 1949b), while the more complete version appeared with the publication of *Manufacturing Business*. However, Andrews could not claim that he had produced a theoretical alternative to marginalism. In particular, his theory lacked a theoretical grounding in a theory of markets, a discussion of industry and markets, an analysis of retail trade and consumer behavior, a discussion of enterprise investment decision-making, and a negative critique of marginalism. Between 1950 and 1966 Andrews repaired these omissions and by doing so transformed his theory of manufacturing business into a theory of industrial markets and then finally into a general theory of markets, which included retail trade and consumer markets, called the theory of competitive oligopoly. Incorporated in the theory were his theories of normal cost pricing and prices (Lee, 1993a).

Andrews' view of the manufacturing business

The manufacturing business that concerned Andrews was a going concern, existed in real time, and whose goals were survival and growth. It did not face internal cost constraints on sales in the short term or on the expansion of the scale of production in the long term. Neither was it impelled to sell at a price determined by the interaction of costs with an external demand constraint; rather, it would decide on a pricing policy and administer its own price. But the absence of such internal constraints did not mean the absence of any constraints at all. The business enterprise existed in an industrial environment, a system of inter-related enterprises, which exerted competitive pressure on pricing behavior which could be ignored only at the risk of the enterprise's own demise.[1] To delineate fully Andrews' view of the manufacturing business a closer look at its average cost structure and at the "environmental" constraints affecting its pricing decisions is required.

First we consider costs. Andrews' explanation of the behavior of the enterprise's average direct and average total costs will first be presented in the context of given plant, equipment, and managerial technique and then extended to the situation where they are variable. Andrews starts his analysis of costs by making the usual assumptions of unchanged product, a single-product enterprise, and fixed material input prices, wages, and salaries. He then proceeds to develop it in a rather novel manner – by discussing the organization of production around a pre-planned maximum flow rate of output. That is, when organizing its production *de novo*, the enterprise would first choose a pre-planned maximum flow rate of output which was greater than what it expected its normal flow rate of output to be, with the amount of extra or reserve output based on the expected frequency of repairs and breakdowns, on normal variations in output, and on the expectation that the enterprise will have a slow but continual increase in sales over time. It would then select a method of producing the normal output that would be both flexible enough to handle disruptions caused by breakdowns and repairs, normal variations in output, and slow secular growth in sales and at the same time be cost-competitive. In this context, the enterprise would select a production technique that consisted of a specific combination of capital equipment, and material and labour inputs to produce a specific flow rate of output. The technique or plant segment would then be duplicated to the extent required to produce the pre-planned maximum flow rate of output. To manage the production of the pre-planned flow rate of output effectively, the enterprise would also employ a particular combination of supervisory personnel, administrators, and associated material inputs organized in a specific manner, which Andrews called "managerial technique." Thus the enterprise's overall productive structure would consist of a single plant made up of x number of identical plant segments and a managerial technique.[2]

Because the plant segments are identical, the enterprise's average direct costs are constant up to full capacity. Moreover, because the managerial

---

[1] Andrews' view of the manufacturing business as a going concern was significantly influenced by MacGregor's own description of the business enterprise. Moreover, Andrews' view of prices as being administered was not dissimilar to MacGregor's own view of prices (MacGregor, 1911, 1934; Lee, 1989, 1993a).

[2] For further discussion of the segmented plant approach to production, see Lee (1986); Dean (1976).

technique is given, average managerial costs decline as the enterprise's flow rate of output increases. Finally, by combining managerial costs with depreciation and interest payments we get indirect costs and, since the latter two components are given for the time period under considera- tion, average indirect costs also decline as the enterprise's flow rate of output increases. Andrews therefore concluded that the enterprise's average total costs, which consist of average direct costs and average indirect costs, decline as its flow rate of output increases up to full capacity (Andrews, 1949a, 1949b, 1952a, 1964).[3]

Now let us shift to the situation in which the business enterprise can alter its entire productive structure in response to a permanent increase in its flow rate of output, as indicated by the actual flow rate of output being consistently larger than the normal flow rate of output. In this context, Andrews begins his analysis by envisaging a spectrum of scale-related plant segments, where the plant segments with the larger flow rates of output have the lower average direct costs. Consequently, when increasing its scale of production or pre-planned maximum flow rate of output, the enterprise would construct a new plant with the appropriate lower-average direct cost plant segments incorporated in it. Thus, Andrews concluded that the enterprise's average direct costs decline as its scale of production increases, with the initial rate of decline being rapid and then falling significantly at larger and larger flow rates of output. As for managerial costs, Andrews argued that they also respond to perma- nent increases in the enterprise's flow rate of output. Because a manage- rial technique can accommodate a wide range of scales of production, the enterprise would initially retain it as its scale of production increased, with the result that average managerial costs at the higher normal flow rates of output would decline. However, at some point the enterprise's scale of production would increase so much that its normal average managerial costs would start to increase. In this situation, the enterprise would employ a different managerial technique that would be more appropriate, that is one which would result in better supervision of production, in better long-range planning, and in a decline of normal average managerial costs.[4] Thus Andrews concluded that, as long as a spectrum of scale-related managerial techniques were available, there was no assignable limit to the fall in normal average managerial costs with respect to increases in the enterprise's scale of production. Adding

---

[3] Constant average direct costs under the conditions Andrews postulated have been substantiated by Dean (1976); Johnston (1960); Koot and Walker (1969–70).

[4] Andrews defined managerial costs to include also cost inefficiencies arising from the production of the output. It is these cost inefficiencies which account for the rising segment of the managerial cost curve as the flow rate of output increases.

average direct costs and normal average managerial costs together and assuming that depreciation and interest payments did not change appreciably, then over time the enterprise's normal average total costs (NATC) would decline continually as its normal flow rate of output increases with the increase in the pre-planned maximum flow rate of output (Andrews, 1944, 1946m, 1949a, 1949b, 1952a; Brunner, 1952; Lee, 1989; Earl, 1993).

The above analysis of costs led Andrews to three significant results. First, the enterprise's production and cost structure does not restrict its ability to grow. On the one hand, when plant, equipment, reserve capacity, and managerial technique are given, the enterprise is "encouraged" to produce as much as possible since its average total costs decline in the process. On the other hand, when plant, equipment, and managerial technique are variable, the enterprise's growth over time is promoted since its NATC decline as its scale of production increases. Moreover, given the general unused capacity embodied in a managerial technique, internal competition among members of management for promotions can push the enterprise towards expanding its scale of production, especially if this route is seen as easier and quicker than other alternatives. Secondly, the enterprise's NATC are the same whether plant and equipment are given or allowed to vary. Thus the enterprise's long-term NATC curve is merely a series of points of short-term NATC. Lastly, instead of being tangent to the long-term NATC curve as in neoclassical theory, the enterprise's short-term NATC curve cuts the long-term cost curve, lying above it when the actual flow rate of output is below normal and below it when the actual flow rate of output is above normal (Andrews, 1948, 1949a, 1952a, 1958; Andrews and Brunner, 1962).

Let us now consider the environmental constraints which the manufacturing business must take into account when making its pricing decisions. The industry and the market together make up the immediate economic environment of the enterprise and impose external constraints on its ability to survive and grow. Andrews saw the individual enterprise as operating within an industry, which he viewed as consisting of all those enterprises which use similar processes and have similar backgrounds of experience and knowledge. This implies that each enterprise in the industry could produce, if it desired to do so, the product of any of the other enterprises. An industry thus comprises many enterprises making different kinds of products. The market, on the other hand, consists of those enterprises currently making products sufficiently similar to be substitutes, though not necessarily perfect ones, in the eyes of buyers or sellers. In short, an industry consists of many markets, each of which had one or more enterprises producing the same kind of product and an enterprise in any particular market could easily produce a product found in a different market, implying that enterprises are potential multi-product producers. Given these concepts, Andrews could now identify and delineate the various kinds of pricing constraints an enterprise faces in its particular market (Andrews, 1949a, 1951, 1952a; Nightingale, 1978).

Because an industry is composed of many markets, each of which can have many enterprises, an enterprise's price-setting behavior, Andrews argued, is constrained not only by its immediate competitors within the market as in previous theories, but also by its not too distant competitors in other markets. That is, Andrews reasoned that enterprises are always cognizant of their own and their competitors' behavior within both the market and the industry. Consequently, because the possibility of cross-entry by established enterprises in related markets was great, enterprises in a particular market felt very constrained in setting their prices. More-over, because the enterprises in the market were aware of each other, no one enterprise could hope to pursue a price policy that would not elicit reactions from the other enterprises. In short, the enterprise was con-strained in its price-setting behavior because it existed in an oligopolistic environment where cross-entry between markets was easy (Andrews, 1958, 1964).

The ability of a manufacturing business to pursue an independent price policy within the market was further constrained in a different manner. Andrews recognized that in industrial (as opposed to consumer) markets goodwill influences the market share of the enterprises. That is, for the sake of convenience of acquisition, the maintenance of easy access to supplies, the maintenance of a regular clientele which permits smooth production runs for the selling enterprise, and the convenience of accounting, buyers and sellers strive to establish mutually rewarding social relationships that go under the title of "goodwill." These relation-ships, in turn, ensure the enterprise a particular share of market sales. However, accompanying goodwill is the possibility that market prices for identical goods may sometimes differ since buyers will maintain their contact with their selling enterprise if they see a higher price as temporary and due to fortuitous events. But if the prices in the market remain non-uniform, pressure will emerge to force the prices to converge to the lowest price in the market. Some of the pressure will come from aggressive sellers, while some will come from the threat of cross-entry into the market by enterprises which inhabit other markets in the industry. The strongest pressure, however, will come from the buying enterprises themselves. Because in industrial markets the product bought becomes part of the costs of another product sold, the buying enterprise will institute routine searches to make sure that the price it pays for the product is, over time, no more than that of its competitors. This is necessary since any alternative form of behavior will increase its cost relative to that of its competitors and therefore place it at a competitive disadvantage. Thus, a buying enterprise will not continue to prefer a higher-priced over a lower-priced product of identical specification. Consequently the selling enterprise will therefore not pursue a pricing policy which will make its price higher than that of its competitors, since if it did so it will lose all its customers' goodwill and cease to be a going concern – once lost, a customer's goodwill cannot be recaptured by a simple elimination of the price differential (Andrews, 1949a, 1951, 1952a, 1964; Andrews and Brunner, 1951; Edwards, 1952, 1955, 1962; Irving, 1978t).

Finally, the enterprise's pricing decision is constrained in inter-related industrial markets because market sales are unresponsive to reductions in the market price. Andrews' argument was that business enterprises will not increase their purchases of an "input" product whose market price has declined if sales of their output are stagnant or decreasing. Further enterprises normally will not reduce their selling prices unless their sales are stagnant or decreasing. Therefore, the market conditions necessary for market prices to decline also ensure that the potential buyers do not want to increase their purchases even at lower prices. Hence Andrews concluded that market sales were not responsive to changes in the market price. Thus, the enterprise is inhibited from pursuing a price policy that would prompt a price war since such an event would lower profits or even generate losses (Andrews, 1949a, 1951, 1952a; Andrews and Brunner, 1951; Brunner, 1952).

To summarize, for Andrews the manufacturing business is a going concern embedded in a system of going concerns. Its average total cost curve declines both when the production and managerial techniques are given as its flow rate of output increases and when they are variable. While the enterprise must necessarily administer its prices to ensure its survival and growth in a non-equilibrium, non-profit-maximizing sense, its pricing choices are restricted because (1) it operates in an oligopolistic industrial environment, and because (2) the nature of industrial buying and selling and the independence of market sales from the market price forces it to set prices which are similar to its competitors. Finally, the degree of competition for the Andrewsian enterprise is not a function of the number of enterprises in the market. Rather, for Andrews, an industrial market would be competitive, irrespective of the number of enterprises actually in the market or whether all the goods in the market were strictly the same or not, as long as entry was relatively easy and competitive forces existed in enough strength to ensure a "single" market price. Thus, the term "competitive oligopoly" aptly captures Andrews' view of the industrial environment in which the manufacturing business enterprise exists (Andrews, 1946, 1966*u*).

The normal cost theory of pricing

Andrews developed his normal cost theory of pricing to describe the pricing procedures used by manufacturing businesses, and to explain why they used procedures which produced stable prices. From his own investigations, Andrews confirmed the position taken by Hall and Hitch that business enterprises set prices by adding a predetermined margin for profit to an average total cost based on a predetermined flow rate of output. However, he chose to describe the pricing procedure in a manner different from that used by Hall and Hitch. Starting with the predetermined flow rate of output, Andrews argued that the enterprise bases its estimate of the flow rate of output on past experience over the trade cycle and on expectations about its likely future sales. This flow rate of output becomes the normal flow rate of output which the enterprise then uses to determine the costs relevant to setting its price. That is, the enterprise chooses a normal flow rate of output and uses this to determine its normal average direct costs, normal average indirect costs, and normal average total costs; to set its price it only has to add to the normal average direct costs a gross costing margin which includes normal average indirect costs and a predetermined margin for profit called the costing margin.[5] Andrews called these pricing procedures normal cost pricing procedures and the resulting price the normal cost price (see figure 5.1) (Andrews, 1949a, 1949b; Brunner, 1975).[6]

The normal cost price that emerged from the pricing procedures was, Andrews observed, stable with respect to short-period variations in the enterprise's flow rate of output. This observation is of interest since it implies that the enterprise has adopted a pricing procedure which does

---

[5] The pricing procedures Andrews described can alternatively be described as marking up normal costs, where the profit mark up on NADC is equivalent to the gross costing margin and the profit mark up on NATC is equivalent to the costing margin (see chapter 11).

[6] In selecting the term "normal cost" vs "full cost," Andrews was trying to make clear that business enterprises cannot always set their prices which would cover their costs and costing margin when the market price is stable. As noted above, Hall, Hitch, and the other members of the OERG never thought that was the case. Consequently, it is not surprising that Hall saw little difference between normal cost and full cost pricing procedures (Andrews, 1951*m*, 1952a, 1952b, 1953*u*; Roberthall, 1979*p*).

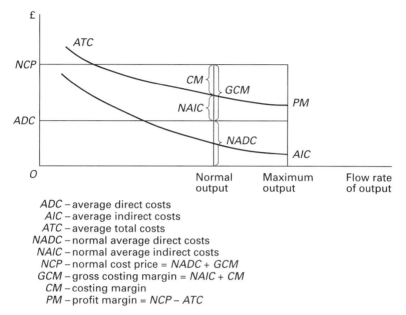

ADC – average direct costs
AIC – average indirect costs
ATC – average total costs
NADC – normal average direct costs
NAIC – normal average indirect costs
NCP – normal cost price = NADC + GCM
GCM – gross costing margin = NAIC + CM
CM – costing margin
PM – profit margin = NCP – ATC

Figure 5.1 Andrews' normal cost price

not let the daily ebb and flow of its flow rate of output affect the price it has set. To explain this, Andrews first noted that changes in the flow rate of output do not affect the costs that make up the normal cost price since those costs are based on normal output. Moreover, the normal average direct and indirect costs are based on the most efficient plant, equipment, and managerial technique appropriate for the enterprise's scale of production. Thus, the costs relevant for pricing are those which represent the fundamental technical forces facing the enterprise, not the ephemeral costs associated with the enterprise running more or less at full capacity.

Next, drawing on the constraints the enterprise faces in the market, Andrews noted that the enterprise would not pursue a pricing policy which, for instance, increases the costing margin – and hence price – in response to an immediate increase in sales, and results in a price higher than its competitors, even if this produces an immediate, albeit tempo-rary, increase in profits. The reason is that such a policy would result in a continuous and permanent loss in sales over time and with it a permanent reduction in future profits and thus would affect the enterprise's ability to remain a going concern. On the other hand, the enterprise would also not pursue a policy that tries to increase the flow rate of output by reducing its price, through reducing its costing margin, below that of its competitors. The reason is that, since the competitors would match the price reduction to prevent the enterprise's flow rate of output from increasing at their expense and since market sales are unresponsive to reductions in the market price, a lower costing margin–price would simply mean a reduction in profits from the level they would have been at if the price reduction had not taken place. Consequently the enterprise would not pursue a pricing policy that linked its price via the costing margin directly to short-period fortuitous variations in its flow rate of output. Such a policy would result in a continuous and permanent loss of sales and profits when sales are potentially high, and in a severe reduction in profits beyond that caused by the increase in costs when the flow rate output is low. In short, such a policy would severely impair the enterprise's ability to be a going concern. Therefore, Andrews concluded that, in order to increase its chances of remaining a going concern, the business enterprise would adopt a price policy of matching competitors' prices only for identical products and employ a pricing procedure that did not connect its costing margin, and therefore its price, to the day-to-day variations in its flow rate of output.

In bringing the above considerations together, Andrews concluded that price stability occurs because the enterprise, as a going concern, must adopt a normal cost price policy and normal cost pricing procedures since these do not link the normal cost price via costs of the costing margin to the short-period variations in its flow rate of output (which implies that the normal cost price is determined by "forces" which lie outside the enterprise's immediate situation). The adoption of any other pricing procedure, such as that found in the marginalist approach, would reduce the chances of the Andrewsian enterprise remaining a going concern. Thus, in explaining why manufacturing enterprises use normal cost pricing procedures, Andrews has clearly produced a theory of pricing – or more specifically a normal cost theory of pricing (Andrews, 1949a, 1949b; Edwards, 1952, 1962; Irving, 1978*t*).[7]

---

[7] Since Andrews developed an explanation for why businessmen use normal cost pricing procedures, it is not correct to label these procedures as "irrational rituals." Normal cost pricing procedures were labeled an irrational ritual and Andrews' theory of normal cost pricing was labeled an irrational ritualistic system of pricing because it appeared that such pricing procedures did not lead to maximum profits. Such criticism assumes implicitly that a demand curve exists for the business enterprise and that an equilibrium price and quantity of sales can be unambiguously and simultaneously determined. However, as noted above, the Andrewsian enterprise does not face a demand curve; moreover, Andrews, while accepting the concept of equilibrium price, did not accept the concept of equilibrium quantity. Hence it is impossible for normal cost pricing procedures to set neoclassical profit-maximizing prices or for the theory of normal cost pricing to be couched in profit-maximizing terms. But this does not mean that business enterprises

The normal cost theory of prices

Andrews developed his normal cost theory of prices to explain the absolute level of the normal cost price, the movement of the normal cost price over time, and the impact of the normal cost price on the structure of the market. Before his theory can be presented, we must first deal with the problem of establishing a single market price. Because of the oligopolistic nature of the market environment, no one enterprise in the market could pursue a price policy that would not affect, and possibly elicit reactions from, the other enterprises in the market. To get around this problem, and hence a cause of short-period market price instability, Andrews stated that the market price would be established either by a price-leader enterprise or by a trade association. In each case, normal cost pricing procedures are used. In the case of price leadership, the enterprise with the largest scale of production and hence the lowest NATC of all the enterprises in the market had the capability of setting a price that could afflict losses on its competitors but not itself. Andrews argued that the smaller-size/higher-cost enterprises in the market would consequently adopt as their price the price set by the low-cost enterprise, thus making it the market price. As for the trade association case, the participating enterprises based the market price on the most efficient enterprise's normal average direct costs and then added on an agreed-upon gross costing margin. In both cases, a single and stable market price would be established. To simplify the subsequent discussion, it will be assumed that the market price is set by a price leader using its own costs and costing margin (Andrews, 1949a, 1950, 1951, 1952a, 1958).[8]

Since for any scale of production NATC are known, the absolute level of the price leader's normal cost price, and hence the market price,

using normal cost pricing procedures do not strive for profits; they do, but in a manner which is conceptually different from that found in marginalism. And as long as normal cost pricing procedures do not impede the enterprise's drive for profits, they can not be called an irrational ritualistic system of pricing (E. A. G. Robinson, 1950, 1980*p*; Andrews, 1949a; Brunner, 1952; Irving, 1978*t*):

> I [Andrews] regard these descriptions of how oncosts are determined as ritualistic – but the essence of a ritual is to get its results. It does not matter in my experience how a business man calculates his overhead costs – he will develop such a rule for this, plus allowance as for new profit, as to give him generally a safely quotable price. The sting of Austin Robinson's "ritualistic" remarks turns against himself, just because he so clearly does not see the purpose of the "ritual". (Andrews, 1951*m*)

[8] In markets where products were quite similar but not identical, Andrews thought of the market price as being a band of prices within a limited range, with the differences in price reflecting real differences between the similar products. Hence the price the price leader sets was not the one other enterprises used, but the one they clustered around.

depends solely on the absolute level of its costing margin. Andrews argued that the magnitude of its costing margin was determined by competition within the market and by the threat of entry by enterprises inhabiting the other markets in the industry. In the former case, the price leader was constrained in determining the magnitude of his costing margin if the enterprises in the market saw the resulting market price as outrageously high and thus preferred a lower one. While this was a possibility, it was secondary in Andrews' view to the principal constraint – the cross-entry of multi-product enterprises from the neighboring markets and industries who could enter quickly in pursuit of higher net profits than they were getting in their other markets and to widen their product range for the sake of future prospects. To forestall these competitive threats, the price leader would set its costing margin just low enough to avoid attracting entry or upsetting its followers. However, this costing margin would generally be greater than zero because of the difficulty of obtaining customers and thus entering the market. That is, since the customers in the market have, at the given market price, attached themselves to their suppliers, the entering enterprise could hope to obtain some of the floating demand only if it adopted the market price. But under this circumstance, it might take the new enterprise a very long time, if it succeeded at all, to obtain enough customers to make its operations cost-efficient and hence profitable. Andrews denoted the entry-preventing costing margin as normal and concluded that it could vary from market to market, as the strength of goodwill and the difficulty of obtaining floating and first-time customers varied. He consequently saw the magnitude of the entry-preventing costing margin as a quantitative measure of the relative difficulties of entry between the various markets. By adding the gross costing margin which included the normal costing margin to NADC, the price leader set the absolute level of the market price. In doing so, the price leader set a price in the short period which was solely determined by its subjective perceptions of long-period forces – such as technology and entry. Thus, we can clearly see why Andrews concluded (1953b) that the normal cost price was a long-period price which ruled in the short period: "the essence of my theory is to call attention to the way long-run or normal factors influence short-term prices" (Andrews, 1949a, 1949c, 1951, 1951m, 1952a, 1952b and 1964; Edwards, 1952, 1955; Brunner, 1975).

With the absolute level of the normal cost market price determined, its movement over time can easily be dealt with. Assuming the price leader's normal costing margin to be constant, changes in input prices over time will result in price changes. If input prices decline, then competition under the pressure of informed buyers will push the price leader to lower his normal cost price and restore his normal costing margin. Conversely, an increase in input prices will eventually result in the price leader raising his price so as to restore his normal costing margin. As for the impact of the price leader's scale of production on his price, assuming his normal costing margin given,[9] Andrews concluded that his price and hence the normal cost market price would decline over time as the scale of production increased (Andrews, 1949a, 1952a).

Given the above discussion, we can now turn our attention to the way Andrews saw the impact of the market price on the structure of the market – i.e. the size distribution of the enterprises producing the good in question. First, for any specific scale of production of the price leader there will exist a normal cost price for the market and a constellation of smaller-size/higher-cost enterprises which can at least survive in the market, given this price, for a short period of time. Thus, the normal cost market price in this context produces a stable market structure by discouraging new entry and preserving the existing population of enterprises. On the other hand, the normal cost market price does not

---

[9] This assumption assumes that changes in interest payments and depreciation that generally accompanies an enterprise's change in the scale of production has no significant impact on the shape of the long-term average total cost curve. It should also be noted that the arguments for falling average total costs in the long term imply a relationship between the scale of production and investment, since changes in the methods of production and managerial techniques require investment expenditures. Andrews' work on capital development clearly establishes this relationship. Whether capital investment involved the replacement of a broken machine or major projects involving the construction of whole plants, re-organization of departments, or the replacement of existing facilities, its basic determinant was the scale of production. In the former case, capital investment is based on maintaining the current scale of production while the latter is based on the expected growth of sales, as opposed to the rate of interest, the marginal efficiency of capital, or the marginal product of capital. To finance their investment projects, Andrews argued, enterprises relied on internal funds – depreciation allowance and net profits. Since depreciation funds were determined by law and external funding was not pursued to a significant degree, enterprises were free only to "adjust" net profits to fit their investment projects. However, since net profits were a residual determined jointly by the actual flow rate of output (or degree of capacity utilization) – which enterprises could not control – and the costing margin, enterprises could "determine" their net profits only by setting their costing margins in reference to normal flow rate of output. Therefore, by implication, one set of the determinants of the costing margin would appear to be the determinants of the investment projects, that is the present and expected future scale of production. Consequently, the movement of normal cost prices in the long term would not only be affected by the impact of the scale of production on average total costs, but also by its impact on the costing margin. So a complete explanation of the movement of normal cost prices would have to contain the effects the scale of production would have on average total costs and on the costing margin. Unfortunately, Andrews did not present an explanation of the relationship between the determinants of the costing margin and investment decisions (Andrews and Brunner, 1950, 1951; Andrews, 1952b, 1953a).

determine the level of market sales or the sales of the individual enterprises in the market. Market sales, Andrews argued, were determined by the level of economic activity of the economy as a whole; and the level of sales of an individual enterprise within the market, given market sales, was determined by the enterprise's goodwill. Hence, the normal cost market price in Andrews' view, produces a stable market structure, but does not determine the level of sales for the individual enterprise or the market as a whole (Andrews, 1949a, 1951, 1952a; Brunner, 1975; Irving, 1978t).[10]

Secondly, since the movement of the normal cost price over time depends directly on the price leader's scale of production, it is easy to conclude that there is an inverse relationship between the market price and the size of the price leader. However, the relationship between the market price and the size of the price-following enterprises is not so easy to state since it involves changes in the market structure. Because the price-following enterprises cannot affect the market price, the same events which brought about the increased scale of production of the price leader – and, hence, a decrease in the market price – can affect the price-following enterprise adversely or favorably. For example, if the events which led to the increase of the scale of production of all enterprises in the market were to permit the price leader to employ a revolutionary new plant segment which reduced its costs significantly, then the resulting market price could eliminate some of the enterprises from the market after a period of some market price instability. Indeed it could constrain their ability to build enough capacity to produce the increase in output which their goodwill warranted them. Hence, the movement of the long-period market price would have a significant impact on the market's structure, including the number of enterprises which inhabited the market and their relative size. While the above scenario implies that an enterprise, once it became a price leader, would eventually monopolize the market, Andrews argued otherwise. He felt that the enterprise's growth could be constrained either by the lessening impact the increased scale of production would have on costs, or by the diminishing ability of the enterprise to stay ahead. But even if the price leader did become a monopolist, which would not have any impact on the market price because the costing margin is determined primarily not by the market's structure, but by the threat of entry (Andrews, 1949a, 1949c, 1951, 1958, 1964; Brunner, 1975; Irving, 1978t).

[10] In freeing the normal cost price from a specific level of output, Andrews felt that his theory of normal cost prices was freed from the static constrictions found in the marginalist approach (Andrews, 1964).

Andrews' theory of competitive oligopoly contains many details on the pricing process, on management and the growth of enterprises, on managerial costs or X-inefficiency, and on the evolution of industrial markets, not to mention the fact that it has been employed in empirical research on pricing, costs, and the linear shipping industry. Yet it is not fully developed. For one, his theory does not provide a satisfactory explanation of the costing margin. In addition, its theoretical analysis of the role codes of behavior and social–economic institutions, such as trade associations and price-leadership enterprises, play in determining the normal cost market price is largely undeveloped. Moreover, as presented, Andrews' theory largely ignores consumer behavior and pays only brief attention to variations in the normal cost price. And finally, although Andrews clearly suggests that his theory operates within the context of historical time, his discussions of the business enterprise and of pricing does not clearly reflect this. What is missing in this regard is the notion of sequential acts of production as a foundation on which to base the enterprise and pricing and prices. Subsequent developments in these areas will be dealt with in chapter 6 (Barback, 1964; Kempner, 1960; Gardner, 1978; Davies, 1984; Earl, 1993).

6   Developments in the doctrine of normal cost prices

After Andrews, the theoretical development of the normal cost prices doctrine took on a rather different form. Instead of being concerned with the larger picture of a non-neoclassical theory of pricing and prices, the subsequent contributors were more interested in particular facets of the doctrine. The purpose of this chapter is to delineate the developments that contributed most to the fleshing out of the doctrine, which includes the analysis of the costing margin; the notion of sequential production inherent in normal cost pricing procedures; the competitive process, social rules and institutions, and the determination of the market price; consumer behavior; and variations in the normal cost price. On the other hand, Kingsley Laffer's (1953) suggestion that a fuller analysis of the implications of reserve capacity for understanding the growth dynamics of the enterprise will be ignored, because it played no part in the doctrine's development. This was due in part to Andrews' unfavorable review of Edith Penrose's book *The Theory of the Growth of the Firm* (1959). Andrews, while agreeing that reserve capacity in management could exist, criticized Penrose's emphasis on it as the main source of growth. The emphasis on internal factors affecting growth was unsatisfactory, he argued, because it ignored the effect of the external environment on the enterprise's ability to grow. However subsequent economists, such as Scott Moss and Peter Earl, have argued that the compatibility of Penrose's work with the normal cost prices doctrine was much stronger than Andrews suggested. For the same reason Alexandre Lamfalussy's discussion of the relationship between normal cost pricing, forms of competition, and investment decisions will be ignored. Finally, Paolo Sylos-Labini's discussion of incorporating normal cost price equations into Piero Sraffa's multi-sector price model will be noted in chapter 9 (Irving, 1978t; Laffer, 1953; Andrews, 1961; Moss, 1981; Earl, 1993; Lamfalussy, 1961; Sylos-Labini, 1962, 1971).

Analysis of the costing margin

As noted above Andrews argued that the magnitude of the costing margin used by the price leader to set its normal cost price was determined by competition within the market and by the difficulty of market entry due to the strength of goodwill and the problem of obtaining first-time and floating customers. He also argued that the magnitude varied from market to market. However, his discussion appeared less than satisfactory to many. Ian Little, for example, remarked in his Oxford tutorials that although it may be true that, as a matter of routine administration, manufacturers applied a given costing margin to their NATC, most of the interesting economics comes under the choice of the margin's magnitude, and this Andrews did not discuss. In addition, a reviewer of *Manufacturing Business* noted that:

It is ... a pity that Mr. Andrews has not given us an analysis of the forces determining the gross profit margin (especially in the long-run development of firms) with the same clarity as his analysis of costs. His answer, if answer there be, to one of the most important questions this subject raises, thus lies hidden. (Leyland, 1950, p. 422; see also Laffer, 1953)

Of the three determinants of the gross profit margin – average indirect costs, the costing margin, and actual output – the enterprise has discretion only over the costing margin, since the determinants of actual output lie beyond the enterprise's control and average indirect costs alter with changes in the flow rate of output. Thus the reviewer's point was essentially a concern about the vagueness with which Andrews discussed the determination of the costing margin and, given normal average total costs, the normal cost price.

Coinciding with the reviewer's comments was an emerging controversy over the normal cost prices doctrine. Generally economists were attempting (and largely succeeding) to make the doctrine compatible with marginalism. The emerging and favorite argument, especially among British economists, in this regard was that full cost and normal cost prices could be viewed as long-period profit-maximizing prices. At this time there also emerged a substantial attack on the notion that enterprises in imperfectly competitive markets were more monopolistic than competitive. To address these issues, and others as well, Harrod began writing an essay in 1951 in which he attempted to revise some of the established doctrines of imperfect competition, especially in light of the findings of the pre-war OERG (Harrod, 1952). In part of the essay, he discussed the extent to which an enterprise's price policy was governed by short-term or by long-term considerations. In particular, drawing on Andrews' published work as well as private correspondence, he noted the role that potential competition and cross-entry had on shaping the enterprise's short-term price policy. This discussion was picked up by John Hicks (1954) and then by Harold Lydall (1955) who introduced the concept of the "no-entry ceiling price" and briefly discussed some of the barriers to entry – such as goodwill, advertising, and cost of capital. Out of this ensuing discussion emerged two monographs – Harry Edwards' *Competition and Monopoly in the British Soap Industry* (1962) and Paolo Sylos-Labini's *Oligopoly and Technical Progress* (1962) – which dealt with the determination of the costing margin among other issues along lines consistent with the doctrine of normal cost prices (Bhagwati, 1970; Lee and Irving-Lessmann, 1992).

Edwards' interest in the costing margin began when he arrived in Oxford in October 1951 with the intent of earning a doctorate in economics. There he met Andrews at Nuffield College and quickly became attached to his work and to Andrews himself, who became his dissertation advisor. In 1952 Edwards, in close consultation with Andrews, wrote an article on goodwill in which he clearly delineated the demand side of Andrews' theory of competitive oligopoly (Edwards, 1952). In Edwards' view, the novelty of the article was found, given Andrews' theory, in setting out the implications that goodwill had for the actual competition between enterprises, and the connections between goodwill, potential competition, new-enterprise entry, and cross-entry of existing enterprises. He further developed this novel analysis in a later article (Edwards, 1955), and introduced the argument that free entry did not mean easy entry. These ideas, however, were most fully developed and explicitly related to the determination of the costing margin and the entry-preventing normal cost price in his doctoral dissertation, "Aspects of the formation of the prices of manufactured commodities" (1957*t*), which was eventually revised and published in 1962 as *Competition and Monopoly in the British Soap Industry*.[1] Sylos-Labini's interest in the determination of the costing margin arose from the dynamic approach he adopted to study economics. Thus when he became interested in the theory of prices,

---

[1] One important contribution Edwards made in *Competition and Monopoly* had to do with his analysis of goodwill as opposed to the costing margin. He argued that goodwill was a structural feature of industrial markets. Thus, embedded in the normal cost prices doctrine is that much of the economic activity in industrial markets is socially conditioned (Edwards, 1962, 1982*p*).

I realized that it was wrong to separate the problem of [price] determination from that of price variations; in fact, marginal analysis was concentrating most of the attention on the former problem and was treating the latter problem in terms of (arbitrary and unexplained) shifts of the demand and supply curves. (Sylos-Labini, 1982p)

In his search for something better Sylos-Labini discovered, at approximately the same time (1953–5), Andrews' *Manufacturing Business* and the volume *Oxford Studies in the Price Mechanism* (1955), which contained an article by Andrews and Hall's and Hitch's 1939 article on full cost pricing. Combining these discoveries with his reading of cost accounting books, and the works of Michal Kalecki, Harrod, Nicholas Kaldor, and others, Sylos-Labini developed an integrated account of price determination and price variation that included normal cost pricing procedures an analysis of the determinants of the costing margin based on the concept of entry (to which he was apparently introduced by Alberto Breglia in the early 1950s). *Oligopoly and Technical Progress* was first published in Italian in 1956, revised in 1957, and finally published in English in 1962. Over the next decade, in a series of articles, Sylos-Labini reiterated many of the book's important themes (Edwards, 1982p; Sylos-Labini, 1966m, 1982p).

Although Edwards and Sylos-Labini developed their analysis of the costing margin independently of each other, taken together they presented a complementary and comprehensive account of the determination of the costing margin, and hence the normal cost price.[2] To lay the foundation of their analysis, they initially assumed that all enterprises in the market produced the same good and had the same NATC, that average direct costs were assumed constant while average total costs fell up to the maximum flow rate of output, that enterprises held reserve capacity, that market demand was not very responsive to changes in the market price, and that market demand was not growing. Since, under these assumptions, each enterprise in the market had the same NATC, the magnitude of the costing margin had to be the same for each enterprise if a uniform normal cost market price was to prevail. Thus the determinants of the costing margin, and hence the normal cost market price, had to be found among those forces which acted upon the market as a whole as opposed to upon individual enterprises within the market (Edwards, 1962, pp. 58–69; Sylos-Labini, 1962, pp. 33–4).

---

[2] In weaving together their analysis of the costing margin, I have concentrated on their non-neoclassical contributions. In particular, this means that Sylos-Labini's use of price elasticity of demand was rejected in favor of Edwards' goodwill.

To begin the analysis, Edwards and Sylos-Labini assumed that entry into the market was free (although not necessarily easy) in that it was unrestricted by law, patents, or market-wide collective agreements designed to inhibit entry. Then they postulated that for a particular normal cost market price, the market would be stable in that there would be no entry or exit of enterprises. The magnitude of this no-entry market price was determined by the magnitude of the uniform NATC and the costing margin. Concentrating their attention on the latter determinant, they argued that the costing margin could be divided into two parts – a part for normal (or minimum) profits, cm_n, and a part for profits due to barriers to entry, cm_b, where $cm = cm_n + cm_b$ and the no-entry normal cost price, $p_e = NATC + cm$. Defining normal profits as that minimum amount of profits which an enterprise must receive at normal output if it was to enter and or stay in the market, cm_n was seen as the minimum value of the costing margin which the enterprise must add to its NATC if it was to stay in the market. In this context, the determinants of normal profits, and hence cm_n, were identified as the rate of interest plus a premium for risk. Because both of these determinants operated with equal force on all enterprises in the market, cm_n was necessarily the same for all the enterprises, but not necessarily the same for all markets due to variations in business risk (Edwards, 1962, pp. 68–76, 88–9; Sylos-Labini, 1962, pp. 39–42, 1967).

Proceeding to the determinants of cm_b, that part of the costing margin due to barriers to entry, Edwards identified two kinds – goodwill and economies of scale.[3] He argued that the principal barrier to an enterprise's ability to enter the market, especially in the context of cross-entry, was the lack of economic space in the market – or, more specifically, the existence of goodwill between customers and existing enterprises. Because the market demand was unresponsive to price changes and the existing floating demand and first-time buyers relatively small, one way an entering enterprise could attract enough attached customers to achieve the scale of production necessary to obtain the prevailing NATC in the market so as to be in a position to earn at least normal profits was to try to lure other enterprises' customers away by lower prices. Such a strategy would work only if the other enterprises in the market maintained the price differential,

---

[3] Edwards identified two additional barriers to entry – systematic cost differentials and large initial capital requirements. However he dismissed them as being insignificant in the face of free cross-entry by existing efficient business enterprises (Edwards, 1962, pp. 78–81).

which was unlikely because of the recognized negative effects on their sales. Another way would be to accept the prevailing market price and to embark upon some kind of marketing campaign for a period of time. But this strategy would increase the enterprise's costs, thus resulting in higher production costs at a time when costs were above normal because of below normal output and, hence, below normal profits. Market entry would be thus forestalled as long as cm_b, and hence p_e, was low enough so as not to tempt enterprises to try entering the market by disturbing the existing goodwill relationships. As for economies of scale, Edwards argued that they constituted an additional but secondary barrier to entry since the scale of production needed to achieve the economies necessary to obtain the NATC prevailing in the market would determine only how intensely the enterprise must carry out its marketing campaign. If the scale of production necessary to obtain the economies enjoyed by enterprises already in the market was large relative to the floating and first-time customers, entry into the market would be more difficult than if it was less large. Edwards therefore concluded that the overall magnitude of cm_b depended primarily on the strength of goodwill and the difficulty of obtaining floating and first-time customers (as Andrews argued) *and* secondarily on the scale of production needed to obtain the cost-equalizing economies (Edwards, 1962, pp. 81–96).

To extend the analysis, the assumption that all the enterprises in the market had the same NATC was replaced with one in which the enterprises' NATC were different. In addition, Edwards and Sylos-Labini assumed that the enterprise with the lowest NATC in the market would be the price leader and set the market price; hence the price leader's costing margin would consist of parts for minimum profits, for profits due to barriers to entry, and for profit due to its differential cost advantage, cm_c. The determinants of cm_c, they argued, were those factors which prevented potential competitors from achieving a flow rate of output and therefore a NATC approaching that enjoyed by the price leader. The factors they identified were (1) the extent to which a reduction in the market price drew first-time buyers to the market and created unattached buyers through the elimination of enterprises to which they were previously attached, (2) the ease with which the entering enterprise could attract these unattached buyers, (3) the absolute size of the market, and (4) the scale of production necessary to achieve a level of NATC which would, at the new lower market price, give the entering enterprise normal profits. Thus, the more difficult it was to create first-time and unattached buyers through a reduction in the market price and to get them as customers, the smaller the absolute size of the market, and the greater the scale of production necessary to achieve a level of NATC which would give normal profits, the greater cm_c, and therefore cm, would be for the price leader. Hence, the no-entry normal cost market price set by the price leader would be $p_e = NATC + cm$ where $cm = cm_n + cm_b + cm_c$. However because cm_c was primarily based on uneven exploitation of technical and organizational developments over time, its magnitude was both historically determined and subject to change as unknown technical and organizational innovations came into play. Therefore, while cm_c was a permanent feature of a dynamic capitalist economy, its magnitude would vary over time (Sylos-Labini, 1962, 1967; Edwards, 1962).

The final step in extending the analysis of the costing margin focused on the impact that intra-market competition of the established enterprises would have on the costing margin. Given the basic assumptions of the analysis, including the one that the market was populated with enterprises with different NATC, Edwards argued that this would produce a constant competitive struggle among the enterprises to get more sales and a greater proportion of market sales relative to their competitors. This urge to grow ensured that the enterprise would be in a perpetual non-equilibrium state and would adopt price policies which could depress the actual normal cost market price below the maximum no-entry market price. Denoting p_e as the maximum no-entry market price and p_a as the actual market price, we have the following:

$$p_e = NATC_{pl} + cm_n + cm_b + cm_c \quad \text{or} \tag{i}$$
$$p_e = NATC_{pl} + cm$$

$$p_a = NATC_{pl} + cm_n + cm_b + cm_c - d \quad \text{or} \tag{ii}$$
$$p_a = NATC_{pl} + cm_a$$

where $NATC_{pl}$ is the normal average total costs of the price leader
cm_a is the actual costing margin
d is the price-dampening effect due to intra-market competition.

Thus the extent to which p_e exceeded p_a depended on the magnitude of d and hence on the factors which determine it.

The factors determining the magnitude of d were, Edwards argued, (1) the characteristics of the product, (2) the number, size, and cost efficiencies of the enterprises in the market, and (3) the responsiveness of market demand to changes in the market price. Therefore if the market was populated with a few equally-sized large enterprises with the same cost efficiencies and financial strength, the product of the market was of a relatively simple and standard character little subject to change, and market demand responded little to price changes, then d would be fairly small and p_a would be close to p_e. If, on the other hand, product innovation was possible, and since product innovation builds goodwill, the market would be continually altered as enterprises competed with each other, with the net result being that d would be large and p_a significantly less than p_e. In fact, the maximum effect of product innovation on d would occur, Edwards noted, when market demand responded well to price changes, the enterprises in the market were of different sizes, and a small enterprise was doing the innovating (Edwards, 1955, 1962, 1982p).

The important advances Edwards and Sylos-Labini made in the analysis of the costing margin were not continued within the context of the normal cost prices doctrine. For example, B. L. Johns (1962) (and also Sylos-Labini to some extent) argued that a steady increase in market demand weakens barriers to entry and the cost differential thus potentially reduces the costing margin. As pertinent was Johns' article with ideas regarding the various ways in which an enterprise could slowly and successfully enter a growing market, they were never examined with regard to their impact on barriers to entry and hence the costing margin. Another and more striking example is the relationship between the financing of investment and the costing margin. As noted previously, Andrews argued that enterprises financed most of their capital investment internally, but he never made a formal connection between the financing of investment and the determination of the costing margin. As a result, the relationship remained unexamined within the context of the normal cost prices doctrine, perhaps because it redirects the normal cost price away from being simply an entry-preventing price to a strategic price which is designed for other things and may, as a result, let some entry occur.

Sequential production through time

Earlier (in chapter 4) it was argued that the full cost price was a price common to many sequential transactions and a price which could exist only in a non-clearing market. Furthermore, it was suggested that a non-clearing market existed only in an economy which fractionally and continually reproduced itself through time. Finally, it was argued that normal cost pricing procedures and normal cost prices embodied the view of the enterprise as a going concern. Thus it would appear that, within the normal cost prices doctrine, production should be depicted as sequential acts and the pricing behavior of the enterprise should be depicted as enabling it to set prices that would permit it to engage in sequential production, reproduction, and growth through time. However, these issues were not developed by Andrews; but they were by Wilford Eiteman in his monograph *Price Determination* (1949) and by John Williams in his article "The Path to Equilibrium" (1967) and in other writings.[4]

Around 1940, Eiteman was teaching marginalism in principles of economics classes at Duke University when it occurred to him that as treasurer of a construction company he had set prices and talked with others who set prices and yet had never heard of any price-setter mentioning marginal costs. He quickly came to the conclusion that a price-setting based on equating marginal costs to marginal revenue was nonsense. Eiteman then began to piece together a critique of marginalism aimed at its production and cost foundations. Although his critique was not accepted by most economists, some did ask that if businessmen did not use marginal costs and marginal revenue to set prices, then how did they set prices? In response to this and to the criticism that he destroyed the existing theory but offered nothing to take its place, Eiteman wrote *Price Determination*, in which he argued that prices were set by cost-plus pricing procedures and that businessmen raised and lowered their prices on the basis of the rate of turnover of their current assets or cash advanced. It was in developing these arguments that he established the relationship between sequential production and normal cost prices (Eiteman, 1949, 1982*p*, 1985*p*; Lee, 1984a, 1984b).[5]

To set out his views on price determination, Eiteman first constructed a model in which the business enterprise was engaged in sequential acts of production and reproduction. Starting at a point in time when the enterprise, by assumption, already had its complement of fixed capital, Eiteman argued that for production to take place the enterprise must have cash on hand to procure the necessary direct and indirect labor and material inputs. Once the necessary productive inputs were obtained, production was undertaken, the output was sold and the revenue was collected. The period of time from the initial buying of the inputs through production to the collection of the revenue, Eiteman called the turnover period. If the amount of revenue

---

[4] In a letter to Andrews, Richard Lester mentioned Eiteman's monograph and noted that it "set forth a theory of business behavior rather different from that involved in the normal textbook explanations" (Lester, 1949*m*). However, it does not appear that Andrews ever read the monograph. On the other hand, as noted in n. 6 in chapter 2 (p. 55), Means did read *Price Determination* and incorporated its important idea of sequential production into his definition of administered prices.

[5] In the monograph, Eiteman never explicitly delineated the pricing procedures used to set the price; however, his examples and other statements clearly indicated that he had a target rate of return pricing procedure in mind. Also see Oxenfeldt (1951, p. 176).

received at the end of the turnover period at least equaled the initial expenditure of cash for productive inputs plus the amount for depreciation, the enterprise could repeat the process again and continually do so as long as the original sum of money advanced was returned and the allowance for depreciation was recovered:

Turnover period 1:
$$M_{ca} \rightarrow TC \rightarrow P \rightarrow S \rightarrow TR = [TC = M_{ca} + D]$$

Turnover period 2:
$$TC \rightarrow M_{ca} \rightarrow TC \rightarrow P \rightarrow S \rightarrow TR = [TC = M_{ca} + D], \text{ etc.}$$

where M_{ca} is the cash advanced
    TC is total costs
    D is the allowance for depreciation
    P is production
    S is selling the output
    TR is the total revenue obtained from selling the output.

Thus, the enterprise could engage in sequential acts of production only when total costs equaled total revenue. If the level of production was normal output, then this would imply that the price equaled normal average total costs (Eiteman, 1949).[6]

To tie the analysis of sequential production and reproduction of the enterprise to normal cost pricing, Eiteman argued that manufacturers used pricing procedures to set prices that would enable the enterprise to reproduce its working capital each turnover period and to make a profit. That is, Eiteman argued that enterprises set prices by marking up costs:

$$(NATC)(1 + t) = p$$

where t is the mark up for profits which will produce the expected rate

---

[6] Utilizing the model, Eiteman noted that the business enterprise could vary its output by working its cash advanced more or less intensely. Using this view of output augmentation, he went on to argue that manufacturers based their price and output decisions upon changes in the rate of inventory turnover. Thus he concluded that:

According to the [marginalist] theory, an increase in the scale of operation is an increase in the quantity of input factor applied. According to the theory [in this monograph], an increase in the scale of operation is a faster turning of existing working capital. On the surface these differences may not seem to be important but close examination proves the opposite. It is apparent that if producers regulate their scale of operations on the basis of inventory policy, then they do not regulate it on the basis of marginal costs and marginal revenue and *vice versa*. (Eiteman, 1949, p. 49)

of return with respect to the value of the enterprise's capital assets.

Assuming that normal output was achieved in each turnover period, the normal cost price would not only permit the enterprise to recover the cash advanced and thus engage in sequential act of production, but also to recover its allowance for depreciation and to make a profit:

Turnover period 1:
$$M_{ca} \to TC_{no} \to P_{no} \to S_{no} \to TR_{no} = q_{no}[(NATC)(1 + t)]$$
$$= TC_{no} + Mp$$
Turnover period 2:
$$TC_{no} \to M_{ca} \to TC_{no} \to P_{no} \to S_{no} \to TR_{no}$$
$$= q_{no}[(NATC)(1 + t)] = TC_{no} + Mp \text{ etc.}$$

where subscript "no" is normal output

q_{no} is the quantity of normal output

$TC_{no} = M_{ca} + D$

Mp are profits and constitute a fund available for capital and other discretionary expenditures.

Thus Eiteman's more sophisticated model showed quite clearly that normal cost prices and pricing procedures enabled the enterprise to engage in continuous sequential acts of production; and conversely, the model implied that if an enterprise was to engage in sequential acts of production, then it must adopt normal cost pricing procedures. The model also implied that the enterprise could expand its output if some of the profits were allocated so as to increase the cash advanced and its fixed capital. Eiteman (1949) did not pursue this point, but John Williams did.

At the same time Eiteman was fashioning his critique of marginalism and developing his explanation of price determination, Williams was beginning to have doubts about the adequacy of marginalism to explain the behavior of business enterprises. In particular, he thought it was nonsense to say that enterprises maximized their profits by drawing their marginal revenue and marginal cost curves and looking to see where these two curves crossed. Believing that he could not get rid of marginalism without offering something to replace it, Williams set his mind to work. Drawing inspiration from Eiteman's articles on production and costs (Eiteman, 1945, 1947), he also developed an explanation of enterprise behavior based on the turnover of current assets or cash advanced. Moreover, after reading Eiteman's (1949) monograph in which Williams found a number of Eiteman's ideas set out, he felt that he could advance his analysis still further. So basing his work on the turnover of cash advanced, he extended Eiteman's analysis of sequential production and normal cost pricing to include the growth of the business enterprise (Williams, 1949u, 1979, 1983p, 1986i).

Working from Eiteman's model and assuming that enterprises continually seek to expand their sales, Williams argued that an enterprise would continue to expand production as long as it was making profits. That is, assuming that the enterprise's price, p^*, and total indirect costs were given and fixed, for an initial amount of output q_1, total costs (TC_1) would equal total direct costs (TDC_1) plus total indirect costs (TIC_1) and the total revenue (TR_1) would equal p^*q_1. If total revenue was greater than total costs or price was greater than average total costs, the enterprise could take this difference and augment its direct inputs and, hence, output in the next turnover period. Now if the total revenue in the next turnover period was greater than total costs, the enterprise would again be able to expand its output in the following turnover period:

Turnover period 1:
$$TDC_1 + TIC_1 = TC_1 < TR_1 = TC_1 + Mp_1$$

Turnover period 2:
$$TDC_2(= TDC_1 + Mp_1) + TIC_1 = TC_2 < TR_2 = TC_2 + Mp_2$$

Turnover period 3:
$$TDC_3(= TDC_2 + Mp_2) + TIC_1 = TC_3 < TR_3 = TC_3 + Mp_3,$$
etc.

Assuming the enterprise had sufficient amount of unused capacity, this expansion process under sequential production would end only when $TR_{n+1} = TC_n$ (or $p^* = ATC_n$), a condition which would occur only if average direct costs were increasing (Williams, 1964u, 1967).

The enterprise's path to the stationary state – or equilibrium, as Williams called it – would not exist, however, if its price was based on normal output. That is, if the enterprise's price was based on NATC which changed as its scale of production increased, then not only would total revenue be greater than total costs at normal output, profits would also be generated which could then be used to expand the cash advanced and to expand plant capacity:

Turnover period 1:
$$M^1_{ca} \rightarrow TC^1_{no} \rightarrow P^1_{no} \rightarrow S^1_{no} \rightarrow TR^1_{no}$$
$$= q^1_{no}(NATC^1)(1 + r)] = TC^1_{no} + Mp_{11} + Mp_{12}$$

Turnover period 2:

$$TC^2{}_{no} + Mp_{11} \rightarrow M^2{}_{ca} \rightarrow TC^2{}_{no} \rightarrow P^2{}_{no} \rightarrow S^2{}_{no} \rightarrow TR^2{}_{no}$$

$$= q^2{}_{no}[(NATC^2)(1+r)] = TC^2{}_{no} + Mp_{21} + Mp_{22}$$

where $q^i{}_{no}$ is the normal output of the ith turnover period

Mp_{i1} is the portion of profits of the ith turnover period set aside for cash advanced

Mp_{i2} is the portion of profits of the ith turnover period set aside for expanding capacity.

So long as $p > NATC$, the enterprise would face no internal constraint to its growth. However, as Williams noted, the enterprise could control the rate at which it grew through the manner which it disposed of its profits and took on external debt. For example, an enterprise could increase its short-term growth rate by increasing its cash advanced through short-term bank borrowing or by relatively increasing the Mp_{i1} share of the profits. On the other hand, the enterprise could reduce its short- and long-term growth rate by distributing some of its profits as dividends. Also implicit in the model was the possibility that the enterprise could control its short- and long-term rate of growth by adjusting the mark up for profit – that is, by adjusting the target rate of return and, hence, the normal cost price. However, this implication was left unexplored by Williams (Williams, 1964u, 1967).

The competitive process, social rules and institutions, and the normal cost market price

As noted in chapter 5, the movement of the normal cost market price involved changes in the number of enterprises which inhabited the market and their relative size. Implied in the movement was a tendency for the price leader to eventually monopolize the market; but the tendency could never work itself out, Andrews argued, because of the lessening impact of the increased scale of production would have on costs and the diminishing ability of the enterprise to stay ahead. Andrews did not proceed beyond this point, but the competitive process underlying the movement of normal cost market prices caught the attention of Jack Downie and Josef Steindl. As will be seen in chapter 10, Steindl used the Andrewsian competitive process to explain the emergence of oligopolistic markets and the eventual economic stagnation of twentieth-century capitalism. Downie, on the other hand, examined the competitive process more fully and its impact on public welfare.

Jack Downie obtained a First in Philosophy, Politics, and Economics at Oxford in 1947. He immediately joined the Economic Section of the Cabinet Office which was under the direction of Robert Hall. In 1954 Downie obtained a Marshall Plan grant which enabled him to spend two years at Oxford investigating the impact of restrictive trade practices on the competitive process and hence on public welfare, the results of which were published in *The Competitive Process* (1958). In the book, Downie argued that the Andrewsian competitive process consisted of the interaction of the transfer mechanism and the innovation mechanism. The former referred to the process by which the lower-cost larger enterprises grew at the expense of the higher-cost smaller enterprises. That is, given the normal cost market price of the price leader, the costing margins of high-cost smaller enterprises would not be sufficient to generate the profits needed to expand capacity in line with their share of the growth of market sales. Therefore, sales which "should" have gone to them by virtue of their existing goodwill would be transferred to the low-cost larger enterprises whose costing margins were sufficient to generate the profits needed to expand their capacity in line with the growth of sales. The relative growth of the larger enterprises *vis-à-vis* the smaller enterprises eventually resulted in the fall of the normal cost market price below the costs of the latter, who then would leave the market with the result that their sales would be transferred to the remaining enterprises. The logical outcome of the transfer mechanism was, Downie concluded, a narrowing of the cost differentials between enterprises and eventually the emergence of a single enterprise in the market.

The innovation mechanism, on the other hand, disrupted the transfer mechanism by altering the cost differences between enterprises. Downie argued that high-cost enterprises which were on the verge of being driven from the market would need to adopt new technological innovations that would reduce their costs. However, the adoptation of such innovations require profits which the high-cost enterprises would not have; therefore in this case the innovation mechanism did not appreciably disrupt the transfer mechanism. In the case of the larger enterprises whose costs differences were minor and declining, the situation was different. As a result of finding their relative dominance over their competitors in the market declining, the larger enterprises turned to technological innovations to improve their relative costs position.[7] The outcome of this cost-reducing innovation-led competi-

---

[7] Downie also noted that enterprises, instead of innovating, could decide to use their profits to enter another market and thereby disrupt the transfer mechanism there.

tion was that the relative cost ranking of the enterprises changed over time, thereby completely disrupting the logic of the transfer mechanism. However, for the innovation mechanism to work, it was necessary that the innovating enterprise was not immediately followed by its competitors. While, Downie argued, such grit in the form of ignorance and uncertainty about precisely what other enterprises were doing was necessary for investment to take place, it reduced the pace at which the productivity of the economy increased, hence affecting public welfare.

Downie argued that the interaction of the two mechanisms explained the cost dispersion among enterprises in a market at a given point in time. More importantly, it provided an insight into the diffusion of innovative production techniques in the economy which was essential for economic progress and increasing public welfare. In this context, he realized that the competitive process based on the interaction of the two mechanisms would have the tendency to produce concentrated markets with large enterprises who adopted trade practices which inhibited price competition, maintained market shares, and promoted co-operative research. As a result of the practices becoming entrenched, both the transfer and innovation mechanisms were disrupted and the competitive process became less intense and more managed. Such a managed competitive economy would, Downie argued, have a lower rate of technical progress and therefore an adverse affect on public welfare. It was consequently necessary to adopt a legal framework governing market activities, which he called "rules of the game," that ensured that the competitive process would not destroy itself. Such a framework would govern the usage of the trade practices noted above (Downie, 1958; Nightingale, 1995*u*).

Downie was not the only economist interested in the Andrewsian competitive process and its social regulation. Both Romney Robinson and George Richardson addressed the issue of the social regulation competition with regard to the determination of the normal cost market price. However, they came to different conclusions than Downie, believing that socially managed competition was necessary if there was to be any economic progress at all. Because of the oligopolistic nature of the market environment, no one enterprise in the market could pursue a price policy that would not affect, and possibly elicit reactions from, the other enterprises in the market. To deal with the problems this creates for the establishment of a stable and uniform market price, Andrews assumed that the market price was set by a price-leader enterprise or by a trade association. Subsequent economists, such as J. N. Wolfe (1954) and Syed Ahmad (1956*t*), working within the context of the normal cost prices doctrine, simply accepted his solution to the problem. However, Andrews' solution obscured the role of the social rules and social institutions in the determination of the normal cost market price. Edwards, with his discussion of the perpetual non-equilibrium state of the enterprise and the depressing effect actual competition had on the market price, clearly suggested the need for social rules and institutions if a chaotic market was to be prevented. But it was Robinson and Richardson who, in their own particular ways, dealt with the theoretical issues surrounding the social determination of normal cost market prices.

Before entering academic life, Romney Robinson had spent nearly 15 years in the business world. When he came into contact with marginalist price theory, he found it a grossly inaccurate description of the pricing behavior which he had experienced. More pointedly, he found the marginalist equilibrium condition

a thoroughly misleading description of real circumstance. At the level of the firm, the firms *I* had known were continually "out of equilibrium," in the particular sense that they were continually striving to do better – or if you like, felt they had to run as hard as they could just to stay in the same place. The marginalist theory of the firm does nothing to convey this sense. (R. Robinson, 1981*p*)

To convey this concept of the enterprise and the price which it sets that keeps it continually out of equilibrium, Robinson wrote three articles, beginning in 1961, arguing that the prices enterprises set were non-market-clearing prices and that they were determined by the social rules and institutions the enterprises faced in the market place.

Robinson argued that there existed two types of prices – those that equaled marginal costs for each transaction and those that lie above marginal costs for each transaction – and that their existence depended on different social–economic institutions and rules of behavior. The former prices existed in markets which were highly organized by an external social–economic institution, were subject to a specific set of rules established by this institution, and contained many buyers and sellers. (For Robinson, the major stock and commodity exchanges in New York, Chicago, and elsewhere were such markets.) The buyers and sellers in the market could not interact directly; rather, they had to interact with the market-maker who ensured that the desires of the buyers and sellers were met. Finally, in such a market, the quantity of output in each exchange was determined by the equation of price to marginal cost, with the consequence that the price in the market fluctuated with fluctuations in output, assuming that marginal costs were not constant. Market equilibrium and the path to market equilibrium was therefore institutionally determined, as opposed to "naturally" occurring in the market, and the prices which emerged in equilibrium Robinson called market-clearing equilibrium prices (Robinson, 1961, 1978, 1981p).[8]

The latter kind of prices existed in markets which were not organized, in which marginal costs were virtually constant and below average total costs until full capacity was reached, in which buyers and sellers formed social (or goodwill-based) relationships to facilitate their market interaction, and in which the roles of socio–economic behavior were determined co-jointly with the competing enterprises within the market. More specifically, these prices existed in oligopolistic industrial markets where enterprises could not pursue an independent price policy and set their own prices. The enterprises in these markets must establish social–economic institutions and rules of behavior that lessen the risk of a debilitating price war which would drive the price below average total costs towards marginal costs and, conversely, ensure that a price acceptable to the other enterprises in the market was established. This code or socially established market price, Robinson argued, would not only be above the marginal costs of each exchange but would also be invariant to short-period fluctuations in output. As long as the rules of behavior on which the market price was based were not violated, the market price would not be forced down to equality with marginal costs and therefore would not vary with short-period variations in marginal costs due to output variations. And if the market price was not equal to marginal costs, Robinson argued, then it would not be a market-clearing equilibrium price. He thus called the socially established and socially sustained market price a non-market-clearing price, or simply a normal cost market price (Robinson, 1961, 1978, 1980u).[9]

The existence of a socially established and sustained market price

---

[8] A fundamental mistake made in conventional price theory, Robinson argued, was the assumption that the markets for manufactured products were "highly organized" in the same manner (even though prices therein may fluctuate less frequently). In fact, he noted, they were not so organized. The rules that govern behavior in manufacturing markets were in part legal, but for the most part conventional. Hence such unorganized markets would yield significantly different results.

[9] In his 1961 article, Robinson used the term "disequilibrium" to describe the price. However, upon reflecting that disequilibrium implied a disruption in the equilibrating process thus suggesting that the disequilibrium was unstable whereas the institutions in place in oligopolistic industrial markets work to sustain the non-market-clearing normal cost price, he discarded the term in favor of "non-market-clearing." It also has to be noted that Robinson used the term "full cost price" in his work; but given his relationship with Andrews and that full cost prices are part of the normal cost prices

brought with it, Robinson noted, a quite different understanding of enterprises' activity in the market. First of all, given the normal cost market price combined with a declining average total cost curve, the enterprise could increase its profits and its sales revenue at the same time. Consequently, so long as the enterprise had unused or reserved capacity, it would be in a constant struggle for business. But how this struggle was carried out depended on the social–economic rules or codes in place. In general, price wars and other unduly disruptive and destructive competitive activities were not considered appropriate means to gain more business; rather, given the formal or informal codes of competition governing market behavior, enterprises would resort to advertising, product differentiation, or changing terms of credit to obtain a larger amount of market demand. In each instance, Robinson noted, the competitive activity was designed to strengthen the goodwill position with current customers and to establish goodwill relationships with first-time and random customers. Secondly, since the social–economic codes govern the establishment of the normal cost market price, it would vary, Robinson argued, as the difficulties imposed by the market environment differed. Thus, what economists needed to do, according to him, was to engage in sociological, behavioral, and economic investigations, in order to discover precisely what were the social–economic rules that governed market behavior and the establishment of normal cost market prices, and to determine how they came about. The outcome of such investigations, Robinson suggested, would be that economists would discover that collusion was largely a social phenomenon in which conflicting individuals had common interests which could be achieved only through establishing a social consensus about the matters at hand. They would also discover that the normal cost market price was neither a profit-maximizing nor an out-of-equilibrium price because those neoclassical adjectives had no meaning in the non-neoclassical environment of the socially determined normal cost price. Finally, they would discover that the code-established prices were enforced by a variety of social–economic institutions – ranging from price-leader enterprises, trade associations, and open-price associations to various government regulatory agencies and legislation (Robinson, 1961, 1978, 1980*u*).

Unlike Robinson, George Richardson was a colleague, although not a close one, of Andrews. During the 1950s, he not only lectured on the normal cost prices doctrines, especially as articulated by Andrews, he also

doctrine, I have substituted "normal cost price" instead (Robinson, 1978, 1981*p*, 1982*p*).

was busily fashioning an analysis of the relationship between social–economic rules and institutions and the market price that was, he believed, compatible and complementary with Andrews' work. After reading Friedrich Hayek's article on economics and knowledge (Hayek, 1937), Richardson became concerned with the theoretical problem of the market conditions under which the enterprise could expect to generate the necessary information on which to base its investment decisions. Approaching the problem theoretically, Richardson first argued that the perfectly competitive model used by economists was incapable of answering the problem. He then argued that the market conditions which enabled the enterprise to obtain the requisite information generally included co-ordination among the market enterprises and social constraints on their market action. More specifically, Richardson argued that the information necessary for making investment decisions could be only obtained in markets where the market price was unchanged for many sequential transactions and did not represent the market conditions peculiar to each transaction. It was in this manner that Richardson came to consider the relationship between social–economic rules and institutions and the market price (Wilson, 1982p; Richardson, 1960, 1981p, 1986i).

Richardson approached the relationship between social–economic institutions and market prices by considering two types of prices with respect to investment decisions – short-period fluctuating prices and long-period stable prices. The former prices, through short-period price competition, were responsive to the conditions surrounding each and every transaction in the market and, hence, were market-clearing prices. Thus, as the short-period conditions continually changed, so would the market price change. However, because of its fortuitous, flexible nature, the short-period market price could not generate the information needed by enterprises for making investment decisions. On the one hand, buyers could not make long-term buying plans, such as the buying of investment goods or consumer durables, based on the goods' relative prices since they could change in a haphazard unpredictable manner; on the other hand, if the total sales of the enterprise were associated with many different prices, then it could not make long-term sales predictions based on sales trend, stock movements, state of orders, or market share. The information needed by the enterprise to make investment decisions would consequently simply not exist.

To eliminate short-period fluctuating prices, Richardson argued, enterprises resorted to developing codes of behavior and social–economic institutions to enforce them. For example, to eliminate secret price shading and therefore the possibility of price wars, a social rule against price cutting would be propagated throughout the market and backed by social–economic institutions such as open-price systems, price notification schemes, cartels, trade associations, or price leaders. Specifically, to eliminate short-period fluctuating market prices, the market enterprises would establish codes of social behavior and social institutions which would establish a single market price based on the normal cost prices of the enterprises in the market that would remain unchanged for many transactions – that is, a stable long-period market price. As a result, sales trends would provide the information enterprises needed to make long-term investment decisions, since the price/quantities combinations which make it up would not be related to short-term market conditions. Thus not only was the socially determined market price stable over time, it also generated the investment information the enterprises required since the indicators would reflect the permanent market conditions (Richardson, 1960, 1965, 1966, 1967, 1969; Foss, 1994*u*).

Consumer behavior

Andrews and other economists who worked within the framework of the normal cost prices doctrine never developed a systematic alternative to neoclassical consumer theory. However, it is possible to argue that interspersed among Andrews' comments on retail trade are enough germane statements on consumer behavior that, when put together in a synthetic whole, do represent an important development in the doctrine. In his work on retail trade (Andrews, 1950, 1964; Andrews and Friday, 1960), Andrews utilized a method of analysis whose roots are found in the Marshallian tradition. But the method goes beyond Marshall and seems best characterized as resembling a prescient bridge between the "utility-tree" notion associated in the neoclassical literature with the work of Robert Strotz (1957), the characteristics analysis proposed by Kevin Lancaster (1966), and the essentially behavioral analysis of contributions to consumer theory made in marketing. Andrews clearly saw consumer choice as an hierarchical process; he did not see consumers as if they possessed well defined brand preferences in an *n*-dimensional goods space. Having engaged in a good deal of enjoyable yet purposeful window-shopping, the Andrewsian consumer decides the budget range within which to look seriously for a particular kind of product – that is to say, the consumer initially is concerned with trade-offs among broadly defined commodity categories, or a particular category against general purchasing power forgone from other unspecified uses. Such budget ranges would be discrete, "conventional" constructs; consumers would not choose between many marginally overlapping rival plans of feasible financial allocations. The budgeting process would consequently leave the consumer with an upper bound for the particular product category, which would exclude as "too expensive" some brands that might otherwise be candidates for serious evaluation and comparison with rival means of meeting the ends in question. The range's lower bound would exclude cheaper goods as likely to be of inadequate quality. With the budget boundaries set, the consumer then engages in a lexicographic ordering process to choose a specific good within these boundaries. Therefore, although the consumers do not have "perfect" information and hence face a certain amount of uncertainty when shopping, the hierarchical process enables them to choose goods that are consistent with their underlying wants.

The use of such attention-confining price bands by consumers – which is empirically well documented by, for example, André Gabor and Clive Granger (1966) – was something that Andrews saw as placing enterprises under competitive pressures to offer products that could safely be priced within conventionally popular ranges. The fact that brand evaluations would be carried out with respect to goods that consumers actually encountered as possible means of producing desired ends led Andrews to emphasize the role of stocks as demand-generating devices, and to be critical of the depiction of incompletely planned consumer spending as irrational "impulse buying." Although Andrews saw consumers as having to focus their attention to cope with potential information overload and uncertainty, he did not see them generally as inconsistent in their underlying wants or incompetent as shoppers.

In Andrews' view consumers, like industrial buyers, would give particular suppliers their goodwill. In embarking on a particular shopping expedition, they would make what we might usefully call "primary patronage choices," according to their assessments of stores' relative competitiveness in respect of the mix of things with which they intended to fill their shopping baskets – not with regard to marginal choices of particular goods. If relative competitiveness did not seem to have changed, they would go to their "usual" store. Having made such decisions and entered particular stores, consumers would then buy as many of the items on their shopping lists as were available and seemed unlikely to be cheaper elsewhere. They would purchase only the residual items in alternative stores. To the extent that this is how retailers also see things, economists should not usually see price competition on particular brands among general stores and super-markets as means of boosting net earnings on the lines in question. Rather, such competition should be seen as aimed at changing primary patronage choices on shopping expeditions (Earl, 1993).

Variations in the normal cost price

Variations in the normal cost price is one facet of the normal cost prices doctrine which has been analyzed extensively by nearly every economist who has taken the doctrine seriously. Hall and Hitch provided an explanation for why enterprises did not change their full cost prices when faced with short-term variations in the flow rate of output. Andrews built on their explanation when explaining the short-term stability of the normal cost price. He also analyzed the movement of the normal cost market price over time in conjunction with any increase in the scale of production of the price leader enterprise. Finally Andrews and other economists, such as Williams (1964u) and Sylos-Labini (1962) argued that, given the assumption of constant costing margin, changes in direct costs resulting from changes in input prices would be eventually passed through into the normal cost price. Beyond this stage of analysis of variations in the normal cost price, little has been done outside of the important work by Sylos-Labini (1962, 1967, 1971, 1974) in which he analyzed normal cost price variations when the costing margin was not assumed fixed. For example, he noted that under the usual assumptions of a given costing margin, if the market experienced a permanent increase in sales, the market price would decrease because of the economies of a larger scale of production accruing to the price-leader enterprise. However, if the change in market output disturbed the existing market share/relative cost dispersion among the enterprises in the market, then the price leader might readjust his costing margin to prevent entry or to re-arrange the existing configuration of enterprises in the market. For instance, if the price leader obtained most of the increase in market sales, only he could reduce his costs through the introduction of larger-scale methods of production. Consequently the price leader could keep the entire cost reduction as profit by increasing cm_c, and hence cm, so as to maintain the same normal cost market price. But if such an action reduced his goodwill with its customers, then cm_c, hence cm, would not be increased beyond the level which would disturb the existing goodwill and thus make entry easier. Variations in the costing margin and the market price become much more complex, Sylos-Labini also noted, if technical change was allowed to occur and to be dispersed unevenly through the market. Not only would the price leader's cost advantage be altered, i.e. cm_c changed, but the barriers to entry, cm_b would also be affected. Variations in market output and technology would thus have a multi-faceted effect on the costing margin and the market price because of the interdependency between cm_b and cm_c.

Sylos-Labini also analyzed the behavior of the normal cost price and costing margin over the trade cycle under various circumstances. He also re-examined direct cost–price variations. For example, if the enterprises in a market were subject to severe international competition, then a "national" increase in direct costs would not be completely passed through into the market price, with the result that the costing margin of the national enterprises in the market would be reduced. On the other hand, if national direct costs fell, then the result might be only a slight reduction in the market price and an increase in the enterprises' costing margins. What emerges from Sylos-Labini's extensive analysis is that understanding and explaining variations in the normal cost price is largely an empirical exercise because of all the market-specific factors which must be accounted for in order to reach any concrete conclusion. What also emerges from his analysis, and which makes it a significant development in the normal cost price doctrine, is the glimpse at the notion that the costing margin is a strategic variable for the enterprise and thus one whose behavior cannot be understood independently of the goals and objectives the enterprise hopes to achieve.

Part III

The doctrine of mark up prices

7 The origin of the doctrine of mark up prices: Michal Kalecki's microanalysis

The origins of the mark up prices doctrine is found in a bundle of ideas and theoretical arguments that Michal Kalecki put together between 1929 and 1945 to provide a foundation for his macroeconomic work on the business cycle and income distribution. The development of this foundation came in two stages – the Polish stage in which Kalecki developed a broad non-marginalist disaggregated framework and the English stage in which he inserted into the center of the framework a marginalist pricing theory. Kalecki set out his disaggregated framework with its marginalist pricing core, or his microanalysis, in articles and books, only some of which were available to the non-Polish reading economists in England; thus personal communication with his colleagues at Cambridge and Oxford was an important route through which his ideas and arguments became known. Whether through the written word or conversations over coffee, Kalecki's microanalysis became recognized as the original core of the mark up prices doctrine. Although he did not present his microanalysis in a schematic manner, it is possible to create one by starting with Kalecki's characterization of a capitalist economy and society, of industry, and of the business enterprise, then delineating his pricing theory and his analysis of the investment decision, and ending by indicating how Kalecki used his microanalysis to examine income distribution, aggregate economic activity, aggregate employment, and, in the end, cyclical growth.

A disaggregated framework: the capitalist economy

As a consequence of being introduced to Marx's economics and his two-department and three-department models at an early age, Kalecki characterized a capitalist economy in terms of categories of goods produced and social–economic classes. The productive side of the economy, Kalecki argued, could be summarized in terms of three

143

departments, one representing the production of investment goods, the second capitalist consumption goods, and the third workers' consumption goods. Moreover, each department was a self-contained productive unit in that, with a given stock of reproducible capital equipment, raw materials such as agricultural and mining products, and labor, a final good could be produced without directly requiring the goods of the other departments as inputs. Consequently, the only flow of goods between the departments which contributed to production was the flow of investment goods to the departments producing consumption goods.[1] Kalecki complemented his tripartite view of the productive structure of the economy with a class view of society. He saw capitalist society as divided into capitalists and workers, where the capitalists, who consisted of rentiers and entrepreneurs, owned and controlled the means of production and had access to finance, and the workers owned nothing but their own labor power. An important consequence of this, Kalecki argued, was that capitalists and workers had different spending patterns: workers, on the one hand, spent all their income on workers' consumption goods, thereby reproducing themselves,[2] while capitalists, on the other hand, spent only a portion of their income on capitalists' consumption goods and saved the rest to spend on investment goods. However, given the special nature of capitalist spending, what the capitalists spent from their income they received back in the form of profits, thereby reproducing the conditions which maintained them as capitalists (Kalecki, 1934a, 1934b, 1936, 1937a, 1938a, 1939a, 1939b, 1943a; Sawyer, 1985; Osiatynski, 1990, pp. 425, 439–40).[3]

[1] To describe production in this manner, Kalecki was clearly thinking in terms of a production model more explicitly developed by Fritz Burchardt (1931, 1932). Moreover, Kalecki assumed that the raw materials were, in some instances, produced outside the economy, but at other times were produced within the department in which they were used. In either case, and given Kalecki's view of the structure of production, raw materials, like labor, were primary inputs to the economy. Consequently, Kalecki nearly always included the role of raw materials (or simply materials in some cases) in the production of any good (Kalecki, 1936, 1937a, 1937b, 1938b, 1939a, 1939b, 1940, 1941a, 1941b, 1942a, 1943a; Burchardt, 1931, 1932).

[2] Kalecki did acknowledge that some workers might save some of their income, but the number of workers who saved were so few compared with the masses of workers, and the amount they saved was so insignificant compared to the savings of capitalists, he felt that workers' savings could be ignored.

[3] The assumption that workers spent what they earned, that is they did not save, was first mentioned by Kalecki in 1930. In 1932 he began an article with the assumption that society was made up of capitalists and workers only. In the same article, his capitalists spent part of their income on consumption goods and saved the rest. The following year he explicitly utilized both of these behavioral–social assumptions in *Essay on the Business Cycle Theory* (Kalecki, 1933a). The assumptions were retained in all his subsequent work

Kalecki assumed that each of the three departments of the economy contained numerous industries, each industry being a self-contained productive unit associated with a distinct final good. He further noted that there was more than one business enterprise in each industry. Finally, Kalecki argued that each industry in the economy could be described as imperfectly competitive due to the existence of market imperfections and oligopoly.[4] Using the marginalist terminology that he adopted when coming to England, he argued that market imperfections were due to positive transportation costs, sensitivity of consumers to price differences, and the lack of organized commodity exchanges which meant that each enterprise in the industry manufactured a slightly differentiated good. This by itself produced some market power for the enterprises, by which they could set their own prices even though the number of enterprises in the industry was very large. Thus, Kalecki concluded, each enterprise in an industry characterized solely by market imperfections faced its own *well defined demand curve with a determinant price elasticity of demand at each point*.[5] Oligopoly existed when the

on business cycles and income distribution. In the *Essay* he also established that, in a closed system, capitalists as a class gain in profits exactly as much as they invest or consume, again a point reiterated in his later work. Finally, in a 1934 essay, he made it clear that capitalist consumption out of profits was assumed to be constant for the analysis. Later, after reading Keynes' *General Theory*, the assumption transformed into a given propensity to consume out of profits. The last transformation was specifying capitalist consumption as consisting of an autonomous component based on past economic and social developments (and therefore given in the short term but changed slowly and proportionally with respect to profits in the long term), and a given marginal propensity to consume out of profits (Kalecki, 1930, 1932a, 1933a, 1934a, 1936, 1937a, 1937b, 1938a, 1943a, 1954, 1968a).

[4] Kalecki's dissatisfaction with the marginalist concept of free competition or perfect competition was based on the simple empirical observation that cartels and monopolies existed, on his work on cartels at the Institute for the Study of Business Cycles and Prices in Poland, and on the fact that nearly all enterprises operated at less than full capacity utilization, which (he felt) demonstrated the widespread existence of market imperfections and monopoly. Thus, in 1932 Kalecki discussed the influence of cartelization of industry on the business cycle; and as early as 1936 he implicitly assumed that the entire economy was imperfectly competitive. In 1939, he explicitly stated the assumption. This meant that raw materials which were produced and sold under conditions of free competition had to be produced outside the economy (Kalecki, 1932b, 1936, 1937a, 1938b, 1939a, 1939b; Osiatynski, 1990, pp. 426 and 433–4).

[5] Kalecki's specification of the industry is not very different from Edward Chamberlin's characterization of what he called a large group of monopolistic competitive enterprises in his *The Theory of Monopolistic Competition* (1962). Moreover, Kalecki's most detailed analysis of market imperfections occurred in an article in which he attempted to establish the conditions, using mathematical formalization (as opposed to words), under which a group supply curve existed for Chamberlin's large group of monopolistic competitive enterprises with product differentiation. Finally, it could be supposed that Kalecki

number of enterprises in the industry declined to the point where the remaining enterprises had significant control over setting and raising their own prices, and faced the problem of how their competitors would react to the price they set. Kalecki overcame this problem of interdependency, and hence the indeterminacy of the enterprise's demand curve, by positing a given degree of oligopoly for the enterprise, which took into account both the power to raise prices and the problem of interdependency.[6] Thus, in an industry characterized by both market imperfections and a given degree of oligopoly, the enterprise faced its own *well defined demand curve* specified in terms of the specific nature of the market imperfections it faced and its own degree of oligopoly.[7] Of the two demand curves, Kalecki felt that the latter was most appropriate for his work because not only was oligopoly pervasive in the economy, it was also the most dominant of the two factors determining the enterprise's demand curve (Kalecki, 1932b, 1933a, 1939a, 1940, 1942a, 1943a; Osiatynski, 1990, p. 467; Sawyer, 1985; Carson, 1993*u*).

Business enterprise, prices, and investment

Kalecki characterized the business enterprise as a self-contained productive unit consisting of a single plant producing a homogeneous good, whose capitalist owners and managers, that is the rentiers and entrepreneurs, received the profits when the output was sold. Furthermore, he classified the costs incurred in the production of the good as prime or direct costs and overhead costs.[8] Direct costs were based on the primary

---

implicitly attempted to generalize Chamberlin's heroic assumption "that both demand and cost curves for all the 'products' are uniform throughout the group." (see pp. 158–60 for further discussion) (Chamberlin, 1962, pp. 81–100; Kalecki, 1940; Carson, 1993*u*).

[6] Kalecki "defined" the degree of oligopoly in the Cambridge way, through implicit or indirect theorizing. That is, denoting the determinant marginal revenue curve of a determinant market imperfections demand curve for a specific enterprise as MR_i, the enterprise's determinant marginal cost curve as MC, and the enterprise's degree of oligopoly as DO, then Kalecki implicitly (indirectly) "defined" the degree of oligopoly as $DO = MR_i/MC > 1$. Thus two determinant variables were used to define a third variable whose purpose was to convert indeterminacy into determinacy. Consequently, the marginal revenue curve of the oligopolistic enterprise can be "determinantly" denoted as MR_i/DO, thereby implying that its demand curve is determinant as well. For a more detailed comment on Kalecki's rather subtle and slippery analysis, see Carson (1991*t*) (Kalecki, 1940, 1942a; Leontief, 1937).

[7] Kalecki's analysis of the degree of oligopoly and the enterprise demand curve was one of the outcomes of attempting to construct the conditions a supply curve would exist for Chamberlin's small group of enterprises under the conditions of oligopoly and product differentiation (Chamberlin, 1962, pp. 100–4).

[8] Kalecki began using the term "prime costs" in 1936 *after* his exposure to economics in

direct inputs used in the production and selling of the good and therefore consisted of raw material costs and labor costs, while overhead costs consisted of salaries, selling costs, depreciation, and interest charges. Finally, given the existing capital equipment, Kalecki argued that average direct costs (and hence marginal costs) were constant with respect to variations in the degree of capacity utilization up to full capacity.[9] On the other hand, since overhead costs were fixed with regard to variations in the degree of capacity utilization, average overhead costs declined as the degree of capacity utilization increased. Average total costs consequently declined as the degree of capacity utilization increased.

Given the enterprise's cost structure and its own demand curve, Kalecki proceeded to argue that the entrepreneur fixed the price for his good such that marginal cost equaled marginal revenue.[10] The difference

England. The term was introduced to British economists by Marshall in his *Principles of Economics* (1920, p. 359). However, Marshall did note that the term was equivalent to the term direct costs; and, moreover, both terms were part of the terminology used by accountants from at least the 1880s to the 1950s. Since both terms are definitionally the same, combined with the need to maintain a common terminology throughout the book, I have substituted "direct costs" for Kalecki's "prime costs."

[9] Kalecki's first arguments regarding the constancy of the average direct cost curve came in the early 1930s when he was working for the Institute for the Study of Business Cycles and Prices. Later, Piero Sraffa's observations on the lack of changes in the ratio of prices to costs with changes in output below full capacity utilization and Joel Dean's research on costs convinced him that his arguments were sound. Thus from 1938 onward Kalecki generally assumed the constancy of average direct costs for all business enterprises in the economy when their degree of capacity utilization was less than 100 percent (Osiatynski, 1991, pp. 483–4; Kalecki, 1939a, 1941b, 1942a, 1943a).

[10] Although Kalecki wrote about costs, prices, and profits in the early 1930s, he did not explicitly utilize the marginalist pricing mechanism (i.e. equating marginal cost to marginal revenue) in his discussion of prices and output until his review of Keynes' *General Theory* in 1936. When he wrote the review he had been in England a few months and had attended seminars at the London School of Economics run by Friedrich Hayek and Lionel Robbins. He utilized the marginalist pricing mechanism again in 1937 in articles on the business cycle and on commodity taxation (Kalecki, 1937a, 1937b). Finally, with his 1938 article on income distribution (Kalecki, 1938b), the marginalist pricing mechanism became the explicit cornerstone of all his subsequent discussions of prices, output, and profit through to 1945. What Kalecki did not utilize in his writings was mark up pricing procedures, although numerous contemporary economists used them to improve the logic and presentation of his microanalysis – see chapter 8 (pp. 153–64). Except for a short piece in 1942 on the excess profits tax and government contracts (Kalecki, 1942b), where he noted that contracts were given on the basis of costs plus percentage profit margin, Kalecki made no reference to enterprises setting prices using mark up pricing procedures until 1943 when he noted the pricing procedures described by Hall and Hitch. But, even then, he dismissed them with the remark that "it is not unlikely that the procedure described by them is not the actual process of fixing prices

between the price and average direct costs (including direct selling costs), Kalecki denoted as the gross profit margin (GPM), which consisted of overhead costs and profits. He then argued that, for given average direct costs (including direct selling costs), the magnitude of the gross profit margin was determined by market imperfections and the degree of oligopoly – or, for shorthand, the degree of monopoly.[11] However, he also noted that the degree of monopoly, and hence also the magnitude of the GPM, could be affected if the enterprise decided to spend more of its income on direct selling costs. Turning to the relationship between the degree of monopoly, GPM, and the price, Kalecki argued that in the short term variations in the degree of capacity utilization due to price iso-elastic shifts in the enterprise's demand curve would not affect the price, the degree of monopoly, or the GPM.[12] On the other hand, because of the existence of sticky prices over the business cycle, the degree of monopoly would vary counter-cyclically. That is, when the economy entered into a slump, wage rates and raw material prices would decline, yet entrepreneurs would attempt to avoid passing on the fall in average direct costs in the form of price cuts so as to avoid destructive price wars. In addition, cartels would become stronger because of the decline of possible new entrants, while tacit agreements to maintain prices would proliferate. Thus the overall result would be that the degree of monopoly for most business enterprises increased, thus preventing prices from declining. Conversely, during the boom the demand for higher wages, combined with higher prices for raw materials, would increase average direct costs which entrepreneurs would not be able to pass on; this would result in a decline in the degree of monopoly, thus

but only a check applied to prices fixed in another way to see whether they make any net profit" (Kalecki, 1943, p. 134) (Kalecki, 1930, 1932b, 1933a, 1933b, 1936, 1942b; Carson, 1993u).

[11] Kalecki first used the term "gross profits" in 1930, and "profit margin" in 1932. He continually used gross profits in his work, but profit margin had a more shadowy existence. In 1937 he stated that gross profits were maximized when marginal cost was equal to marginal revenue. Then, in the 1938 article on income distribution (Kalecki, 1938b), he introduced the term "degree of monopoly" but did not mention the profit margin. While the connection between the three terms appears obvious, Kalecki did not explicitly state it until 1942 when he introduced the term "gross profit margin," identified its place within the degree of monopoly formula, and argued that it was determined by market imperfections and oligopoly which constituted the degree of monopoly. Finally, in 1943 he altered the term "gross profit margin" to "gross margin" while still maintaining that it was determined by market imperfections and oligopoly (Kalecki, 1930, 1932b, 1937b, 1938b, 1942a, 1943a).

[12] This marginalist interpretation of the relationship between Kalecki's degree of monopoly, GPM, and the price was first made by Joan Robinson in a 1939 memo with which, one can assume, Kalecki was familiar (see pp. 158–60).

preventing prices from increasing. Lastly, Kalecki argued that the degree of monopoly had a tendency to increase in the long run because the secular increase in industrial concentration increased the degree of oligopoly far more than economic development reduced market imperfections (Kalecki, 1936, 1938b, 1939a, 1939b, 1939c, 1940, 1941a, 1942a, 1943a; Sawyer, 1985).[13]

In addition to fixing prices, Kalecki's entrepreneur also made investment decisions which led, at a later date, to the enterprise purchasing investment goods. Complementing the goal of maximizing profits when fixing prices, the motive for an entrepreneur to consider undertaking any investment project was its expected profitability. Kalecki argued that the entrepreneur would invest in, and hence enter, another industry if the expected rate of profit upon entry was greater than the normal rate of profit. Moreover, the factors which determined whether an investment plan was acceptable for implementation was whether its expected rate of profit was greater than the interest rate plus the risk premium. Finally, Kalecki argued that the entrepreneur accepted investment plans up to the point where the expected rate of profit of the last plan equaled the interest rate plus the risk premium. More specifically, he argued that the entrepreneur ranked the prospective investment plans in order of their diminishing expected rate of profit, although the rate at which it declined would be gradual as long as the investment plans were spread across many products. Thus with a given long-term interest rate and a gradually declining marginal expected rate of profit, there would not be a significant restriction on the number of investment plans the entrepreneur would accept and hence no reasonable limit to the size of the business enterprise. Finding this conclusion unacceptable, Kalecki introduced the "principle of increasing risk," which stated that the larger the investment in fixed plant and equipment undertaken by the entrepreneur with

---

[13] Kalecki's discussion of the stability, variability, and long-term movement of the degree of monopoly was derivative of what he considered to be the stylized facts of capitalism. In 1932, he noted that, in non-cartelized industries, profit margins fluctuated over the business cycle, whereas in cartelized industries they were constant (Kalecki. 1932b). The next year he extended the idea of constant profit margins to constant or sticky prices in monopolistic and cartelized industries. Finally, in 1935 Kalecki hinted that cartelized industries could be associated with rising profit margins, and later argued that

the degree of monopoly has undoubtedly a tendency to increase in the long run because of the progress of concentration. Many branches of industries become oligopolistic; and oligopolies are often transformed into cartels. (Kalecki, 1938b, p. 17)

Thus Kalecki did not really explain sticky prices and stable or increasing GPM; rather, he simply took them as stylized facts and "marginalized" them (Kalecki, 1933a, 1933b, 1935).

borrowed capital relative to his own capital, the greater his risk of making severe losses if the rate of profit on investment fell below the rate of interest. Thus, given the gradually declining marginal expected rate of profit and the sharply increasing degree of risk with each additional investment plan financed by borrowed capital, the total number of investment plans accepted by the entrepreneur and hence the total amount of investment undertaken would have a well defined limit, implying also a limit to the size of the individual enterprise.[14]

Since the expected rate of profit was the crucial factor determining investment decisions and the volume of investment undertaken by an enterprise at any point in time, Kalecki went on to note that it was a function of national income and the capital stock.[15] Thus, if past investment decisions were such that current national income was high then, Kalecki argued, entrepreneurs would increase their expectations about the future rate of profit for any investment plan, thus increasing the number of investment projects they found acceptable for execution. On the other hand, if the capital stock increased while national income remained fixed, then the degree of capacity utilization would decline and this would reduce entrepreneurs' expectations about the future rate of profit and the number of projects they found acceptable for execution (Kalecki, 1936, 1937a, 1939a, 1943a; Sawyer, 1985; Feiwel, 1989).[16]

Microanalysis and macroeconomics

Kalecki used his microanalysis as a prop on which to build his macro-economic theory of economic dynamics. In particular, he used it to examine the impact of changes in the degree of monopoly on the

---

[14] Kalecki also argued that the principle of increasing risk would apply to corporate enterprises as well where entrepreneurial capital was not relevant.

[15] Kalecki believed that the long-term interest rate was the relevant interest rate for affecting investment decisions. Since it varied so little over time, Kalecki argued that it could be taken as fixed and therefore could be ignored as a factor producing cyclical variations in investment decisions. Moreover, if a significant reduction in the long-term rate did occur quickly, there would be numerous undesirable consequences, one being that many financial institutions would suffer severe losses and another being that stocks, shares, bonds, land, and houses would greatly increase in value (Kalecki, 1944b; Schumacher, 1944a; Sawyer, 1985).

[16] In 1932, Kalecki stated that the incentive to invest was expected profitability, and he repeated the argument in 1933 (Kalecki, 1932a, 1933b). In 1936, he complained that Keynes did not take sufficient account of the influence of current profitability on investment. And finally in 1937 he argued that investment decisions were a function of the expected rate of profit, risk, and the interest rate. Thus, expected profitability always played the dominant role in Kalecki's views on the decision to invest (Kalecki, 1936, 1937a).

distribution of income, aggregate economic activity, and aggregate employment. As a comparative basis for his other arguments, he repeatedly noted that, given the volume of investment, economy-wide increases (or decreases) in money-wage rates would not alter the distribution of income between workers and capitalists, the workers' real wage, or the level of aggregate economic activity if the degree of monopoly for all enterprises remained fixed; all that would happen would be an increase (or decrease) in money prices sufficient to offset the increase in the money wage rate and hence any demand impact on economic activity.[17] This argument became known as the "iron law of wages." In contrast, Kalecki argued, for a given volume of investment, changes in the degree of monopoly would have an impact on the distribution of income, the workers' real wage, and aggregate economic activity. For example, if money-wage rates increased and the degree of monopoly declined so that prices did not change, then workers' real wages would increase (along with the wage share in national income), which in turn would increase the demand for workers' consumption goods, thereby increasing aggregate economic activity. In the case where technical change increased the size of the business enterprise and hence increased the degree of industrial concentration, Kalecki noted that this would increase the degree of monopoly and therefore also have a negative impact on income distribution, workers' real wages, and aggregate economic activity.

Kalecki argued that when the historical development of capitalism reached an advanced stage, there would be a significant increase in enterprise size and hence in industrial concentration. This in turn would produce a long-term permanent progressive increase in the degree of monopoly and a fall in the growth of workers' real wages and in the wage share of national income. The immediate impact would be a reduction in the rate of growth of national income, and with it a reduction in the entrepreneurs' profit expectations and hence in their investment decisions. The decline in investment would reinforce the depressive effects of the rise of the degree of monopoly on aggregate economic activity, with

---

[17] On the other hand, as Kalecki also noted, if raw material prices increased economy-wide, while money-wage rates and the degree of monopoly remained constant, the wage share in national income and the workers' real wages would decline and with it the level of aggregate economic activity. Kalecki saw the external raw materials sector as being competitive and hence governed by the Marshallian laws of supply and demand. The interaction between the competitive raw materials sector and the imperfectly competitive manufacturing economy, and the resulting impact on prices, employment and aggregate economic activity, Kalecki described in a manner quite similar to Gardiner Means, as delineated in chapter 2 (pp. 58–61) (Kalecki, 1932b, 1933a, 1935).

the consequence that the economic system would tend towards economic stagnation and its corollary of rising unemployment. In this context, Kalecki argued, the capitalist state, under political pressure to do something, would engage in deficit spending in order to directly reduce unemployment as well as to stimulate private investment. But attaining and maintaining full employment would generate a political backlash from the capitalists, in part because they would lose the power of the "sack." Thus the capitalist state would be subject to "stop–go" political pressure which would ultimately prevent it from stopping the drift towards economic stagnation and the corresponding secular increase in unemployment. Kalecki concluded that either capitalism must be fundamentally reformed if it was to be made able to sustain full employment or, if it proved incapable of adjusting to such reforms, it must be replaced (Kalecki, 1935, 1938a, 1938b, 1939a, 1939b, 1941a, 1941b, 1943a, 1943b, 1944b; Barna, 1945; Dobb, 1973; Bellamy, 1981p; Sawyer, 1985; Henley, 1988; Feiwel, 1989).

By the early 1940s, Kalecki had developed his microanalysis to the point where other economists could draw upon it for their own work, and thereby intentionally or unintentionally extend and develop it. As delineated in chapter 8, during the war years, economists linked with both Oxford and Cambridge made some significant contributions to the microanalysis and, more importantly, set the stage for the subsequent post-war developments. These post-war developments took two different but complementary paths. One involved piecemeal developments and transformation of Kalecki's microanalysis, which began in 1952 and ended in the early 1980s, by various economists, including Piero Sraffa, Geoffrey Harcourt, Peter Riach, Joan Robinson, Nicholas Kaldor, Athanasios Asimakopulos, Adrian Wood, Alfred Eichner, and Kalecki himself, and is delineated in chapter 9. The second involved the development of the microanalysis from 1945 to the early 1980s to explain why capitalist economies were prone to economic stagnation. The stagnation thesis was pursued by Josef Steindl while he was at Oxford in the 1940s and later by Sylos-Labini, Paul Baran, Paul Sweezy, Harry Braverman, and David Levine and is delineated in chapter 10.

8   Kalecki's microanalysis and the war years

Oxford

With the outbreak of war in September 1939, economic research at Oxford quickly transformed itself into war-related research. On the one hand, the OERG decided to become inactive for the duration of the war; on the other, the Oxford Institute of Statistics wound down its pre-war activities and embarked upon research which examined the impact of the war upon the various sectors of the economy. Since most of the pre-war Oxford economists had left Oxford for military service or to take up appointments in the war-time administration, it was necessary to replace them, and this meant hiring many refugees from occupied Europe. Thus a group of economists was brought to Oxford in 1940 and stayed together for most of the war. In particular, Kalecki, Steindl, Fritz Burchardt, and G. D. N. Worswick were brought together. Out of their interaction came important contributions to Kalecki's microanalysis (Young and Lee, 1993).[1]

---

[1] Both Kalecki and Worswick had no previous research connection with Oxford or the Institute of Statistics, although Worswick was an Oxford graduate with a degree in mathematics in 1937 and the Diploma in Economics and Political Science in 1938. Soon after Hitler seized power in Germany in 1933, Balliol College became active in providing a refuge for displaced German (and later Austrian) scholars. In 1938, it gave refuge to Steindl; he stayed on at Balliol as a research lecturer until 1941, and during this period he gave lectures on the economics of risk and uncertainty, economic problems of socialism, and recent publications in economic theory, as well as publishing an article on risk. After returning from internment in 1940, he became a research worker at the Institute until 1949, when he returned to Austria. Burchardt had been at Oxford as a research scholar at All Souls College since 1935 when he fled Hitler's Germany. From 1936 to 1940 he was involved with the OERG and a member of the project on public works and the trade cycle which was housed in the Institute. The interaction of Steindl, Worswick, and Burchardt with Kalecki can be gathered from the introduction to *Studies in Economic Dynamics* (Kalecki, 1943a) where Kalecki acknowledged their contribution, and the introduction to *Small and Big Business* (Steindl, 1945b) where Steindl acknowledged Kalecki's and

Kalecki had an enormous impact on his colleagues at the Institute. While this was partly due to his published writings, much of it came from long hours of discussion; Burchardt, Worswick, and Steindl utilized aspects of his microanalysis in their own work and also extended and developed what they used. In their analysis of the economics of full employment, Burchardt and Worswick drew extensively upon Kalecki's microanalysis; in fact Burchardt's delineation of the theory of effective demand was done entirely in Kaleckian terms. Burchardt's "left-Keynesian" arguments for government regulation of demand and Worswick's suggestions for avoiding inflation under full employment were drawn directly from Kalecki's own views on these issues. Of particular interest was their analysis of the impact of a change in wage rates on workers' real wages. Burchardt and Worswick started with the novel argument that under imperfect competition entrepreneurs marked up their average direct costs to set their prices.[2] Denoting the mark up as the gross profit margin, they then stated that it was determined by the degree of monopoly. Finally, Burchardt and Worswick concluded that if the degree of monopoly, and hence the mark up, remained fixed for the short-term, then any increase in the money wage rate, given the mark up pricing procedures, would result in prices increasing sufficiently to keep the real wage constant, that is the "iron law of wages" prevailed. When delineating the argument, Burchardt did not explicitly relate the pricing procedure, the mark up, or the degree of monopoly to marginalist pricing or to the price elasticity of demand; Worswick, on the other hand, felt that the mark up pricing procedures agreed closely with marginalist pricing theory of equating marginal cost with marginal revenue. Both the introduction of mark up pricing procedures and the possible questioning of the marginalist explanation of the mark up

Worswick's contribution (Young and Lee, 1993; J. Jones, 1988; *Oxford University Gazette*, 1938–41; Steindl, 1941b, 1952; Lowe, 1959).

[2] Although Kalecki had previously argued that enterprises did not use cost-based pricing procedures when setting prices (see n. 10 in chapter 7, pp. 147–8), he had changed his mind by 1944 when he stated

If, as is plausible to assume, firms fix their prices normally by "marking up" prime costs, i.e. costs of materials and wages, overheads *plus* profits increase roughly in the same proportion as prime costs. Thus, if raw material prices rise more than wages, overheads *plus* profits also increase more than wages. (Kalecki, 1944a, pp. 139–49)

In general, it could be said that as Kalecki, Steindl, Worswick, and the other economists at the Institute became more aware of the many different price-setting rules used when awarding government contracts, they became more inclined explicitly to use mark up pricing procedures in their work (Steindl, 1941a, 1942; Worswick, 1945).

represented novel and disjunctive developments in Kalecki's micro-analysis (Worswick, 1944, 1977; Burchardt, 1944).

Steindl's wartime activities at the Oxford Institute of Statistics included covering the war effort of the United States and those dominions and countries in the British Empire that made major contributions to the war. He paid special attention to the United States' war effort, on which he contributed 10 articles to the *Oxford Institute of Statistics: Bulletin* from 1942 to 1944. In other articles he wrote for the *Bulletin*, Steindl dealt with topics such as fixed prices, cost-plus and target price contracts, variations in efficiencies of business enterprises, and profit margins. In 1943, his work at the Institute took on a new direction when he became involved in the Courtauld Inquiry on the relative efficiency of small- and large-scale business enterprises. In setting up the Inquiry, the supervisory committee decided that the theoretical investigation into the optimum size of plants and enterprises should be carried out by someone from the Institute, and Steindl was given the job. Thus in October 1943 he presented a memorandum to the committee outlining his proposed research project. After setting out the theoretical issue under considera-tion, Steindl argued that it would be important to discover whether there was a systematic connection between the size of enterprises and the profit rate, the cost per unit of output, productivity of labour, profit margins, capital in relation to output, sales cost, and capacity utilization. He then went on to discuss what was meant by "large-scale economies" and some of the problems of using cost studies to demonstrate their existence; and concluded by noting the role of imperfect competition in protecting the existence of small enterprises, and mentioning efficiency, rate of profit, and risk. The committee accepted the proposal and eight months later, in May 1944, Steindl submitted to them his report entitled "Inquiry into the Size of Firms" (Steindl, 1944*m*). The committee accepted the report; however, it was unacceptable to Courtauld because he disagreed with Steindl's conclusion that oligopoly led to a reduction in the rate of technical progress. Steindl reacted to the criticism by strengthening his analysis of oligopoly and technical progress, and had the revised report published in 1945 as *Small and Big Business: Economic Problems of the Size of Firms* (Young and Lee, 1993; Steindl, 1941a, 1942, 1943*m*, 1945b, 1981*i*; Worswick, 1986*i*).

In *Studies in Economic Dynamics* (Kalecki, 1943a, p. 137), Kalecki advanced the argument that "if there is a rise in capital intensity of production and the degree of utilization does not increase, the rate of profit falls, while the percentage gross margin is stable. Working with Kalecki's microanalysis Steindl, combining the argument with (1) Ka-lecki's beliefs in the secular rise of oligopoly and that technical progress increased the degree of monopoly and (2) his suggestion that a fall in the rate of technical progress would eventually lead to economic stagnation, fashioned the proposition that the secular rise of big enterprises made possible by technical progress would paradoxically result in the long-run stagnation of technical progress. The implication of the proposition was that economic stagnation would follow. Specifically, Steindl argued that as a business enterprise increased in size (measured in terms of sales), the large-scale economies it reaped, combined with the oligopoly power it acquired, meant that its profit margin[3] expressed as a proportion of total costs increased. On the other hand, the production techniques which embodied large-scale economies were capital-intensive (i.e. had high capital–sales ratios); thus as the enterprise acquired greater large-scale economies, its degree of capital intensity would increase. Using these two arguments, Steindl then argued that the continued exploitation of new large-scale economies and newly obtained oligopoly power by the enterprise would result in an increase in its profit margin and hence in its rate of profit, despite the fact that its capital intensity had also increased. But this positive relationship between the profit margin, rate of profit, and large-scale economies was limited, in that a point would eventually be reached where, if further exploitation of scale economies occurred, the enterprise's profit rate would fall. Utilizing Kalecki's argument that an entrepreneur would continue to invest in capital-intensive techniques and reap their large-scale economies only if their introduction resulted in an increase in its rate of profit, Steindl concluded that once the enterprise approached the maximum profit rate (as indicated by a progressive decline in the rate at which its profit rate increased after the introduction of each new relatively more capital-intensive technique), the entrepreneur's desire to reduce costs by introducing even more capital-intensive techniques would decline.

To escape this potential technical stagnation, it would, in principle, be necessary to squeeze the profit margin and hence reduce the rate of profit for all enterprises; but such action, Steindl argued, would result in small business enterprises being eliminated, thus increasing the oligopoly power and hence the profit margins and profit rates of the remaining enterprises. More generally, he argued that the manufacturing sector could be divided into those less important industries which were dominated by small enterprises and those more essential industries dominated by relatively larger enterprises. The small-enterprise industries were, for

[3] Steindl defined "profit margin" as the difference between total revenue and total costs divided by total costs, where total revenue and total costs were calculated at normal output or the normal degree of capacity utilization (Steindl, 1945b, pp. 25–6).

various reasons, not conducive to technical progress, while the continuous progress of absolute and relative concentration in the large-enterprise industries, with the resulting increases in the profit margin, progressively weakened the desire of entrepreneurs to introduce new capital-intensive techniques.[4] Thus Steindl concluded that as the essential industries became more concentrated, the rate of technical progress in the capitalist economy would decline and eventually stagnate at a lower rate. By basing his proposition on Kalecki's microanalysis, Steindl contributed to a fuller characterization of the Kaleckian business enterprise, to Kalecki's analysis of entrepreneurial investment behavior, and to Kaleckian macroeconomics (Kalecki, 1941b, 1943a, pp. 135–8, 187–90, 1945; and Steindl, 1945b).

In additional to these contributions, Steindl also further articulated and developed Kalecki's principle of increasing risk.[5] He first formalized the relationship between the rate of profit received on the entrepreneur's own capital (r_e) net of interest payments, investment, and the interest rate (i):

$$r_e = g(r - i) + i$$

where r is the rate of profit on the capital invested in the enterprise and g is the gearing ratio and represents the ratio of the total amount of capital invested in the enterprise (including borrowed money and bonded debt) to the entrepreneur's capital.[6]

Next Steindl argued that according to the equation the higher the gearing ratio, given the interest rate and the rate of profit, the greater would be r_e. However, because the higher gearing ratios were due to

---

[4] Steindl noted that as enterprises grew in size the desire of entrepreneurs to introduce capital-intensive techniques could decline for a variety of other reasons as well:

The large and growing concerns, having at their disposal those means of turning their greater size to advantage, will not only use them, but they will tend, in the conditions so created, to neglect cost reduction and technical progress. They are able to acquire a greater share in the market by the buying up of existing plant. Once they have secured a substantial part of the industry's equipment they are less keen on technical progress and the replacement of old plant by new large scale plant, because this implies scrapping their own equipment. As long as industry had not reached the stage of "oligopoly," technical progress was much more likely to occur, because in a rapid expansion of an enterprise under these conditions, the equipment which was displaced and rendered valueless was largely the equipment of competitors. (Steindl, 1945b, p. 64)

[5] Burchardt contributed as well, by introducing Keynes' distinction between borrower's and lender's risk (Burchardt, 1944).

[6] Following Kalecki, Steindl defined "entrepreneurial capital" in the case of a private entrepreneur as his private capital, and in the case of a corporation as the sum of ordinary share capital and capital reserves (Steindl, 1945a).

increases in the amount borrowed and invested in the enterprise, the risk of either severe losses or very high profits rate for the entrepreneur increased. Thus an increasing gearing ratio was the basis for the principle of increasing risk.[7] Finally, Steindl used the principle of increasing risk to explain why the empirical phenomenon of small enterprises with positive incomes having higher rates of profit than large enterprises with positive income did not undermine the positive relationship between enterprise size and profit rates necessary for his technical progress stagnation argument in *Small and Big Business*. He also used the principle to help account for the growth of big business and the resulting increase in absolute and relative industrial concentration (Steindl, 1941b, 1945a, 1945b).

Cambridge

The propagation of Kalecki's microanalysis outside Oxford was tied up with the National Institute of Economic and Social Research (NIESR) and with certain Cambridge economists. In August 1938 a Cambridge committee consisting of Austin Robinson, Piero Sraffa and David Champernowne recommended to their Faculty Board a research project that would investigate the intensity of the effects of the 1930–5 Depression and the subsequent period of recovery upon various parts of the economic system in the United Kingdom. The Board approved the project, which was then submitted to the recently founded NIESR, which accepted it. Christened the "Cambridge Research Scheme," the project was supervised by a committee consisting of Sraffa, Austin Robinson, Champernowne, Richard Kahn, and Keynes, who was its chairman. The remit of the Scheme included the study of the relation of prices to costs and of employment to output in a number of industries at different dates and at different levels of activity. It was hoped that the study of these topics would throw light on the factors determining changes in real wages per head as between prosperity and depression, the operation of diminishing returns in the short period, changes in degree of monopoly, rigidities and flexibilities of prices, and other theoretical aspects of the supply curve. Kalecki was employed as the principal researcher and was assisted by numerous individuals.

Although work was carried out on the demand for imports and on retail sales, Kalecki and his assistants spent most of their time and energy from October 1938 to June 1939 compiling statistical data on prime

---

[7] Thus, for Steindl as well as for Burchardt and Kalecki, risks arose as a consequence of borrowing money from financial institutions for investment purposes.

costs, output, and proceeds of six industries: pig-iron, tobacco, ship-building, coal, cotton, and steel. This statistical work attracted much attention within Cambridge, with Joan Robinson and Richard Stone examining the concept of the degree of monopoly, Kahn and Joan Robinson pointing out the need to separate the factors determining the degree of monopoly from among those determining the ratio of proceeds to direct costs, and Kahn arguing that the real objective of the Scheme should be the theoretical and empirical construction of the industry supply curve. Joan Robinson's discussions of the degree of monopoly is of particular interest for three reasons. First, she argued strongly that the degree of monopoly was not a thing in itself but depended on market imperfections, the number of enterprises, monopoly agreements and tacit agreements, wage changes, and the state of market demand; thus a simple claim that the degree of monopoly had changed could never be the final account of what actually happened in the market. Second, Robinson discussed a constant degree of monopoly in terms of "price iso-elastic" and "output iso-elastic" shifts in individual demand curves, based on the assumptions that oligopoly effects were negligible and that enterprises maximized their profits. Lastly, she noted that in practice price was equal to average direct costs plus a conventional percentage, and this "practical" method of determining prices would have an important role in determining the degree of monopoly.[8]

When the data were presented to the committee overseeing the Scheme in the form of interim reports, Keynes and Kahn began to have serious misgivings about the entire project. For example, Keynes felt that the statistical work on retail sales by Erwin Rotbart needed a bit more work; however, he saved his most truculent criticism for Kalecki, questioning his statistics, his flair for carrying out the research, and even the aim of

---

[8] Joan Robinson also posed the question of how far the material on pricing and the degree of monopoly can be interpreted in a manner independent of marginalist assumptions. Although she was willing to entertain the possibility that pricing and the degree of monopoly could be interpreted independently of marginalism, Robinson and her Cambridge colleagues quickly discounted the possibility, as evident in the marginalist controversy, and maintained their marginalist interpretation for the next 15 years or more (Lee and Irving-Lessmann, 1992).

Many of Robinson's arguments were articulated by Oscar Lange in his review of Kalecki's *Essays in the Theory of Economic Fluctuations* (Lange, 1941). He also brought together, in a simple analytical "model," full cost pricing and Kalecki's degree of monopoly and, rejecting the price elasticity of demand definition, defined the latter in terms of the custom and competition determined full cost pricing profit mark up. Lange then went on to argue that in this re-formulation of Kalecki's degree of monopoly "we obtain a social-power theory of distribution according to which the average degree of monopoly actually determines the distribution of incomes" (Lange, 1941, p. 281).

the scheme. Kahn, for his part, when relaying Keynes' comments to Kalecki, added comments of his own and referred to some of Joan Robinson's comments on whether the ratio of proceeds to direct costs always measured the degree of monopoly. Although Kalecki and his assistants responded in detail to Keynes' and Kahn's comments, he was stung by the criticisms and so asked Kahn if he could discontinue the research and spend the rest of the year correcting the omissions and writing a theoretical interpretation of the results. Given the criticisms and Kalecki's feelings, combined with the coming of war, the research project was discontinued; however Kalecki did write up the results, which appeared in 1940 as his article on the industry supply curve summarizing his work on the project (K. Jones, 1988; Robinson *et al.*, 1938*m*; "Cambridge Research Scheme," 1938*m*; Keynes, 1939a*m*, 1939b*m*; J. Robinson, 1939*m*; Kahn, 1939a*m*, 1939b*m*; Kalecki, 1939a*m*, 1939b*m*; Osiatynski, 1991, pp. 522–6).

Although the Cambridge Research Scheme was not a complete success, it did apparently confirm in Joan Robinson's mind the importance of Kalecki's microanalysis, especially the concept of the gross profit margin, for the theoretical underpinnings of the theory of effective demand and economic growth.[9] This became evident in 1942, when the NIESR established a major research project on the distribution of the product of British industry and a committee to supervise it. The all-Cambridge economists' committee consisted of Joan Robinson, Nicholas Kaldor, Brian Reddaway, and J. R. N. Stone and they formulated the problems and issues to be investigated, while the project was carried out by Laci Rostas.[10] The core of Rostas' work concerned productivity and, secondly, its relationship to prices, profit margins, and distribution. In this latter area, Rotas took up the Cambridge agenda and carried out an empirical investigation to

discover the structure of prices, the relations of different elements of costs and, in particular, the ratio of the selling value of output to the prime costs of production in the different branches of industry and of their movement through time. (Rostas, 1948, p. 1)

which he hoped would shed light on the factors that determined prices

[9] Robinson drew upon Kalecki to interpret Marx when writing *An Essay on Marxian Economics* (J. Robinson, 1942), although Maurice Dobb felt uneasy about it. Of particular interest was that Robinson defined the gross profit margin solely in terms of the price elasticity of demand (Dobb, 1941a*m*, 1941b*m*; Flanders, 1943).

[10] The London School of Economics (LSE) was relocated to Cambridge for the duration of the war. Consequently, although Kaldor was on the staff of the LSE, he was able to develop closer contacts with the Cambridge economists; hence his inclusion with them. The project was completed in 1946, but not published until 1948.

and the distribution of the product of industry between wages and profits.[11]

As an introduction to the research, Rostas noted that the issue at hand revolved around what determined the gross profit margin. Without referring to Kalecki or Hall and Hitch, he proceeded to delineate their arguments regarding the determination of the gross profit margin. In the case of an industry characterized solely by market imperfections, Rostas accepted Kalecki's argument that the gross profit margin was determined by the price elasticity of demand. On the other hand, in the case of an industry characterized by market imperfects and oligopoly, he rejected Kalecki's claim that the business enterprise faced a uniquely determined demand curve. It was not possible to explain the gross profit margin in terms of the price elasticity of demand, except in those particular cases of price leadership, joint profit maximization, or monopoly. Turning to the Hall and Hitch case, where the determination of the gross profit margin was not based on the assumption that the enterprise tried to maximize profits, Rostas delineated two hypotheses: the first was the "fair-price policy" hypothesis where enterprises tried to fix a gross profit margin which covered overhead costs and provided a normal rate of profit on capital when operating at full capacity utilization; the second was the "conventional margin" hypothesis that gross profit margins were determined by historical factors, such as custom and tradition, rather then by any precise calculation of current costs or current market conditions.[12] Although Rostas concluded that the empirical evidence supported only the case of the price elasticity of demand determination of the gross profit margin, his survey of the various arguments was important to the subsequent development of Kalecki's microanalysis for two reasons. One was that he questioned the determinacy of Kalecki's market imperfections–oligipoly demand curve and hence the theoretrical soundness of his microanalysis, the second was that he posed a non-marginalist explanation of the gross profit margin as a counter-explanation to Kalecki's price elasticity of demand explanation of the gross profit margin (K. Jones, 1988; Rostas, 1948).

At the same time as the NIESR was undertaking its research project on distribution, the Advertising Association approached it about under-

---

[11] Not only was Joan Robinson skeptical of Kalecki's explanation of the degree of monopoly, Reddaway (1994p) was not convinced by Kalecki's explanation of its level and what caused it to change. In particular, he wanted to know whether the degree of monopoly was a true causal force, a convergence of the state of the economy, or a bit of both.

[12] Rostas also argued that conventional profit margins were used in the setting of "full cost" prices.

taking an inquiry into the economic effects of advertising. The offer was accepted and in 1943 a research project on advertising was launched under the supervision of the Cambridge-dominated advisory committee which included Kahn, Austin Robinson, Reddaway, R. F. Fowler, and Henry Clay, with Nicholas Kaldor as the primary investigator. The aim of the investigation was

> to establish the economic facts about advertising and to examine the effects of advertising, or of particular methods of advertising, on social welfare in all its aspects. (Kaldor and Silverman, 1948, p. xiii)

One of Kaldor's first activities was to write a memorandum on the economic issues connected with advertising. In it, he argued that when an enterprise was small, advertising would increase its sales so that the more the enterprise spent on advertising the greater its sales would be. Since this process of advertising-driven growth resulted in increased industry concentration, the now large enterprise found itself in an oligopolistic industry. The features of the large business enterprise were that it could take advantage of all available economies of scale, was less likely to suffer from a shortage of retained earnings, was able to borrow cheaply from financial institutions, and was capable of engaging in risky activities such as research and development. The consequence of these features, combined with its goodwill *vis-à-vis* its customers, was that the large enterprise had a significant degree of monopoly power which meant that it could set a price, p, which would exceed its own average total costs plus "normal profits", c, without attracting new competitors into the industry. The measure of the degree of monopoly would be, in this case, $(p - c)/p$ which, Kaldor noted, was different from the one based on price elasticity of demand.[13] Finally, he suggested that the large enterprise would spend the bulk of its above normal profits on advertising and other sales-producing methods to try to enlarge its share of the market relative to its competitors and on increasing its degree of monopoly power by strengthening its goodwill with its customers. However, the precise amount that the entrepreneur should spend on advertising was not theoretically determinable because of the problem of oligopolistic indeterminacy (Kaldor and Silverman, 1948; Kaldor, 1950).

By 1943, the issue of post-war full employment dominated the thinking of Oxford and Cambridge economists. Joan Robinson articulated the left-Keynesian position that full employment was not possible without common ownership of the means of production, national economic

---

[13] Kaldor never accepted Kalecki's price elasticity of demand-based degree of monopoly because he felt that the demand curve on which it was based was invalid due to its oligopolistic component (Kaldor, 1986).

planning, price controls, and (particularly) a national investment policy. The microfoundations of her arguments were drawn from Kalecki's microanalysis; thus when explaining why increasing wage rates was a false reason for unemployment, she used the same arguments as those utilized in Kalecki's "iron law of wages" argument. However, like Worswick and Burchardt, and following her previous acknowledgment of the existence of practical pricing, Robinson based her argument on mark up pricing where the gross profit margin was rigid. Moreover, since the gross profit margin directly affected employment, she carried out a campaign calling for the control of monopolies and the regulation and abolishment of cartels and other restrictive trade agreements because of their inherent tendency to set high gross profit margins. The issue of post-war full employment also caught the attention of William Beveridge. After establishing an inquiry to investigate the issue, Beveridge formed a technical committee to assist him in carrying out the inquiry. Both Joan Robinson and Kaldor were members of the committee and they pushed the view, which was widely accepted by Barbara Wootton, Frank Pakenham, and Fritz Schumacher, the other members of the committee, and became part of Beveridge's *Full Employment* report (Beveridge, 1994), that monopoly and price-fixing cartels needed to come under public control so as not to endanger full employment (J. Robinson, 1943a, 1943b, 1943c, 1943d, 1943*m*, 1945*m*; Harris, 1977; Technical Committee, 1943–4*m*).

Assisting Kaldor in his work for Beveridge on the quantitative aspects of full employment was Tibor Barna. Although primarily a statistician, Barna had a good understanding of economics, due partly to his association with Kaldor and Joan Robinson on Beveridge's study. As a result he accepted some of Kalecki's theories as mediated by Robinson. After the completion of the Beveridge inquiry, Barna wrote a pamphlet for the Fabian Society on the stability of the share of wages in national income and its relation to full employment (Barna, 1945). To explain the microfoundations of this stability, Barna adopted Kalecki's micro-analysis, with two important contributions.[14] The first, following on from Robinson, Burchardt, and Worswick, was the use of mark up pricing procedures in that enterprises set their prices by marking up average direct costs, where the mark up or the gross profit margin was to cover overhead costs and profits. The second was a clear delineation of the left-Keynesian economic policy implications associated with a stable

---

[14] Barna also noted that in the absence of imported raw materials, all prices could be completely resolved in wages and profits. Robinson had earlier explicitly made the same argument (Robinson, 1943d).

wage share, mark up pricing and a rigid gross profit margin. In particular, Barna argued that the "iron law of wages" property of mark up pricing meant that direct action by the state in reducing gross profit margins and prices or maintaining prices while wage rates increased was necessary if real wages were to increase and full employment were to be reached and maintained. Moreover, he suggested that, since higher prices were not necessarily the consequence of higher wage rates but rather the results of entrepreneurs maintaining rigid gross profit margins, state action to control and reduce profit margins was necessary if inflation was to be avoided. Thus it was the control of the gross profit margin rather than wages that was the essential micro key to full employment (Barna, 1945, 1990p; Bellamy, 1981p).

9 Kalecki and the Cambridge contributions

There were numerous references to Kalecki's microanalysis during the early post-war years. In general, they summarized Kalecki's pricing analysis and its relation to private enterprise and profits, income distribution, and price policies. Although no significant theoretical developments occurred at this time, the economists generally interpreted Kalecki's degree of monopoly in terms of price elasticity of demand, while at the same time noting that it was an intermediate concept which was based on a range of more basic influences. Moreover, economists continued to discuss the relationship between Kalecki's pricing analysis and full cost pricing, which led to considerable progress towards formalizing the monopoly–full cost pricing model. Finally, there were various comments throughout the period, and on both sides of the Atlantic, to the effect that enterprises preferred satisfactory or reasonable profits, sought security, and did not aim for profit maximization; that enterprises' pricing policies produced empirically stable gross profit margins; that marginal cost curves were mostly linear and deviated little from average direct costs; and that oligopoly conditions undermined the determinant nature of the enterprise demand curve. This interlude in the development of the mark up prices doctrine had come to an end by the early 1950s. Although there was the publication of Kaldor's memorandum on advertising (Kaldor, 1950) and Ron Hieser's analysis of the degree of monopoly (Hieser, 1952), the development of Kalecki's microanalysis did not really begin until 1954 with the publication of *Theory of Economic Dynamics* (Kalecki, 1954). After Kalecki's piecemeal revision, numerous economists associated with Cambridge, England, further revised and developed his microanalysis, concentrating on its representation of production, pricing and the degree of monopoly, and on investment decisions (Dunlop, 1944; Rothschild, 1947; Tsiang, 1947; Rostow, 1948; T. Wilson, 1948; Cheek, 1949; Streeten,

1949; Phelps Brown and Hart, 1952; Keirstead, 1953; Lee, 1984b; Lee and Irving-Lessmann, 1992).

The theory of economic dynamics and after

Although Kalecki turned his attention to the economics of socialist and developing economies in the post-war years, he did revise and develop various aspects of his microanalysis in *Theory of Economic Dynamics* (Kalecki, 1954) and in subsequent articles on economic growth and the distribution of income. He continued to utilize his Burchardt-type three-department model of a capitalist economy where each of the three departments production was fully integrated, starting with raw materials and labor and ending with final goods, and there were only inter-department flows of investment goods. Consequently, Kalecki increasingly ignored intermediate manufactured goods and concentrated more of his attention on the prices, production, and competitive conditions of final investment and consumption goods industries. He also continued to argue that each industry in the economy could be described as imperfectly competitive due to the existence of market imperfections and oligopoly, and that each enterprise in the industry produced a differentiated good and therefore possessed some degree of market power, and that average direct costs were constant. In addition, Kalecki slightly modified his analysis of the entrepreneurial investment decision by adding the arguments that investment decisions were an increasing function of savings and profits instead simply of national income; that the distribution of some profits to rentiers in the form of dividends had a negative influence on investment decisions; that innovations had a positive influence upon the decision to invest, comparable to an increase in profits; and that the expected rate of profit of the last investment plan equaled the standard or normal rate of profit.[1] Finally, Kalecki repeated his pre-1954 arguments regarding the effects of changes in the degree of monopoly on the distribution of income, aggregate economic activity, and aggregate employment, but also introduced a new argument for the tendency of capitalist economies to drift towards economic stagnation. Acknowledging the importance of innovation for economic growth, Kalecki argued that in its later stages, the entrepreneurs of a capitalist economy would experience a decline in the intensity of innovations due to the emergence of assembly industries, to the diminishing importance of opening up new sources of raw materials, and to the increasingly monopolistic character of capitalism. As a result, they would become

---

[1] Kalecki also introduced for the first time an analysis of investment in inventories.

relatively more disinclined to approve investment decisions (Kalecki, 1954, 1968a, 1968b, 1968c, 1971).[2]

The changes that Kalecki made in his microanalysis centered primarily on his analysis of price determination and the degree of monopoly. In particular, he ceased to state explicitly that the business enterprise faced its own well defined demand curve, even though at times he carried out his analysis of price formation as if the enterprise demand curve actually existed.[3] Moreover, as noted previously, Kalecki was aware that enterprises used mark up pricing procedures, that his Oxford colleagues had introduced such procedures into his microanalysis, and that various economists were explicitly modeling his marginalist explanation of price determination in terms of a mark up pricing equation. However, in *Theory of Economic Dynamics* he did not rely on mark up pricing procedures when stating how enterprises determined their prices; rather he simply stated that the enterprise would take into consideration its average direct costs and the prices of its competitors while ignoring its overhead costs when setting its price. Kalecki eventually rejected this imprecise description of price-setting by the late 1960s at the very end of his life, when he began describing price determination by the business enterprise in terms of mark up pricing procedures:

Each firm in an industry arrives at the price of its product p by "marking up" its direct costs u, consisting of average costs of wages plus raw materials, in order to cover overheads and profits. (Kalecki 1971, p. 99)

Finally, Kalecki introduced an industry price equation into his micro-analysis. Although each enterprise in the industry produced a differentiated good and set a different price, he argued that they could each be represented in terms of a price equation which had as a common denominator the average industry price. The industry price equation was then derived from an aggregation of the individual enterprises' price equations. At this point, Kalecki argued that the industry price equation could then be used to examine the impact of changes of individual enterprises' prices on the average industry price and hence on the economy as a whole. Thus the industry price equation connected the

[2] Kalecki also noted that a secular trend towards larger dividend pay-outs also contributed to the tendency for capitalist economies to drift towards stagnation (Kalecki, 1954).

[3] Given that by 1954 Steindl had rejected the concept of price elasticity of demand, Rostas, Kaldor, Chamberlin, and many other economists rejected the existence of a determinant enterprise demand curve under conditions of oligopoly, and the lack of empirical evidence that enterprises set their prices by reference to price elasticity of demand or to maximize profits, it is not surprising that Kalecki stopped using the term in his writings (Feiwel, 1975, pp. 472–3n.).

micro activity of the individual enterprise to its macroeconomic outcomes.[4]

Kalecki subjected his analysis of the degree of monopoly to ambiguous changes which did not, however, have any effect on his arguments for the relationship between the degree of monopoly, GPM, and the price for short-term variations in the degree of capacity utilization, over the business cycle, or in the long run. Since he did not explicitly state that the business enterprise faced its own well defined demand curve, Kalecki did not argue that when determining its prices, the enterprise attempted to maximize its profits, although his description of what the entrepreneur would consider when selecting a price could easily be interpreted as attempting to do precisely that. Consequently, he made no reference to the price elasticity of demand as a determinant of the degree of monopoly. Instead, responding to Joan Robinson's criticism that the degree of monopoly was a derivative concept encapsulating the impact of more fundamental economic forces, Kalecki went behind his usual phrase of "market imperfections and degree of oligopoly" to identify industrial concentration, sales promotion, the ratio of overhead costs to direct costs, and trade union power as the fundamental factors which determined the magnitude and changes in the magnitude of the degree of monopoly and hence determined the GPM and the ratio of price to average direct costs.[5] Later, when he described price determination in terms of mark up pricing procedures, Kalecki adapted his previous arguments and argued that the mark up was determined by the degree of monopoly. But he did not take the next step of grounding the degree of monopoly, and hence the mark up, in all the major fundamental factors noted above. Instead Kalecki repeated his pre-1954

---

[4] Prior to 1954, Kalecki utilized industry supply curves or derived industry gross profit margins to establish a causal connection between the activities of the individual enterprise and macroeconomic outcomes. He later modified his (1954) industry price equation by replacing it with a system of individual enterprise price equations and an average industry price. Peter Kriesler (1987) has strongly argued that Kalecki's concept of industry was poorly developed and thus vitiates his analysis of price determination at both the enterprise and the industry level; on the other hand, Liliana Basile and Neri Salvadori (1984–5) and John Carson (1994) have examined whether the system of equations has a unique solution. While their arguments are of interest, they have in fact missed the real theoretical importance of Kalecki's (1954) industry price equation: it was the handle by which economists were able to integrate Kalecki's microanalysis with the Sraffian price model (see below).

[5] Kalecki initially attempted to delineate the fundamental economic forces that determined the degree of monopoly in 1939–40. It is also of interest to note that in 1952 Robinson argued that the impact of increasing monopoly on the degree of thriftiness could be counteracted by the emergence of powerful trade unions (Kalecki, 1940, 1941a; J. Robinson, 1952; also see J. Robinson, 1956, 1957, 1965).

arguments that the degree of monopoly was determined by market imperfections and the degree of oligopoly, and then argued that class struggle mediated through trade union activity could affect the degree of monopoly and, more broadly, its economic environment. Examples of the latter would be, Kalecki suggested, trade unions pushing for price controls or a profit tax used to subsidize the prices of wage goods (Kalecki, 1954, 1968a, 1968b, 1968c, 1971; Feiwel, 1975; Jossa, 1989; Carson, 1993u).[6]

Production as a circular process

Of the production schemes utilized by economists in the 1930s, one of the most common was the "one-way street" associated with the Austrian economists. Production, in this scheme, begins with original non-produced inputs, usually labor and raw materials, and continues through various intermediate stages to the eventual production of final consumption goods. The defining feature of the scheme is that the intermediate capital goods used for further production were not themselves produced by capital goods at a later stage in the production process. A second and less popular production scheme was the one advocated by Fritz Burchardt. He argued that the stock of fixed capital goods necessary for production in a capitalist economy could be maintained and expanded only within the context of circular production where they acted as their own inputs. On the other hand, Burchardt felt that the one-way street captured very well the role of working capital in production. He therefore concluded that the latter should be integrated with the former in order to depict the maintenance and reproduction of fixed capital which ensured the one-way flow of working capital from original resources to final consumption and capital goods (Burchardt, 1931, 1932; Nurske, 1935; Clark, 1984b).

Although the Burchardt model of production was different from the Austrian one-way street model of production and Kalecki clearly utilized the Burchardt model, those economists who dealt with Kalecki's work in the 1940s failed to see the distinction and utilized the Austrian model in their analysis.[7] The failure to see the distinction was often repeated in the post-1954 Keynes–Kalecki-inspired analysis of growth and distribution.

---

[6] Given Kalecki's pre-1954 description of the determination of the degree of monopoly and the fact that his 1971 mark up pricing equation was mathematically equivalent to his 1940 marginalist pricing equation, Carson may well be correct that Kalecki's formal analysis of price determination was marginalist to the end (Carson, 1993u; Basile and Salvadori, 1984–5; but, for an opposing view, see Kriesler, 1987).

[7] See for example, Barna (1945) and Tsiang (1947).

Many economists remained faithful to the Burchardt production model underlying Kalecki's microanalysis, while others utilized the Austrian model. But neither group critically considered whether the production model they were using was deficient in its representation of production.[8] For example, in the 1930s Hugh Gaitskell argued that circular production occurred among intermediate or working capital goods as well as among investment goods, and that in a circular production model it was not possible to reduce intermediate goods to dated quantities of original inputs. Therefore he concluded that circular production and the inter-industry flow of intermediate and investment goods were the ultimate data of the economic system. Gaitskell also noted that the most basic circular production model was one in which a single good was produced and used directly in its own production – that is, what later became known (following Piero Sraffa) as a "corn model" (Gaitskell, 1936, 1938). At the same time Wassily Leontief developed his multi-industry input–output model in which only the flows of intermediate goods were present (Leontief, 1941, 1991). In light of these theoretical and empirical criticisms, the Burchardt production model was modified to include circular production and explicit inter-industry flows of intermediate capital goods and to include more than three sectors (Screpanti, 1993; Kurz and Salvadori, 1995).

The most significant contributions to the development of the circular production model were made by Piero Sraffa when he developed his corn model to explain Ricardo's theory of value and later when he developed his circular production multi-industry price model. In particular, Sraffa confirmed Gaitskell's (and Leontief's) argument that in a circular production model intermediate goods could not be entirely reduced to dated quantities of labor because a commodity residual existed; introduced the distinction between basic and non-basic goods with regard to production and inter-industry flows of goods; and grounded the existence of positive prices and profit rates in the production of surplus goods over what was used up in production. Most importantly, he developed a multi-industry price model whose individual industry price equations bore a close resemblance to mark up

---

[8] The former group of economists included J. Robinson (1952, 1956, 1960, 1962), Kaldor and Mirrlees (1962), Kregel (1973), Asimakopulos and Burbidge (1974), Asimakopulos (1975a, 1977), Halevi (1978), Rowthorn (1981); and the latter group includes Kaldor (1958, 1959), Davidson (1960), D. Harris (1974). Both groups also assumed integrated industries or business enterprises, thereby merging all the stages of production. Again, neither group critically considered whether integrated industries and enterprises adequately reflected economic reality. However, the assumption did permit them to use labor-based pricing equations.

pricing equations and to Kalecki's industry price equation.[9] Hence only a short step was needed to integrate Sraffa's circular production price model with the Kaleckian pricing model, thereby transforming the production schema underlying Kalecki's microanalysis (Sraffa, 1951, 1960).[10]

Although hinted at by Robinson, the first step in this direction was undertaken by Geoffrey Harcourt (1965), when he combined a corn model with a non-basic good and mark up pricing to examine the issues of income distribution and employment in the short run. Then Sylos-Labini argued that non-uniform rates of profits due to differential degrees of monopoly could be easily incorporated in Sraffa's price model (Sylos-Labini, 1971); his arguments were subsequently supported by Alessandro Roncaglia (1978) and Ian Steedman (1977). Later Lynn Mainwaring (1977), applied mark up pricing with differential profit mark ups to a corn model with a non-basic good and ran that model alongside a Sraffian price model with differential rates of profit. Finally, beginning in the middle 1970s various economists began inserting mark up and normal cost pricing equations directly into Sraffian price models in order to produce an alternative Post Keynesian model of general equilibrium, to examine wage–price spirals, and to examine the conditions under which actual prices in the market converged to long-period prices. Consequently, by the early 1980s the integration of the Sraffian circular production model with mark up (or normal cost) pricing equations had been completed, laying the foundation for a model of general microeconomic analysis (Robinson, 1956, 1962, 1965; Moss, 1976; Nikaido and Kobayashi, 1977; Boggio, 1980; Kotz, 1982; Eichner, 1983; Vicarelli, 1984; Semmler, 1984; Sawyer, 1985; Lee, 1985).[11]

---

[9] Sraffa delineated his industry price equation in terms of a profit mark up on circulating material inputs plus labor inputs, whereas Kalecki depicted his industry price equation in terms of a gross profit mark up on average direct material and labor costs (suitably weighted). In both cases, the profit mark up was applied to costs determined at the level of the industry. Thus, the merging together of the two industry price equations involved the relatively simple task of specifying the appropriate industry level average material and labor costs to be used.

[10] Both Robinson and Kaldor utilized corn models and multisector circular production models in their work on economic growth in the 1950s and early 1960s. Although they discussed prices, neither actually developed an explicit and formal link between such models and cost-plus pricing equations during this period (J. Robinson, 1952, 1956, 1962; Kaldor, 1957, 1958).

[11] Willi Semmler (1984) also developed a pricing model which integrated a Sraffian circular joint-production model with mark up pricing.

Pricing and the degree of monopoly

Because of the ambivalent manner with which Kalecki dealt with the concepts of enterprise demand curve and profit maximization, he left his analysis of price determination, and indeed his microanalysis open to various interpretations. Nearly simultaneously with the publication of *Theory of Economics Dynamics*, Ashok Mitra published a small book in which he re-examined the concept of degree of monopoly (Mitra, 1957). Basing his analysis on Kalecki's pre-1945 writings, he reiterated Joan Robinson's point that the degree of monopoly was based on the price elasticity of demand, which itself was a synthetic concept derived from fundamental "pure" data, such as wage rates, raw material costs, technical factors of production, slope of the demand curve, and the volume of aggregate output. Although believing that his analysis was firmly located within the marginalist framework, Mitra's analysis did open the possibility that the degree of monopoly could be based on fundamental data that could themselves be interpreted in a non-marginalist manner. Thus the implication of Kalecki's ambivalent position towards demand curves and profit maximization, and Mitra's concern with fundamental data, was that the degree of monopoly and indeed Kalecki's microanalysis could be interpreted and developed either along neoclassical or non-neoclassical lines.

The economists who opted for the neoclassical interpretation of Kalecki's microanalysis argued or implied that *Theory of Economic Dynamics* remained firmly within the marginalist framework of his pre-1954 writings. They particularly argued that enterprises set prices to maximize profits and that the degree of monopoly and hence the gross profit margin was determined by the price elasticity of demand along with market share and collusion.[12] However, others with a more heretical bent of mind quickly argued that in *Theory of Economic Dynamics* Kalecki had dropped the price elasticity explanation of the degree of monopoly and hence the assumption of profit maximization. Kaldor argued that in *Theory of Economic Dynamics* Kalecki had abandoned the link between the degree of monopoly and the price elasticity of demand and simply defined the ratio of price to average direct costs as the degree of monopoly (Kaldor, 1956). He then deprecated Kalecki's tautological approach to analyzing the relation between prices and costs and suggested that it needed to be grounded in market relationships, such as

---

[12] See for example, Reder (1959), Rothschild (1961), Nuti (1970), Bronfenbrenner (1971), Dobb (1973), Johnson (1973), McFarlane (1973), Cowling (1982), and Sawyer (1982a, 1985).

cross-elasticities of demand.[13] Four years later, Paul Davidson argued, in a similar vein, that Kalecki had abandoned his marginalism in 1954 and simply defined the degree of monopoly as the ratio of price to average direct costs (Davidson, 1960). Finally, Sydney Coontz simply asserted that Kalecki maintained the position that monopoly power in modern capitalism was such as to ensure a fixed mark up over average direct costs so that the ratio of total revenue to total costs at the industry was constant (Coontz, 1965).

But it was Peter Riach's (1971) analysis of the degree of monopoly in that it was pivotal in making economists aware that Kalecki's (1954) analysis could be plausibly interpreted as a "short-run" non-marginalist behavioral relationship between price and average direct costs. In particular, Riach argued that Kalecki's attempt to ground the degree of monopoly in the more fundamental independent longer-run economic forces of market concentration, sales promotion, ratio of overhead costs to direct costs, and trade union power constituted a non-marginalist explanation that was amenable to empirical testing. That is, changes in the short-run relationship between price and average direct costs could be explained in terms of changes in the degree of monopoly that arose from changes in one or more of the fundamental economic forces. Riach's argument became accepted by numerous economists (see citations below), with the result that his non-marginalist explanation of the degree of monopoly had become an accepted component of the mark up prices doctrine by the early 1980s. This is clearly evident, for example, in Peter Reynolds' examination of the degree of monopoly (Reynolds, 1980u, 1983, 1984a) where he essentially reiterated Riach's arguments but couched them in the more pregnant expression of environmental/ institutional factors, while at the same time extending them to include economies of scale and diversification (Ferguson, 1969; Harcourt, 1972; D. Harris, 1974, 1978; Asimakopulos, 1975a; Feiwel, 1975, 1989; King and Regan, 1976; Mainwaring, 1977; J. Robinson, 1977; Reynolds, 1980u, 1984a, 1987; Semmler, 1984; Seccareccia, 1984; Kriesler, 1987).

The drawback to the Riach–Reynolds explanation of the degree of monopoly was that it did not explain the process by which the business enterprise decided upon the mark up it used when setting prices. However, at the same time as the Riach–Reynolds explanation was being

---

[13] In his writings on economic growth, Kaldor utilized the concept of a long-term minimum profit margin, which he also called "degree of monopoly." He argued that it was determined by competition under conditions of less than full employment and by the level of aggregate demand (and hence investment) at full employment. In either case, the profit margin/degree of monopoly was not based on the price elasticity of demand (Kaldor, 1956, 1957, 1958, 1959; Kaldor and Mirrlees, 1962; Riach, 1969).

articulated, a different longer-term enterprise-specific explanation arising from the growth theory work of Robinson and Kaldor was being developed. Beginning in the late 1930s, Joan Robinson began work on economic growth by trying to generalize the *General Theory* to the long period. This involved synthesizing ideas from both Keynes and Kalecki (as well as Roy Harrod). Hence her analysis of economic growth was grounded in part on the Keynes–Kalecki view that investment generated the profits that it required; consequently, investment decisions were closely related to the accumulation of gross profits. This view was also quite similar to Steindl's argument that, under oligopoly, investment decisions were based primarily upon the volume of internal accumulation of funds out of current profits. Robinson therefore stressed the role of the profit margin in affecting economic growth. In particular, starting in 1952 she argued that the degree of monopoly could be measured by the ratio of the gross profit margin to average direct cost, but did not claim that it was determined by the price elasticity of demand (J. Robinson, 1952). Rather, she hinted that it was determined by the investment needs for steady-state growth.

Over the next decade, Robinson developed the point in more detail, but failed to clearly connect the profit margin required for growth to pricing by the business enterprise. Instead she articulated the doctrine of the "subjective normal price" based on mark up pricing procedures, where the mark up for gross profit or the gross profit margin was calculated to cover overhead costs, depreciation, and the ruling rate of profit when the enterprise was operating at normal capacity utilization. The magnitude of the mark up was conditioned, Robinson argued, by the ruling degree of competition and the rate of investment. Thus, when comparing the effects of different investments, she concluded that the greater the rate of investment, the greater the gross profit mark up, subjective-normal prices, and the rate of profit (J. Robinson, 1956, 1957, 1960, 1962, 1969a, 1969b, 1969a*m*, 1969b*m*).[14] However, by 1970 she had begun to note that price leaders when setting prices would directly adjust their profit mark up in the light of the profits needed to finance their planned investment projects. But the explicit linking of the profit mark up to investment was carried out by others (Kalecki, 1943a,

---

[14] Robinson also argued that, for a given degree of competition and rate of investment, the resultant magnitude of the gross profit mark up would eventually become accepted by entrepreneurs as conventional. Thus, if money-wage rates increased, the entrepreneurs would maintain the existing mark up, resulting in prices increasing and real wages remaining constant. Therefore, the Kaleckian "iron law of wages" was due, Robinson argued, to the rate of investment being unaffected by changes in money-wage rates rather than by the pricing decisions of entrepreneurs.

1954; J. Robinson, 1970, 1970a*m*, 1970b*m*, 1971a*m*, 1971b*m*, 1971c*m*, 1971, 1974*m*, 1977; Eichner, 1970b*m*, 1971a*m*; Kregel, 1971; Hamouda, 1991).

In 1952, Ron Hieser wrote an article extending Kaldor's analysis of the degree of monopoly power (Hieser, 1952). Accepting Kaldor's suggestion that monopoly power was present only when the enterprise's entry-preventing price was greater than its average total costs plus normal profits, he argued that the "monopoly" profit margin, $p - c$, was a function of three barriers to entry – economies of scale, cost of marketing, and secret or patented techniques of production.[15] However, Kaldor did not incorporate Hieser's contributions into his writings on economic growth. Instead, he focused his attention on the business enterprise and the concept of a minimum profit margin which, he argued, would determine the lowest price an enterprise would set but did not necessarily set the price, especially in the context of full employment. In the short term the profit margin, Kaldor argued, was relatively stable and took on the characteristic of being customary and hence historically determined, but was ultimately determined by long-term investment requirements and savings propensities.[16] However, in the long term, under conditions of full employment, it was "thermostatically" tied to the level of aggregate demand and hence to investment (Kaldor, 1956, 1957, 1958, 1959; Kaldor and Mirrlees, 1962; Riach, 1969; Kregel, 1971; D. Harris, 1974).

Issues of economic growth, administered prices, full cost pricing, ownership and control, and the motivation of the business enterprise were popular with economists in the 1960s. Thus, even without Robin-son's and Kaldor's particular approach towards growth theory, the idea that there was a link between investment, pricing, and the profit mark up was certainly an issue economists were concerned about. Illustrative of this general concern was James Ball's analysis of the profit mark up

---

[15] Hieser's work on Kaldor's degree of monopoly and barriers to entry was quite far ahead of any work being done at the time. He also wrote an interesting review (Hieser, 1954) of Steindl's book *Maturity and Stagnation in American Capitalism* (Steindl, 1952). However, this promising academic beginning was not maintained and he slowly faded away. Hieser was born in 1921, was a member of the Australian army in the Second World War, obtained his undergraduate degree and masters degree in economics in 1949 and 1953, respectively from the University of Adelaide, and wrote his master's thesis on "The Degree of Monopoly and the Theory of Value" (Jennings, 1991*p*).

[16] Kaldor argued that the

long-term investment requirements and savings propensities are the underlying factors which set the standard around which these customary levels are formed, and which are responsible for the gradual levels are formed, and which are responsible for the gradual change of these levels in any particular economy. (Kaldor, 1957, p. 298)

(Ball, 1964).[17] Ball acknowledged that business enterprises utilized mark up pricing procedures to set prices which they administered to the market and kept stable for the short term. He also accepted the popular view at the time that enterprises were interested in long-term growth in sales instead of short-term maximum profits. Ball argued that, since investment in fixed capital was necessary if enterprises were to experience a growth in sales, a relationship between price and investment decisions therefore was essential.[18] To establish this point, he first assumed that the enterprise retained a fixed proportion v of its profits P as retained earnings and that it financed all investment in fixed capital out of retained earnings, that is $I = vP$.[19] He then argued that the enterprise based its investment plans on its expected long-term growth rate of sales g; so, given the incremental capital–output ratio x, the amount of investment the enterprise needed to undertake was

$$I = g \times Q$$

where Q was output. Finally, since total profits equaled the profit mark up times total costs, the volume of planned investment determined the mark up, which in turn was determined by the expected growth rate in sales.[20] Ball concluded his analysis by noting that, with price policies and investment plans made in conjunction with long-term expectations of

[17] Also see Cyert and George (1969).

[18] As Ball acknowledged, Jack Downie had reached the same conclusion six years earlier:

> the rate of profit which a firm earns will, given its costs and capital employed, depend on the prices which it charges. And the rate at which its market will be growing will also depend on its prices. Both the means to finance new capacity and the market to employ it will, therefore, vary, in opposite directions, with the prices it charges. And there will be some level of prices at which the rates of growth of capacity and the market price are equal ... I shall call the level of prices at which the firm's capacity and market are equal and increasing in step the equilibrium. (Downie, 1958, pp. 66–7)

[19] Ball recognized that enterprises might also use external sources to help finance investment projects.

[20] Ball's argument can be set out in the following set of relationships:

$$P = r[(Q)(ATC)] \tag{1}$$

$$I = vP = vr[(Q)(ATC)] \tag{2}$$

$$g \times Q = I = vr[(Q)(ATC)] \tag{3}$$

$$\frac{g = vr[ATC]}{x}. \tag{4}$$

So given, v, x, and ATC (which Ball assumed to be constant), the expected growth rate of sales decided by the enterprise determines the amount of investment to be undertaken and hence financed out of retained earnings, which in turn determines the profit mark up r.

future growth in sales, short-term variations in sales would not prompt the enterprise to alter its price or investment plans, hence resulting in the observed phenomena of stable, short-term, non-market-clearing prices.

Robinson's and Kaldor's work on economic growth inspired two different approaches to linking investment, pricing, and the profit mark up. The Robinsonian approach minimized the role the enterprise and ignored the role of finance in determining its mark up, while the Kaldorian approach placed greater emphasis on both these factors in determining the mark up. The former approach is represented by the work of Athanasios Asimakopulos, while the latter is represented by Jan Kregel, Harcourt, Peter Kenyon, Adrian Wood, and Alfred Eichner. In 1969 Asimakopulos wrote an article recasting Robinson's analysis of economic growth in terms of a one-sector growth model. Since the growth model was based on a Burchardt production model, he argued that production involved both direct and overhead labor and that labor-based mark up pricing prevailed. Asimakopulos then showed that if all plants were operating at full capacity utilization, the mark up for gross profit was a function of the rate of investment and thriftiness while the rate of profit was a function of the rate of accumulation. If, on the other hand, there existed under-utilized capacity, the mark up was determined by the existing degree of monopoly and was related to a customary rate of profit at an average degree of capacity utilization.[21] Extending this latter point in an exposition of a Kaleckian theory of income distribution, Asimakopulos argued that the enterprise included in the gross profit mark up the target rate of return which it used when formulating its long-range investment plans. Consequently, an increase in the degree of monopoly due to an increase in industrial concentration, for example, would result in the mark up increasing, and hence in an increase in the actual rate of return experienced by the enterprise. The higher actual rate of return would, in turn, encourage the enterprise to increase its target rate and this would increase the number of investment projects to be implemented. By tying the target rate of return to the mark up, and hence to the price, the enterprise, he argued, was able to generate the profits needed to finance its investment plans (Asimakopulos, 1969, 1970, 1975b, 1977, 1978, 1980–1; Asimakopulos and Burbidge, 1974; D. Harris, 1974; Reynolds, 1983).

Although Asimakopulos linked investment decisions to a component

---

[21] This point was initially made by Joan Robinson (J. Robinson, 1969a, 1969b). Two years later Riach argued that, since the corporate business enterprise formulated long-term planning and profit objectives in terms of profit on invested capital, Kalecki's degree of monopoly could be reinterpreted as determining the desired rate of profit (Riach, 1971).

of the gross profit mark up, the determinants of the mark up were still located outside the enterprise in its environment/institutional milieu. A second – (less Robinsonian and more Kaldorian) – attempt to link the profit mark up to investment decisions was carried out by Kregel (1971). When examining the generality of the assumptions underlying the treatment of profit rates and distribution in Robinson and Kaldor growth models, he noted that an increase in an enterprise's degree of monopoly resulted in higher prices and greater gross profits; that the enterprise could adjust its distribution of profits between dividends and retained earnings; and that the enterprise used retained earnings to finance its investment plans. Assuming the Robinsonian link between investment decisions and profit rates, Kregel suggested that, for a given rate of investment, an increase in the enterprise's degree of monopoly would permit it to increase its dividend pay-out ratio as well as its gross profit margin so as to generate the retained earnings necessary to fund its investment plans. But a higher gross profit margin also increases the rate of profit, which in turn stimulates a higher rate of investment. This complex and at times opaque interplay between gross profit margins, retained earnings, profit rates, and investment decisions implies that a more direct relationship between investment decisions, financing those decisions, and profit mark ups could be articulated.

Kregel subsequently addressed this point in his book on Post Keynesian economics (Kregel, 1973). He argued that the enterprise would attempt to ensure that its actual rate of capacity utilization tended to hover around its targeted normal rate of capacity utilization. Therefore, when the enterprise expected its actual rate significantly to exceed the normal rate, it would formulate and then implement investment plans to correct the imbalance. It would then determine the magnitude of the profit mark up such that the accrual of profits would be sufficient to finance the investment project. The profit mark up and the price were thus linked, Kregel argued, to the enterprise's expectations about the future and the rate of investment that it thought it would be profitable to carry out. The implication of this investment-based pricing strategy was that short-term changes in sales would be accommodated by changes in actual capacity utilization, not by changes in price or investment plans.[22]

A third attempt to link the profit mark up to investment decisions primarily along Kaldorian lines was carried out by Harcourt (1972).

---

[22] Kregel also noted that a multi-product enterprise would pursue various pricing strategies, possibly related to the life-cycle of each product, so that the composite decisions over all the profit mark ups would generate profits sufficient to finance its various investment projects. The projects would include increasing the productive capacity of the existing products at different rates as well as introducing new products.

Although Kaldor grounded his growth models in the behavior of business enterprises, especially with regard to pricing and investment behavior, he did not clearly specify the short-term relationship between pricing, the profit margin, and investment that was necessary for them to work. In the early 1960s, Harcourt undertook a study of Kaldor's work on the trade cycle, income distribution, and growth theory (Harcourt, 1963). He paid particular attention to the long-term flexible profit margin, arguing that it must also be flexible and thermostatically tied to investment in the short term if Kaldor's growth models were to work. Utilizing a Burchardt production model and labor-based mark up pricing procedures, Harcourt showed that Kaldor's models worked when changes in profit margins and prices in the short term were determined by the pattern of planned investment. Subsequently, in a two-sector corn model with a non-basic good used to analyze the distribution of income and the level of employment in the short term (Harcourt, 1965), he employed industry mark up pricing equations in which the mark up was a function of demand for investment goods. Harcourt further extended the argument in a draft paper in 1966, which was rejected for publication and set aside; and in 1972 when he made the price level of the economy a function of the level of planned investment expenditure and then argued that

The businessmen who make the investment decisions, i.e. set the level of [planned investment] may also be the principal price-makers, via price leadership, in the economy ... If, then, the level of [planned investment] is, in part, an index of the current state of their confidence, it may also be a proxy for the profit margins that they wish to set and feel that they can get away with. This view seems all the more reasonable if we posit as well a longer-run link between profits arrived at and investment plans which are *internally* financed. (Harcourt, 1972, p. 211)

By postulating a connection between long-term investment plans with short-term pricing and profit margins through the agency of the price leader, Harcourt provided the basis for a long-term explanation of the mark up for profit which is used to set short-term prices.

In 1976 Harcourt with Kenyon returned to the issue of investment and the mark up in order explicitly to develop the direct causal relationship between them at the level of the business enterprise (Harcourt and Kenyon, 1976). Assuming the enterprise to be a price leader and that it used cost-based pricing procedures, Harcourt argued that it set its mark up for profit so as to accrue the amount of retained profits necessary to finance its investment plans. The investment plans, in turn, were based on expected growth of future sales, with the objective that the new investment in capacity would restore the normal degree of capacity utilization. With investment decisions made in the short term, but based on long-term expectations, the short-term profit mark up, and hence the short-term market price, were determined by long-term factors; moreover, the long-term determination of the short-term profit mark up and market price provided the mechanism by which long-term commitments and expectations were integrated with the short-term day-to-day concerns of the enterprise. Thus, by tying together long-term expectations and investment commitments with the short-term profit mark up, Harcourt provided an interesting theoretical argument which made sense of Kaldor's supposition that long-term investment requirements and saving propensities were the ultimate determinants of the short-term customary mark up for profit, and hence influenced the level and rate of change of short-term prices. As such, then, Harcourt's explanation clearly indicated why the short-term price elasticity of demand had no role in determining the short-term mark up for profits (Harcourt, 1972; D. Harris, 1974; Rimmer, 1993; King, 1995).

Both Kregel and Harcourt related the financing of investment plans to the determination of the profit mark up. In doing so, they implied that it was the availability of finance via retained earnings, external borrowing, and new share issues which permitted investment plans to be implemented. Such a view de-emphasizes the role of saving propensities of capitalists and workers as constraints on investment. Kaldor initiated the move explicitly to consider the role of finance in determining the mark up with his neo-Pasinetti theorem, in which prices were determined by enterprise investment, financial policies, and the technical conditions of production. Drawing upon Downie's and Ball's work, the implications of Kaldor's neo-Pasinetti theorem, and Robin Marris' suggestive comments on finance and growth, Adrian Wood developed an explanation of the enterprise's long-term profit margin in which he integrated finance with investment decisions (Kaldor, 1966; Moss, 1978; Rimmer, 1993; Marris, 1964; Wood, 1975).[23]

Wood argued that the amount of profits the business enterprise planned to earn was determined by the amount of investment which it intended to undertake; and the profit plans were expressed in terms of a long-term targeted profit margin. He then defined "profit margin" as the ratio of the enterprise's total profits from all product lines to total sales revenue from all product lines. Wood also defined the "long term" as a

---

[23] Wood's interest in the profit margin stemmed from his attempt to fashion a theory of the long-term share of profits in national income. The explanation for the determination of the profit margin was designed to provide the micro-foundation for the theory. Wood was a post-graduate student and research fellow at Cambridge and his work on the profit margin constituted part of his doctoral dissertation which he completed in October 1972.

three–five-year period; thus the long-term profit margin was defined concretely as a three–five-year moving average of yearly or short-term profit margins. Given the definitions, he proceeded to explain the magnitude of the profit margin in terms of an enterprise objective function – maximizing sales revenue – subject to three constraints – growth of demand, capacity, and availability of finance. The constraints, in turn, were restated as the opportunity frontier and the finance frontier. The former defined the maximum profit margin attainable, given any expected rate of growth of sales revenue, g_s, and expected investment–output ratio (or investment coefficient), k: $pm \leq z(g_s, k)$. The latter, on the other hand, defied the minimum profit margin needed to provide finance for any g_s, given k:

$$pm = (1 + f - x)g_s k/r$$

where f is the financial asset ratio, x is the external finance ratio, and r is the gross retention ratio.[24] Given values for f, x, and r and assuming a value of k, a static solution for pm and g_s exists in which growth of sales revenue is maximized and the magnitude of the profit margin provides the finance needed for the investment in additional plant capacity. If a range of values for k are assumed, a solution for pm and g_s still exists but, in this case, the enterprise would pick the investment coefficient where the pm and g_s solutions gave it the highest rate of growth of sales revenue (Wood, 1975).

Wood clearly brought finance and investment decisions together to explain the magnitude of the profit margin. However, the drawback of his explanation was that it was enterprise-specific instead of product-specific; hence Wood did not actually explain the magnitude of the product-specific profit mark up. On the other hand Alfred Eichner, using a similar argument, advanced a product-specific explanation for the magnitude of the profit mark up. After finishing his doctoral dissertation on the emergence of oligopoly in the US sugar refining industry in 1966, Eichner embarked on a research project to develop a realistic

theoretical understanding of how prices are determined in the oligopolistic sector

[24] The financial asset ratio is a long-term target liquidity ratio whose size is determined by the enterprise's expectations about the extent of future short-term deficits on the capital account in relation to the availability of short-term credit facilities. The external finance ratio is determined by the maximum gearing ratio the enterprise wants to work with, by the initial level of outstanding debt, and by the extent of the growth in the value of its total physical and financial assets. Finally, the gross retention ratio specifies the amount of internal finance that would be generated by any particular level of profits.

of the American economy and how those prices, so determined, affect the growth and stability of the economy as a whole. (Eichner, 1976, p. 1).

The project culminated with the publication of *The Megacorp and Oligopoly* (Eichner, 1976). Central to the project was the development of a satisfactory theory of oligopolistic pricing, which in Eichner's mind meant cost-plus pricing and a satisfactory explanation of the profit mark up.[25] To articulate the theory, he assumed the existence of an oligopolistic sector and the presence of large multi-product business enterprises who were price leaders and whose management wanted to maximize growth of sales. Further, focusing on one product of a price leader, Eichner assumed that the price leader's share of market sales was stable and that market sales were growing. Finally, Eichner assumed that the enterprise attempted to finance its growth primarily with retained earnings and secondarily with external finance. Eichner thus sought to explain the profit mark up which generated the retained earnings by linking it to investment planning by way of the pricing decision and therefore the financing decision.

Accepting the existence of target rate of return pricing procedures, Eichner modified standard average total costs (SATC) so as to include dividend payments and interest payments to fixed debt holders, and to exclude depreciation. Consequently, the profit mark up on SATC, or rSATC, covered depreciation and profits which the enterprise retained for discretionary expenditures on research and development, advertising and other competitive activities, and investment on plant and equipment.[26] If the business enterprise was growing steadily over time, the existing mark up would, he argued, be sufficient to generate the gross profits required for financing the steady growth. But if, for some reason, it expected a change in its steady growth, the enterprise would alter its mark up, and hence its price, to match the change in need for investment funds.[27]

---

[25] Eichner first articulated his theory of oligopolistic pricing in a paper titled "Monopolistic Practices and Inflation" in 1968. He submitted the paper to *The American Economic Review* and the *Quarterly Journal of Economics*, but with no luck. In 1972, Eichner submitted it to *The Economic Journal* where it was accepted and published in December 1973. Wood was one of the referees for the paper and he suggested that its title be changed to "A Theory of the Determination of the Mark-Up Under Oligopoly." Eichner duly and perhaps wisely, accepted the recommendation (Eichner, 1969a*m*, 1969b*m*, 1973; Borts, 1972*m*; Wood, 1973*u*).

[26] Eichner called rSATC the average corporate levy because he wanted to emphasize its planned role of securing for the corporate enterprise financial resources for capital accumulation (Eichner, 1969d*m*).

[27] Eichner approached his explanation of the profit mark up from a historical perspective. Starting with a single-product competitive industry with many enterprises, he argued

More specifically, to explain the change in the magnitude of the mark up, Eichner assumed an initial position in which the price leader had set its price by marking up its SATC, with the magnitude of the profit mark up sufficient to finance the investment plans necessary to ensure that, in the long term, the actual rate of capacity utilization did not diverge significantly from the standard rate. However, if the price leader experienced an increase in its actual capacity utilization above the standard rate which it believed represented a permanent increase in its growth rate of sales, it would have to initiate additional investment plans; and to finance these additional plans, the price leader would increase its profit mark up. Thus the change in the mark up, Eichner argued, was a function of the demand for additional finance over time required for the additional investment, subject to the marginal investment plan generating a minimally satisfactory rate of return; the supply of internal fund over time generated by the increased mark up tempered by the substitution effect, threat of entry, and government intervention; the market rate of interest; and the implicit interest rate on the additional investment funds generated internally through an increase in the mark up. Depending on the demand for additional investment funds, the change in the magnitude of the profit mark up therefore would vary between zero and a positive value at which the implicit interest rate equaled the market rate; if additional investment funds were needed, they would be obtained via external fund raising, such as issuing additional stocks and bonds and borrowing from financial institutions (Eichner, 1969, 1969a*m*, 1969c*m*, 1970a*m*, 1970b*m*, 1971a*m*, 1971b*m*, 1972b*m*, 1972*u*, 1973, 1974*m*, 1976).

The enterprise–investment explanation of the profit mark up both corrected an omission in the Riach–Reynolds explanation of the degree of monopoly and gave a more specific meaning to it. In subsequent work

that as long as the demand for the industry's product continued to grow at a pace which exceeded the growth rate of the economy as a whole, its structure would not change. But once the growth of sales failed to keep pace with increases in industry capacity, the competitive industry would be transformed into an oligopolistic one. At this point, the industry would emerge as a mature oligopoly dominated by a few large enterprises, one of whom would be the price leader. The profit mark up the price leader applied when pricing its product would, at this initial stage, be a product of the past historical experience of the industry. From this point onward, however, changes in the mark up depended on changes in aggregate demand conditions which determined the need for internally generated funds. Consequently, Eichner explained the initial mark up in his analysis in terms of past historical experience and the financial needs for steady growth, and the subsequent changes in the mark up in terms of changes in the need for investment finance in light of planned changes in growth. Because the former was grounded in history and therefore given to the analysis, he centered his attention on explaining the change in the profit mark up (Eichner, 1972b*m*).

on the mark up by Nina Shapiro, Nai-Pew Ong, and Scott Moss, for example, environmental and institutional factors were combined with enterprise-specific investment requirements and business strategies to explain its magnitude in the light of various pricing strategies an enterprise might consider. Thus, from the middle 1980s onward, the synthetic Post Keynesian explanation of the profit mark up was in wide use, largely because of the insights it offered for understanding enterprise behavior and pricing decisions (Eichner and Kregel, 1975; Shapiro, 1981; Ong, 1981; Moss, 1981).[28]

Investment decisions

The foundations of Kalecki's analysis of entrepreneurial investment decisions was the implied assumption that entrepreneurs had a natural propensity, whether it be weak or strong, to invest and accumulate capital. Consequently, his analysis of the investment decision centered on the factors which encouraged or discouraged entrepreneurs to formulate and implement them, relative to a given base of investment decisions in the process of being implemented. Similarly, Keynes with his "animal spirits" assumed that entrepreneurs had a natural propensity to invest and then made actual investment decisions a function of future profit rates. Since the assumption implied that economic growth under capitalism was "natural,", it was central to the Keynes–Kalecki economic growth project initiated by Kaldor and Robinson in the 1950s. However, only Robinson clearly acknowledged the existence of the assumption when she argued that the propensity to invest in productive capacity was based on Keynes' animal spirits, a concept which in turn was based on the innate characteristics of human nature – moral sense of duty, spontaneous optimism, and the spirit of emulation. Given animal spirits and hence the urge to grow, Robinson then argued that the decision to formulate and enact investment decisions for the purpose of capital accumulation was a function of the expected level of profits and the degree of competition. Finally, she noted that the assumption also implied that the entrepreneur was motivated by the innate desire for survival and growth, not the desire for profits *per se*; rather, profits were desired only for their contribution to survival and the growth process. Consequently, Robinson concluded that while entrepreneurs preferred more profits to less, they did not attempt to maximize profits in the neoclassical sense (Robinson, 1952, 1956, 1960, 1962).

---

[28] Support for this last remark is found in Tables IA.1 and IA.2 in the appendix to the Introduction (pp. 11–16).

Like Robinson, Kaldor in his work on economic growth accepted the "animal spirits'" assumption (although he christened it "technical dynamism") and its implication that survival and growth was the principal motivation of the entrepreneur. Kaldor also accepted the argument that entrepreneur's decision to formulate and enact investment plans was in part a function of the expected rate of profit relative to a predetermined satisfactory rate of profit; in addition he argued that it was also a function of the growth of sales *vis-à-vis* normal capacity utilization.[29] In accordance with the "acceleration principle," the growth in sales would induce the entrepreneur to implement additional investment plans so as to expand capacity in line with the increase in sales without requiring a higher expected rate of profit. Kaldor's acceptance of the principle prompted other economists to include it in their own work. Both Harcourt and Wood referred to the principle when describing the process by which the entrepreneur determined the profit mark up. Eichner, on the other hand, synthesized Robert Eisner's modification of the principle – that investment depended on changes in industry sales distributed over several years previously – with the price leader's objective to maximize sales, and directly incorporated his lagged-sales accelerator investment function into his explanation of the change in the profit mark up. However, in spite of Eisner's empirical evidence supporting the position that entrepreneurs based their investment decisions on expected future sales as indicated by the change in sales over previous years, the Kalecki–Robinson view that investment decisions were primarily a function of expected profit rates was still widely adhered to in the 1980s (Kaldor, 1957, 1958; Kaldor and Mirrlees, 1962; Eichner, 1969b*m*, 1969c*m*, 1970a*m*, 1971b*m*, 1971c*m*, 1976; Eichner and Kregel, 1975; Eisner, 1956, 1963, 1978; Rowthorn, 1981; Dutt, 1984).

---

[29] Kaldor also argued that the entrepreneur's investment decision was affected by the length of the pay-back period required to repay the cost of the investment (Kaldor and Mirrlees, 1962).

10   Josef Steindl and the stagnation thesis

Before leaving Oxford, Kalecki suggested to Steindl that he examine the puzzle as to why capitalism ceased to function in the inter-war period. Steindl took up the suggestion and after completing *Small and Big Business* (1945b) turned his attention to the puzzle. In particular, he sought to contribute to the mature economy controversy initiated by Alvin Hansen through a concrete examination of the rise, decline, and eventual stagnation of capital accumulation in the American economy from 1869 to 1939. Believing that the explanation of economic stagnation required the articulation of a long-term theory of growth, Steindl developed Kalecki's theory of investment into a theory of growth centered on the propensity of entrepreneurs to invest, where this propensity was a function of past savings, relative indebtedness, and the degree of capacity utilization. Furthermore, he argued that the degree of capacity utilization was dependent on the magnitude of net profit margins *vis-à-vis* the given level of investment. Steindl therefore began his investigation by examining the forces which determined the net profit margin. The outcome of this work was a microanalysis of the net profit margin, which was completed by 1947. He then turned his attention to developing his theory of growth based on this microanalysis, which was completed in 1949. The completed manuscript was sent to the printers in January 1950, but the printing of *Maturity and Stagnation in American Capitalism* was delayed until 1952. The importance of the microanalysis in *Maturity and Stagnation* was that it developed Kalecki's microanalysis and thus contributed to the development of the mark up prices doctrine (Young and Lee, 1993; Oxford Institute of Statistics, 1945, 1947, 1948, 1949, 1950; Steindl, 1952, 1984, 1990a).[1]

---

[1] Its importance is also found in its congruence with Andrews' analysis of the movement of the normal cost market process and Downie's analysis of the competitive process.

Steindl and stagnation

Central to Steindl's analysis was the distinction between corporate and non-corporate business enterprise. Drawing on his previous sketch in *Small and Big Business* as well as Kalecki's work, Steindl characterized the enterprise as a technique of production defined in terms of the labor and raw material inputs, the degree of capital intensity, and the product produced. Further, each technique embodied particular production economies depending on its scale of production, and these were encapsulated in the degree of capital intensity, with the greater degree of capital intensity implying that more production economies embodied in the technique. Finally, the costs of the enterprise were categorized into direct and overhead costs. Average direct costs were assumed constant, while average total costs declined with respect to increases in capacity utilization. Given this general characterization of the business enterprise, Steindl then discussed four of its features that directly connected the enterprise to external market activities: the degree of capacity utilization, cost differentials, investment decisions, and prices. He noted that each technique of production had a "practical" full capacity, that the entrepreneur chose a planned degree of capacity utilization on which pricing and investment decisions were based, that the planned degree of capacity utilization (PDCU) was less than full capacity utilization, and that planned excess capacity was held to deal with seasonal and unexpected variations in sales and with a secular increase in sales.[2] Steindl also noted, that at the same PDCU, enterprises with greater degrees of capital intensity had lower average total costs due to the economies of scale associated with the more capital-intensive production techniques. Finally, drawing upon his discussion in *Small and Big Business*, Steindl assumed that entrepreneurs had a basic urge to increase the productive capacity of their enterprises, that is to accumulate capital, and therefore argued that they based their investment decisions on the level of retained profits (past savings), the degree of capacity utilization, the gearing ratio, and the rate of profit. In particular, the partial accelerator impact of capacity utilization on investment combined with the rigidity of outside savings, propelled the entrepreneur to adjust his capacity-expansion investment decisions in an effort to restore the PDCU and to maintain a financially sound gearing ratio.

[2] Steindl defined practical capacity as the "output achieved with normal length of working time, with sufficient shut-downs to allow for repairs and maintenance, and without disturbance of the smooth running of the production process" (Steindl, 1952, pp. 7–8). He also noted that if practical capacity was exceeded, the enterprise would incur extraordinary costs so that its marginal costs would rapidly increase.

Regarding prices, Steindl had to place the enterprise within a close community of enterprises, that is an industry.[3] Within the industry, he argued, there were a number of enterprises, each with a specific but not necessarily equal share of industry sales, with a different degree of capital intensity and hence with different average total costs at planned degree of capacity utilization (PATC), and with its own view of an acceptable profit margin. The growth of a particular enterprise's sales was, Steindl argued, mostly dependent on time and hence on the accumulation of goodwill:

Whatever [the entrepreneurs] might do within a restricted period in the way of advertisement, price cuts, or by whatever method, he will not be able to increase his sales above a certain level; whereas with the lapse of time the mere existence of the firm will bring a gradual extension of goodwill; and advertisement and other methods of stimulating sales will only gradually bring results as time goes by. (Steindl, 1952, p. 10)

The same argument was extended to the growth of industry sales, with the reinforced conclusion that sales at the level of the enterprise or the industry in the short term and over the trade cycle were highly or virtually inelastic with regard to changes in the industry price.[4] Consequently, any attempts by an individual enterprise to increase its share of market sales in the short term or over the trade cycle by reducing its price when production techniques, and hence costs, were given would result in

---

[3] Steindl viewed the industry in terms of imperfect competition. That is, the industry consisted of many markets that were imperfectly related. Thus it was possible in his view to conceive of the representative good produced in the industry and hence talk about an industry price which would govern the dispersion of prices for the various markets. Consequently, it becomes possible to carry out analysis in terms of a single price and a single good, while at the same time referring to issues in the context of a single market.

[4] As Steindl stated:

It can be argued that in the short run the demand for the products of an industry is very inelastic, because the possibilities of substitution for other products are very limited. The substitution of one consumer's good for another, for example, rayon for silk, or rayon staple for wool, is a process which takes considerable time. The consumers are attached to the product of a particular industry in a much greater degree than to that of a firm. A whole series of traditions and prejudices has to be changed until a considerable shift of demand can occur, and propaganda continuing over a long period will often be necessary. In the case of producers' goods a similar role will be played by technical traditions and inertia, and by quite objective technical difficulties, which make substitution again dependent on the lapse of time. The substitution may require changes in outlay and equipment which cannot be quickly effected and which must be decided on permanently. Just as in the case of the individual firm, the growth of the market of an industry is, therefore, dependent on time. We conclude that in the short run the demand for the products of an industry is in most cases probably very inelastic, whereas in the long run this is less likely to be the case. (Steindl, 1952, p. 16)

an industry price war with virtually no compensating increases in the degree of capacity utilization. In this context, the industry price had to be set by a cartel or price leader, and was then accepted by the other enterprises in the industry.[5] The industry price set had two important properties, that it was rigid or stable in the short term and over the trade cycle and that it was set at a level

which just keeps potential competitors out; or, in some other cases, it may be fixed at a level which is sufficient to squeeze out some existing competitors, whose markets the price leaders want to take. (Steindl, 1952, p. 17)[6]

Given an industry price, Steindl argued that there would exist within an industry a spectrum of different-sized enterprises with correspondingly different PATCs and different net profit margins.[7] There would consequently exist at any point in time a group of the smallest enterprises that operated at the margin of the industry and as a group earned no profits, and hence had, on average, zero net profit margins, whereas the larger lower-cost enterprises would have positive net profit margins. The questions that Steindl sought to answer were: What regulated the competitive pressure within the industry which was the very force that determined who were the marginal enterprises? How did net profit margins move over time? The framework used by Steindl to examine the questions involved analyzing the pattern of competition within an industry where there were many small enterprises and entry was easy, and where there were fewer and larger enterprises and entry was more difficult.[8] To establish the basis of his analysis, he assumed that technical change was continuous, that enterprises invest only in their own industry, that increases in the entrepreneur's own capital were an important

---

[5] Steindl did not provide any details as to how the cartel or price leader actually set their price, which became the industry price. However, in the last chapter of the book he described mark up pricing in the context of discussing the "iron law of wages" (Steindl, 1952, p. 236).

[6] In stating both of these properties, Steindl made it quite clear that the concept of price elasticity of demand was particularly ill designed to explain both of them; consequently, he simply made no recourse to the concept in *Maturity and Stagnation* (Steindl, 1952, pp. 17, 67, 71).

[7] Steindl argued that a spectrum of different size/cost enterprises in an industry was a permanent and universal characteristic of capitalism; and that it was due, in part, to the relative scarcity of big units of capital. Steindl defined the net profit margin as price minus PATC; the gross profit margin he defined as consisting of the net profit margin plus depreciation and the "salary" of the entrepreneur (Steindl, 1952, pp. 38–9).

[8] Steindl identified the former industry type as competitive and the latter as oligopolistic. Oligopolistic industries, he suggested, were characterized as having very high four-enterprise concentration ratios and/or minimum capital requirements (Steindl, 1952, p. 72).

inducement to invest, and that the growth rate of the industry was given. Steindl also assumed that enterprises could affect their own growth rates through their sales effort, in that the sales effort would be positive if the enterprise wanted to grow faster than the industry growth rate (Steindl, 1987, 1990a).[9]

Starting with the case of the small-enterprise, easy-entry competitive industry, Steindl assumed that an industry price was given. Since the PATC differed among the enterprises in the industry according to their size, their net profit margins would differ as well, with the marginal enterprises having a zero net profit margin. Given that industry sales are growing, the marginal enterprises whose PATC equaled the industry price would be unable to grow; consequently, the increase in industry sales would be taken up by the larger enterprises in the industry or by the entry of new enterprises. The scenario which Steindl argued happened historically was that the progressive enterprises in the industry found that their actual capacity utilization was greater than their PDCU. With an increase in their net profit margins, and the consequent flow of greater amounts of profits into the enterprises, resulting in an increase in their rates of profit,[10] the progressive entrepreneurs would, in light of their "investment function," undertake investment in new larger-scale techniques of production which brought with them new scale economies.[11] The new techniques would restore production in the progressive enterprises to their PDCU and at the same time reduce their PATC. If the industry price remained unchanged, the progressive enterprises would find that sales had not increased sufficiently to ensure that the new techniques operated at the PDCU. This would inspire the entrepreneurs to engage in sales effort with the result that the industry price would fall, in line with costs, the consequence being that the existing marginal enterprises would be driven from the industry and their sales acquired by the progressive enterprises.

This competitive process would continue, Steindl argued, as long as actual capacity utilization was greater than planned, the price–net profit

---

[9] Steindl defined sales effort as a sacrifice, in the form of reduced prices, or increased PATC, or increased selling costs, that is undertaken by an enterprise for the purpose of increasing its sales. He also noted that the efficiency of the different forms of sales effort varied with different market circumstances. Finally, Steindl noted the theoretical possibility that a progressive enterprise could increase its selling cost and finance this cost by a corresponding price increase, but only up to the point where selling methods ceased to be superior to price cutting as a way to increase sales (Steindl, 1952, pp. 42, 55–66).

[10] See pp. 155–8 for Steindl's discussion of the relationship between the net profit margin and the rate of profit.

[11] Steindl defined "progressive enterprises" as those enterprises which took the lead introducing technical innovations (Steindl, 1952, p. 45).

margin at PDCU generated excessive profits, and the rate of profit on new investment was expected to increase so that the progressive entrepreneurs would be continually propelled to invest in larger-scale capital-intensive techniques of production. As the process of lowering PATC and increasing sales efforts resulted in continual declining industry price, there would be a continual exit of marginal enterprises from the industry and an increase in the size of the progressive enterprises. The process would continue in the long term until the net profit margin had adjusted to the declines in PATC and increased sales effort, so that it was just sufficient to provide investment funds to enable the progressive enterprises to accommodate its portion of the growth of industry sales, taking into account the progressive increases in the degree of capital intensity and any changes in the gearing ratio. Thus, as long as the industry remained competitive, the level of net profit margins and prices would be limited by growth and technical requirements, net profit margins would remain relatively stable (as would the wage share) over time, the rate of profit for the progressive enterprises would continually increase, and the actual degree of capacity utilization would be continually gravitating towards PDCU for each enterprise.

The competitive process noted above could have a different ending if the process of creating larger enterprises resulted in the existence of relatively large "marginal enterprises" which had positive net profit margins and financial resilience and hence greater staying power. In this case, the increased sales effort by the progressive enterprises would, if successful in eliminating the marginal enterprises, be so costly that success would result in a decline in the rate of profit, unless it was offset by significant cost reductions achieved by the introduction of new technology. Consequently, the net profit margin at the PDCU would be more than sufficient to provide investment funds for growth, taking into account increases in the degree of capital intensity. Thus the progressive enterprises would have to reduce investment so as to prevent the emergence of unwanted excess capacity. Moreover, the entrepreneurs of the progressive enterprises would not, Steindl argued, find it easy to re-direct their surplus investment funds to other industries, since cross-entry into other similar industries would not appear any more attractive than its own, while entry into competitive industries would take a significant amount of money and time to acquire the customer goodwill necessary for entry to be a financial success. The level of the net profit margin, and hence also the rate of profit, would thus not, in the long term, be shaped and limited by the growth and technical requirements of the industry or of the economy as a whole; rather, Steindl concluded that a significant degree of arbitrariness in the long-term determination of the new profit margins existed in oligopolistic industries dominated by few relatively large business enterprises.[12] As a result, the net profit margin and the rate of profit would increase while the wage share would decline over time as more industries became oligopolistic (Levine, 1975; Shapiro, 1988; Norton, 1983*u*).

Steindl argued that over time the industrial structure of a capitalist economy would alter as the competitive process resulted in the emergence of big enterprises and oligopolistic industries. Since the net profit margins in the oligopolistic industries could provide more investment funds than were needed to expand capacity in line with the growth of sales, the progressive entrepreneurs would reduce their investment expenditures. Consequently, the progressive emergence of oligopolistic industries had a damping effect on aggregate economic activity and hence on the degree of capacity utilization throughout the economy. The reaction of the entrepreneurs in the competitive industries to a reduction in the growth of sales would be to cut prices by reducing their net profit margins, while the enterprises in the oligopolistic industries reduce their investment expenditures but maintain their new profit margins. As long as the positive stimulus of price reductions outweighed the depressing impact of investment expenditure reductions, the capitalist economy would continue to grow, albeit at a slower rate. However, the secular trend towards more oligopolistic industries would, in Steindl's view, mean that the capitalist process would decline and eventually stagnate. Thus the competitive process, which had created impressive growth in the early stages of capitalism, also produced, as an inherent consequence of its own action, economic stagnation at a latter stage. Steindl later acknowledged that the above scenario implied that it was not legitimate to assume the industry growth as given. He also acknowledged that his theory did not deal adequately with the disruptive effects of a new entrant to the industry who uses a new technology or produces a new product (Steindl, 1976, 1979, 1987, 1990a; see also Shapiro, 1981).

Developments in the stagnation thesis

The subsequent developments of the Kalecki–Steindl stagnation thesis were undertaken by economists who had no direct association with Kalecki and Steindl, but were attracted to the message of the thesis

---

[12] Steindl dismissed the effectiveness of the classical assumption of the tendency towards a uniform rate of profit as the long-term determinant of the structure of prices and net profit margins in the economy on the grounds that the long-term mobility of capital did not hold (Steindl, 1952, pp. 67–8).

itself.[13] Coming from the Alvin Hansen school of economic stagnation, Sylos-Labini developed similar arguments for stagnation based on increasing profit margins and grounded on the normal cost prices doctrine.[14] He began his analysis by stating that the economy could be divided into two sectors – one in which all the industries were competitive and a second in which the industries were oligopolistic and hence imperfectly competitive. When faced with cost-reducing innovations, enterprises in the competitive sector would respond with matching price reductions whereas the enterprises in the oligopolistic sector would respond by partially off-setting wage increases, by widening their profit margins, and by some price reductions. Since cost-reducing innovations also contributed to progressive industrial concentration and hence to the continual spread of oligopolistic industries, the fruits of technical progress, Sylos-Labini argued, were distributed by rising consumer and enterprise money incomes. Consequently, the absorption of the workers made redundant by technical progress depended primarily on the expansion of effective demand to create the investment opportunities on which large enterprises could spend their "extra profits" and entice consumers to spend their "extra income."[15] However, Sylos-Labini argued, there existed no inherent mechanism within an oligopolistic capitalist economy that would always ensure that effective demand expanded sufficiently, so that economic stagnation and growing unemployment was the general tendency of an oligopolized capitalist economy, unless an external stimulus was forthcoming from growing public expenditure (Sylos-Labini, 1962; Roncaglia, 1994).

The most ardent admirers and developers of the thesis, however, were the Marxists of the monopoly capital school, especially Paul Baran and

---

[13] The stagnation thesis was a recurring theme in Robinson's analysis of economic growth. However, her discussion of it was restricted to identifying the "effect of a rise in thriftiness" and then to suggesting that whatever might cause it to rise, such as the growth in monopoly, would be counteracted by other powerful forces, such as trade unions. In short, economic stagnation was a theoretical possibility, but not very likely (Robinson, 1952, 1956, 1957, 1960, and 1962; see also Asimakopulos, 1969).

[14] Although many of his arguments corresponded quite closely to many of Steindl's, Sylos-Labini was not influenced by *Maturity and Stagnation*. A principal but subtle theoretical difference which separated them was that Sylos-Labini worked with the concept of a competitive uniform rate of profit whereas Steindl was not concerned very much with the concept or about the determination of relative prices (Roncaglia, 1994).

[15] Sylos-Labini noted that enterprise investment incentives in a competitive economy were also generated by a fall in the prices of direct and overhead inputs and in the interest rate for investment borrowing. But, under oligopoly, price reductions were not frequent and most enterprises financed their investment with retained earnings. He also noted that if enterprises did not spend their extra profits on capital investments, they would probably devote them to financial investments and this would weaken effective demand.

Paul Sweezy. Although a Marxist theory of monopoly capitalism was first broached at the turn of the century, none of the theorists examined the impact of the large corporate enterprise on the operation of a capitalist economy with any degree of thoroughness.[16] After this initial phase the theory remained in a rather dormant state until it was revived in the 1950s and early 1960s and eventually tied to the Kalecki–Steindl stagnation thesis by Baran and Sweezy. Central to the Marxist arguments in the 1950s and early 1960s was the view that the emergence of large corporate enterprises since 1900 had gradually altered the nature of competition under capitalism, with the result that there was a gradual reduction in the profitability of competitive industries, widening profit margins in the oligopolistic and monopolistic industries, and leading to a decline of investment opportunities due to increase in the introduction of capital-saving technology. These changes would lead to the eventual stagnation of the capitalist economy, unless some way was found to increase investment to match the potential profits generated by the widening of profit margins. While broadly compatible with the Kalecki–Steindl stagnation thesis, the arguments of the monopoly capital school were not as "tight" and incisive as those of Kalecki and Steindl. However, the Marxists did succeed in explicitly locating the question of economic stagnation in the characteristics and complex behavior of the large business enterprise, in raising the question of what form the utilization of the potential profits would have to take if stagnation was to be avoided, and in showing the need to delineate the relationship between the large business enterprise and the state (Howard and King, 1992; Sawyer, 1988; Gillman, 1957, 1965; Baran, 1957; Sweezy, 1972, 1991; Semmler, 1984; Foster and Szlajfer, 1984b).

The arguments of the monopoly capital school were integrated with the Kalecki–Steindl stagnation thesis by Baran and Sweezy in their book *Monopoly Capital* (1966). In their synthesis, the austerely described business enterprise of Kalecki and Steindl comes alive with characteristics and a sense of self-importance and destiny. The large corporate enterprise of mid-twentieth-century America, Baran and Sweezy argued, was controlled and directed by management whose goal was growth, that is the accumulation of capital, funded through profits. Those who made up management were drawn from the middle and upper-middle classes and identified with the enterprise to the extent that its goal was their

---

[16] Sweezy also argues that the early theorists also did not consider whether the rise of the large business enterprise and its consequent monopolization of markets affected the theoretical concepts and arguments they were using. Sweezy felt that it was illegitimate to use theoretical concepts fashioned to examine competitive capitalism to examine monopoly capitalism.

goal. Consequently, management ceased to be composed of individual business leaders but was now a team dedicated to the advancement of the enterprise. Because the corporate enterprise dominated many markets and was able to control prices and production, management was capable of generating enough profits to finance all its planned investment and to maintain a moderately steady dividend policy to satisfy all stockholders. Freed from "outside" stockholder meddling and from financial dependence on banks and other financial institutions, the corporate enterprise became an island of power which the management could direct as it deemed appropriate.

Although the corporate enterprise was an island of power, management could not fully control its destiny because of the existence of other large corporate enterprises. Adopting a conservative long-term view, management embraced a non-aggressive attitude *vis-à-vis* its competitors. In particular, to avoid costly price wars and to maintain orderly and profitable market operations, market prices were set, Baran and Sweezy argued, by an acknowledged price leader at a level that maximized profits for all. However, enterprises would compete for larger market shares as this would lead to declining costs and since management in their pursuit for profit and growth would not pass on the cost reductions through lowering prices, to widening profit margins.[17] In choosing to widen its profit margins, the management of the corporate enterprise behaved rationally within the context of monopoly capitalism but, as Baran and Sweezy argued, this rational behavior pushes the economy towards stagnation. The pursuit of profits could not in fact be successful if the increased potential profits from the widening of profit margins were not realized. Since the management of the large corporation were not risk-takers, they would not increase their investment expenditures *pari passu* with the widening of profit margins; moreover, because they maintained a stable payout ratio for dividends, increasing capitalist consumption to match the increased profit margins was also not possible.[18] However, management would undertake sales efforts to create demand for their products and to produce new wants and, hence, new products.[19] In

---

[17] The widening of profit margins is the basis for Baran and Sweezy's law of the rising surplus under monopoly capitalism (Baran and Sweezy, 1966, pp. 71–2).

[18] Steindl also assumed a stable pay-out ratio for dividends. As Bruce Norton has noted, this assumption essentially assumes that capitalists cannot correct the tendency to stagnation by transferring increasing amounts of retained profits to consumption (Norton, 1983*u*, 1986, 1988, 1988*u*).

[19] Sweezy (and Steindl – see Steindl, 1990a) later extended this point to argue that the limited sales growth of existing products, in part, drove the business enterprise "to move outside of and beyond its historical field of operation, to penetrate new industries and

addition, Baran and Sweezy argued, government expenditure on social consumption and on the military absorbed some of the potential profits from the widening of the profit margins. But even these possibilities were limited, thus leaving the tendency towards stagnation not completely checked. It was in this context that Baran and Sweezy argued that the large corporate enterprise and the state established a relationship in an attempt to stop the drift towards stagnation (Baran and Sweezy, 1966; Sweezy and Magdoff, 1972; Sweezy, 1979; Norton, 1983*u*; Lebowitz, 1990).

Developments in the stagnation thesis continued after the publication of *Monopoly Capital*.[20] Sweezy explicitly connected the thesis to labor force participation rates and unemployment rates, while Harry Braverman (1974) connected it to the deskilling of the labor process and the degradation and polarization of working conditions. In particular, Braverman argued that management's drive for cost reductions within the context of expanding sales increasingly took the form of taking control of the labor process away from workers, leaving them only with unthinking working motions. Furthermore, with Harry Magdoff, Sweezy explicitly introduced the financial sector and financial enterprises into the thesis (and hence into the mark up prices doctrine) and argued that their presence in a stagnant economy promoted demand through their extension of consumer credit and their own purchases of investment goods. However, the positive effect on demand was counteracted since the financial assets promoted by the financial enterprises enabled industrial business enterprises to spend their surplus profits on financial investments rather than on plant, equipment, and research; and this move to making money as opposed to making goods further reinforced, Sweezy and Magdoff argued, the stagnation tendencies in the economy.[21] Finally, David Levine (1975) argued that to assume entrepreneurs had a natural propensity to accumulate capital, as Steindl and Baran and Sweezy did, implied that capital accumulation was a self-sustaining process and that the widening of profit margins was a direct outcome of the process.[22] But the widening profit margins created a barrier to the

---

new markets – in a word, to go conglomerate and multinational" (Sweezy and Magdoff, 1972, p. 100). Sweezy also noted that the move to being a multinational enterprise was assisted by the existence of an unused pool of managerial talent within the enterprise.

[20] Keith Cowling's work on monopoly capitalism and stagnation is not considered because of its neoclassical foundations (see n. 12 in chapter 9, p. 172) (Cowling, 1982; Sawyer, 1988).

[21] Steindl (1990a) has also put forward a similar argument.

[22] The issue of whether basis of capital accumulation can be reduced to a self-sustaining activity based on the natural propensities of capitalists is questionable (see Norton, 1983*u*, 1986, 1988, and 1988*u*).

accumulation process. Therefore, Levine argued, entrepreneurs would overcome the barrier and hence avoid economic stagnation through product innovation, which becomes, in his view, the representative form of competitive and investment activity under monopoly capitalism (Sweezy and Magdoff, 1972, 1988; Sweezy, 1991; Foster, 1994; Magdoff and Sweezy, 1987; Lebowitz, 1990).

Part IV

The grounded pricing foundation of Post Keynesian price theory

11   Pricing and prices

The administered prices, normal cost prices, and mark up prices doctrines contain numerous theoretical insights and arguments useful for the development of a Post Keynesian theory of prices, especially its pricing foundations. The purpose of this and the following chapter is to draw upon the three doctrines to develop an empirically grounded pricing foundation for Post Keynesian price theory. Chapter 11 will examine and empirically ground the analytical costing, pricing, and price components of the pricing foundation. That is, over 100 empirical studies on costing, pricing, and prices will be used to establish the appropriate analytical delineation of the costing and pricing procedures and price policies of the business enterprise and price-setting market institutions and to delineate the properties of the prices based on the pricing procedures. Then, drawing on the formal and mathematical methods associated with the mark up prices doctrine, the enterprise and market pricing equation which can be derived from the pricing procedures will be formalized and mathematized. Chapter 12 continues the development of the pricing foundation and discusses its implication for Post Keynesian price theory.

Costing and pricing procedures

Each price doctrine postulated that prices were set in connection with costs in that the pricing procedures used by the business enterprise are based on the cost accounting system it uses to collect product costs. In general, enterprises use cost accounting systems that collect direct material and labor costs; however, beyond direct costs, the systems will differ in their collection of shop expenses[1] and enterprise

---

[1] "Shop expenses" are defined as those expenses related to the production of a particular product line and generally include the salaries of foremen, support staff, and supervisors; the materials needed to maintain the support staff and the technical efficiency of the plant

expenses[2] which comprise the overhead costs of a product. Some cost accounting systems collect the labor cost, material cost, and depreciation components of shop expenses, while others collect the same cost components for both shop and enterprise expenses. In addition, the depreciation component in shop and enterprise expenses is determined by using historical costs for valuing plant and equipment and the straight-line or declining charges methods for calculating the depreciation allowance.[3] From the product cost base generated by the cost accounting system, the enterprise develops the costing procedures[4] which it will use to determine a product's costs at normal, estimated, standards, or budgeted output or

and equipment used directly in production; and the depreciation allowance associated with the plant and equipment.

[2] "Enterprise expenses" are defined as those expenses which are common to all product lines but specific to none and are necessary if the business enterprise is to stay in existence as a going concern. In general, these costs are associated with those activities in which the enterprise must engage in order to co-ordinate the production flows of the various product lines, to sell the various products and to develop and implement enterprise-wide investment and diversification plans, and which include the salaries of management, office expenses, insurance, selling costs and the depreciation of the central office buildings and equipment.

[3] It is important to note that not all businesses make regular deductions for depreciation and in some cases capital is maintained by expenditures out of revenue (J. R. Edwards, 1980; Wale, 1990). Furthermore, the tax codes in the United States, Germany, and France stipulate that business enterprises must use historical costs for valuing plant and equipment, while the tax code in the United Kingdom states that enterprises can use either historical or current costs, although most use historical costs for valuing plant and equipment. For evidence supporting the historical costs approach to depreciation, see appendix A costing studies A2, A10, A12, A13, A14, A16, A17, A20, A22, A23, A26, appendix B pricing studies B6, B16, B22, B33, B44, and Grant and Mathews (1957). The implication of these two points is that the Sraffian treatment of depreciation is inconsistent with economic reality, not to mention in violation of the law as symbolized by the tax code. Moreover, because nearly all business enterprises either do make deductions for depreciation or value their fixed capital assets at historical costs, the target rate of return (whether it be a reasonable or fair, high or low) which is utilized in setting prices is simply not the same as the rate of profit found in Marxian and Sraffian studies. Hence to equate the two and then argue that business enterprises are directly setting long-period prices (as, for example, Clifton, 1983, and Semmler, 1984 do), is incorrect.

[4] There exist two general types of costing procedures, estimated costing and standard costing. In the former, costs are determined by methods that range from a perfunctory guess to a very careful computation based upon past experience; in either case, past costs are used as the basis to determine the costs of a good that will be produced in the future. In the latter, costs are determined by a process of scientific fact-finding which utilizes both past experience and controlled experiments in advance of production. However, in spite of the differences, both estimated and standard costing arrive at the costs of producing a good that will be used in setting the price in the same way. Hence in the following discussion, reference will be made only to costing.

capacity utilization.[5] The normal costs will then be used to set the actual selling price of a good before actual production takes place, and hence the *actual* costs of production are known.[6]

The activities of costing and pricing are aspects of business leadership and hence are carried on within the business enterprise by an individual, such as its owner, or by a committee made up of business administrators or managers drawn from different departments and levels of management. In either case, costing and pricing are activities that are administered by the administrators, which implies that the kind of costing and pricing procedures used within the business enterprise, including how depreciation and normal output or capacity utilization are calculated, are administratively determined. The administratively determined actual selling prices are then administered to the market, hence the name "administered prices." Pricing administrators utilize costing and pricing procedures as a medium through which they can administer their prices to the market (Costing studies A7, A12, A14, A17, A24, A26; Pricing studies B1, B19, B20, B21, B22, B23, B28, B30, B31, B32, B33, B38, B40, B44, B55, B63, B64, B67; Capon *et al.*, 1975; Farley *et al.*, 1980).[7]

For those cost systems which generate only direct material and labor

---

[5] The specific figure for normal, estimated, standard, or budgeted output or capacity utilization is administratively determined and its determinants range from anticipated sales for the period under review, anticipated sales for a period of years into the future, average sales experience for a number of past years, to the practical capacity of the enterprise – see costing studies A3, A4, A12, A20, A23, A26 and pricing studies B1, B5, B6, B7, B8, B10, B14, B16, B17, B43.

[6] Since the costs used for pricing are based on normal output or capacity utilization and hence are known before production takes place, the question of the shape of the average direct cost curve is immaterial for *pricing purposes*, contrary to the view found in those studies in table IA.2 in the Introduction (pp. 12–16) which assumed for pricing purposes constant average direct labor costs or constant average direct costs.

[7] Not all administratively determined prices are based on costing procedures. In the case of destructive price wars, especially associated with rapid technical change and innovation, administrators frequently set and re-set prices without regard to costs, as in the case of the tractor price war between Ford and International Harvester.

Late in January [1922], Henry Ford telegraphed all dealers that the retail factory stripped price of the Fordson tractor had been reduced $230 to a new low selling price of $395. The market was stunned. When Alexander Legge, President of International Harvester, was 'phoned the news he exploded:

What? What's that? How much? Two hundred and thirty dollars? Well, I'll be ... What'll we do about it? Do? Why, damn it all – meet him, of course! We're going to stay in the tractor business. Yes, cut two hundred and thirty dollars. Both models – yes, both. And say, listen, make it good! We'll throw in a plow as well! (Conant, 1949*t*, p. 65)

There are, of course, prices which are not administered, such as those found in auction markets and commodity exchanges.

costs, the direct costing procedures determine only the normal average direct costs for pricing purposes;[8] for those systems which generate direct costs and shop expenses, the costing procedures determine normal average factory costs for pricing purposes; and for those systems which generate direct costs, shop expenses, and enterprise expenses, the costing procedures determine normal average total costs for pricing purposes.[9] Starting with the costs determined by its costing procedures, the business enterprise then adds a costing margin or mark ups the costs to set the price. Depending upon the costing procedures used by the enterprise, the pricing procedures used by it will ensure that the costing margin or mark up will cover overhead costs and produce a profit.[10] More specifically, mark up pricing procedures consist of marking up average direct costs based on normal or estimated output to set the price, with the mark up being sufficient to cover shop and enterprise expenses and produce a profit. Normal cost pricing procedures consist of marking up average direct costs based on normal output to cover shop expenses which gives normal average factory costs, then marking up normal average factory costs to cover enterprise expenses which gives normal average total costs, and then marking up normal average total costs to set the price, with the mark up producing a desired margin for profit. Finally target rate of return pricing procedures consist of marking up normal or standard

[8] When direct labor and material costs are classified as variable costs, the costing procedures are called variable costing.

[9] Empirical evidence for the relationship between cost accounting systems and costing is somewhat difficult to come by; but it can be inferred. It is clear that if the enterprise does not collect overhead costs, then it cannot use costing procedures in which overhead costs are an explicit component. On the other hand, it is possible for an enterprise to collect overhead costs, but then use a costing procedure in which they are not a part. However, there is little support for this latter possibility. For example, Black and Eversole (A5) found in their study of cost accounting in American industry that of the 20,282 enterprises which used a recognizable cost system to calculate their costs, nearly 90 percent of them could calculate their average total costs. It can then be argued (see Simon et al., 1954; Chandler, 1962) that the enterprises would use the developed cost base when engaging in costing. Therefore if the latter possibility is to have any support, then the costing procedures used by enterprises must be restricted primarily to direct costs. But this is clearly not the case, as can be gathered from the costing and pricing studies in Appendixes A and B. The connection between cost accounting systems and costing can consequently be taken as indirectly empirically grounded.

[10] This implies that business enterprises do not consider profits as part of costs. Consequently, the typical statement made by Sraffians and Marxists that prices equal their costs of production (which includes a uniform rate of profit) in long-period positions has no conceptual correspondence to the concepts of costs and prices used by business enterprises. Without this link, the Sraffian and Marxian theory of prices cease to be grounded in the real world inhabited by actual business enterprises and their costing and pricing procedures.

average total costs (which include shop and enterprise expenses) by a certain percentage that will generate a volume of profits at normal or standard capacity utilization which will produce a specific rate of return with respect to the value of the enterprise's capital assets. These pricing procedures can be formalized in the following manner:[11]

Labor and material-based mark up pricing:
$$[NADC][1 + k] = \text{price}$$

Normal cost pricing: $[(NADC)(1 + g)][1 + h][1 + r] = \text{price}$
$$[(NAFC)(1 + h)][1 + t] = \text{price}$$
$$[(NATC)(1 + r)] = \text{price}$$

Target rate of return pricing: $[NATC][1 + t] = \text{price}$
$$[SATC][1 + t] = \text{price}$$

where $NADC$ is normal average direct costs
  $NAFC$ is normal average factory costs
  $NATC$ is average total costs
  $SATC$ is standard average total costs
  k is the mark up for overhead costs and profits
  g is the mark up for shop expenses
  h is the mark up for enterprise expenses
  r is the mark up for profit
  t is the mark up for profit which will produce the target rate of
    return with respect to the value of the enterprise's capital assets.

Thus the differences between mark up pricing, normal cost pricing, and target rate of return pricing procedures are due to the different cost accounting systems underlying them.[12]

---

[11] As noted in Table IA.2 (pp. 12–16), many Post Keynesians utilize a mark up pricing procedure which consists of marking up average direct labor costs based on normal or estimated output to set the price, with the mark up being sufficient to cover material costs (if any), shop and enterprise expenses, and produce a profit. This labor-based mark up pricing procedures can be delineated as follows:

$$[W][1 + s] = \text{price}$$

where W is average direct labor costs based on normal output and s is the mark up for material costs, overhead costs, and profits. However, of the 71 pricing studies in Appendix B (pp. 235–40), only two reported the existence of labor-based mark up pricing procedures, which suggests that they are generally not used by business enterprises.

[12] It is particularly important to note that for normal cost and target rate of return pricing procedures, business enterprises first identify and quantify their shop and enterprise expenses which are generally joint costs and then decide on how they will be allocated to their various products. The allocating procedures used range from applying a predetermined mark up on direct labor costs, on direct material costs, or on both to

The empirical evidence clearly indicates that the three pricing procedures postulated by the doctrines are used by business enterprises. However, it is possible to roughly ascertain the extent to which the different pricing procedures are in fact used by business enterprise. Of the 71 pricing studies in appendix B, only 24 reported the use of mark up pricing procedures (see table 11.1). Further, of the 26 costing studies in Appendix A, 12 reported the use of direct and variable costing while 18 reported the use of direct and overhead costing; but in terms of numbers, only 21 percent of the 1,600 enterprises surveyed utilized direct and variable costing procedures.[13] Finally, the costing and pricing studies indicate that many of the enterprises which utilized mark up pricing procedures restricted their usage to *secondary and strategic* pricing decisions and special cases, such as pricing by-products, sub-contracting, repairs, disposing of obsolete and out-dated production, determining price floors in extreme price-cutting situations, market penetration, and new products (see costing studies A9, A11, A12, A23, A26 and pricing studies B31, B60, B64, B66). Thus, while all three pricing procedures are used by business enterprises, normal cost and target rate of return pricing procedures are the most prevalent.[14]

using machine hours. In all cases, the methods used are based on past experience and scientific fact-finding. Consequently, enterprises use normal cost and target rate of return pricing procedures to arrive at a product's average total costs on which they then apply a mark up for profit to set the price. Therefore, it is conceptually inappropriate to algebraically reduce normal cost or target rate of return pricing procedures to a mark up pricing procedure, since the latter is used only by enterprises who cannot (or do not) identify, quantify, and allocate their overhead costs among their products and who cannot (or do not) separate costs from profits. Since enterprises differentiate between mark up, normal cost, and target rate of return pricing procedures, they will retain their separate identities throughout this and the following chapter. For further discussion on this issue, see Lee (1994b, 1996); Downward and Reynolds (1996); Downward *et al.* (1996).

[13] It is also important to note that costing studies A4, A7, A10, A11, A23, A26 show that the predominant form of pricing is normal cost pricing. Further, the costing evidence suggests that establishments which operated under government management, such as Royal Ordnance Factories and Admiralty Dockyards, use quite sophisticated systems of cost accounting when costing fixed price and cost-plus contracts (see Select Committee on National Expenditure, 1941, and costing study A25).

[14] The implication of this is that 42 of the 47 studies cited in table IA.2 in the appendix to the Introduction are not very useful to Post Keynesians and the 32 studies which only used labor-based mark up pricing should be completely discarded. Further, studies, such as Kregel (1973); Harcourt and Kenyon (1976); Ong (1981); Dutt (1988); Sawyer (1990b), which combine mark up pricing, large business enterprises, and growth, are empirically and theoretically misleading in that mark up pricing is more likely to be associated with small enterprises – of the pricing studies involving small enterprises and delineating pricing procedures, most of them reported the use of mark up pricing –

Table 11.1 *Distribution of pricing procedures reported in appendix B*

	LMBMUP	NCP	TRRP
Number of studies reporting the pricing procedures	24	51	15

Notes: LMBMUP Labor and material-based mark up pricing.
         NCP   Normal cost pricing.
         TRRP   Target rate of return pricing.

Turning to the market, common to the three doctrines is the view that most markets are inhabited by more than one business enterprise. Consequently, co-ordination is required among the enterprises if destructive price competition is to be avoided and an acceptable, single market price established. Business enterprises have therefore utilized a range of private market institutions, such as cartels and price leadership arrangements, buttressed by an array of ancillary conventions, traditions, and restrictive trade agreements to establish an orderly market with a single market price. When the private market institutions have failed to control price competition, enterprises have turned to quasi-government or purely government organizations, legal decrees, and laws in order to establish an orderly market with a single market price. In cases where a cartel is involved in fixing the market price, the price administrators may take an average of the average total costs of the member enterprises with the lowest costs adjusted for share of market sales; or they may take an average of costs of all their member enterprises. In either case, a mark up for profit is applied to the costing equation to set the market price. Finally, a cartel may simply specify the costing and pricing procedures, but not specify a particular market price, with the consequence that there will not be a single market price. As for price leadership, the pricing administrators within the price-leader enterprise utilize its pricing procedures to determine the price which it then administers to the market and which the price-following enterprises accept as the market price and therefore adjust their mark ups for profit accordingly given their costing base. Finally, in the case of a government agency determining a market price, the costing and pricing procedures its pricing administrators used are the same as used by private business enterprises.

The empirical evidence regarding the existence of market institutions setting market prices and the extent of their activities within a corporate

whose goals and objectives are survival, satisfactory profits, and customer satisfaction (see pricing studies B11, B25, B26, B29, B36, B39, B40, B48, B57, B68).

economy is evident within the pricing studies. Pricing studies B6, B14, B15, B19, B21, B22, B33, B34, B35, B44, B51, B60 reported that the pricing administrators within the cartel utilized mark up and normal cost pricing procedures buttressed by ancillary conventions and agreements when determining market prices. Similarly, pricing studies B1, B15, B31, B34, B51, B62, B71 establish that the pricing administrators within the price-leader enterprises generally utilize normal cost and target rate of return pricing procedures when setting their prices, while pricing studies B7, B8, B11, B15, B31, B39, B44, B62 indicate that the price-following enterprises adjust their profit mark ups in order to set the same price as the price leader. Finally, in situations in which government agencies determine prices, they use mark up and normal cost pricing procedures and the extent of their activities varies from the economy as a whole, such as during wartime, to a few particular markets depending on the political situation (see costing studies A7, A25 and pricing studies B22, B44, B69, B70). Corroborating evidence beyond the pricing studies can also be found in various industry, enterprise, and government studies.[15] Thus the existence of market institutions and their pricing activities are well documented.

Pricing policy and prices

Common to the three doctrines is the view that the business enterprise utilizes mark up, normal cost, and target rate of return pricing procedures to set prices that would enable it to engage in sequential acts of production over time and thereby reproduce itself and grow.[16] Because the market conditions facing the enterprise's many products are not uniform and change over time, its price administrators necessarily utilize a variety of multi-temporal, open-ended pricing strategies designed to achieve time-specific and temporally undefined goals. The compendium of pricing strategies is known as the enterprise's pricing policy and the prices which it administers to the various markets are based on one or

---

[15] For studies on trade association price-fixing activities in capitalist economies in the twentieth century, see Ripley (1905); Nelson (1922); Levy (1944); Political and Economic Planning (1957); Galambos (1966); Wilberforce et al. (1966, Appendixes IX, XIV); Swann et al. (1974); Fickle (1980); Yamazaki and Miyamoto (1988); Mercer (1995). For studies on price-leader enterprises and price-following enterprises, see Burns (1936); Wilcox (1940); Stocking and Watkins (1951); Adams (1961); Hazledine (1979u); White (1980). For studies on government involvement in determining prices, see Lyon and Abramson (1936); Fisher and James (1955); Grant and Mathews (1957); Hawley (1966); Rockoff (1984).

[16] For a theoretical analysis of this point, see Lee (1985, 1990–1).

more of these strategies. Thus the administered prices of a business enterprise are strategic prices whose common and overriding goals are often survival and growth (see pricing studies B1, B18, B19, B20, B21, B22, B25, B27, B31, B32, B34, B37, B40, B41, B44, B50, B53, B54, B55, B60, B62, B63, B64, B67, B68, B71).[17]

Essential for the success of the pricing strategies is that the administered prices remain stable for a period of time and sequence of market transactions. Since the pricing process can be labor-intensive and time-consuming (see Capon *et al.*, 1975; Farley *et al.*, 1980), it is not surprising that 25 of the pricing studies in appendix B report that enterprises and market institutions which use mark up, normal cost, and target rate of return pricing procedures, adopted pricing policies designed to maintain prices for a period of time, such as a selling season.[18] Moreover, pricing studies B1, B6, B9, B22, B24, B30, B31, B33, B36, B37, B40, B41, B43, B44, B45, B48, B52, B55, B61, B65 show that enterprises and market institutions used the pricing procedures to set prices that remained stable for three months or longer. In addition, as shown in table 11.2, mark up, normal cost, and target rate of return pricing procedures are associated with prices of products which remain stable over periods of time.

Finally, the stability of prices for a period of time implies that numerous market transactions take place at the same price. Direct evidence for this is found in the sales records of business enterprises[19] and indirectly found in pricing studies B1, B2, B5, B9, B10, B11, B13, B14, B16, B21, B24, B26, B30, B32, B35, B38, B40, B44, B47, B48, B53, B65, B68. The connection between pricing procedures, price stabilization policy, and price stability implies that, conversely, prices of products which change infrequently have been set by enterprises and market institutions using mark up, normal cost, and target rate of return pricing procedures. The widespread use of such pricing procedures within a capitalist economy implied above is affirmed in tables 11.3 and 11.4. Thus it can be concluded that a significant proportion of industrial and consumer products in a capitalist economy have prices based on mark

---

[17] For example, business enterprises may also administer their prices to achieve social and political objectives, such as Esso Standard's attempt to slow down the post-Second World War inflationary price rise (see Hansen and Niland, 1952).

[18] Blinder (1991) and Hall *et al.* in pricing study B65 noted that the enterprises thought that the use of cost-based or normal cost pricing procedures was an important factor in explaining infrequent price changes.

[19] Examples of such records are found in the records of E. I. Du Pont de Nemours and Co., especially in the monthly sales agents' reports and in agents' sales books – see Lee (1997*u*).

Table 11.2 *Pricing procedures and price stability*

Study	Product group	Pricing procedure	Range of average lengths (in months) of price stability		
			Means[a]	Carlton[b]	Other
B3	Fertilizer	NCP	2–4		
B3 B16 A4	Shoes	NCP	4–10		Riley[c]: 5–35
B3	Men's clothing	NCP	3–95		Riley: 6–35
B5 B8 B16	Agricultural implements	NCP	16–95		
B8	Cosmetics	NCP	12–18		
B8	Candies	NCP	7–12		
B8	Heating equipment	NCP	2.6–12		
B8	Office equipment	NCP	4–12		
B16	Apparel–Men's suits	NCP	5–10		
B16	Woollen fabrics	NCP	3–6		
B16	Tobacco	NCP	10–45		Riley: 35
B16	Paperboard	NCP	2–4		Riley: 35
B16	Dry batteries	NCP	24		Riley: 7–35
B8	Household appliances	NCP	12–45		Riley: 1.5–4
B16	Paper bags	MUP		7.5	Riley: 2
B16	Fiber containers	NCP		11.6	
B16	Yarns	NCP			Riley: 1–35
B16	Hosiery	NCP	2.7–4		Riley: 7–35
B16 B8	Paper cartons	NCP			Riley: 5–35
B16 B8	Glass products	NCP	7.3–32		Riley: 12–18
B16	Gray-iron casts	NCP			Riley: 1.3
B8 B31	Steel	NCP	2–45	12–22	Riley: 3.6–12
B31	Aluminium	TRRP	7		Kaplan[d]: 8–9 Riley: 5–7
B31	Industrial gases	TRRP		16.8	Riley: 7
B31	Antifreeze	TRRP			Kaplan: 12.5 Riley: 12
B31	Cellophane	TRRP			Kaplan: 14–18
B31	Rayon and nylon	TRRP			Kaplan: 12–38 Riley: 35

Notes:

[a] Means (1939a) – the average length of price stability for a particular product is calculated by dividing the 95 possible monthly price changes by the number of price changes that occurred; the range of average length of price stability is given in terms of the shortest and the longest average length of price stability of the products in the product group.

[b] Carlton (1986) – the range of average length of price stability is taken from Table 5, column 3.

[c] Riley (1958) – the average length of price stability for a particular product is calculated by dividing the 35 possible monthly changes in its price index by the number of changes in the price index which occurred, except when there were no changes in the price index, in which case 35 was used as the average length of price stability.[20]

[d] Kaplan – the data comes from Kaplan et al. (1958); and the method of calculating the average length of price stability is the same as used for Means.

Table 11.3 *Product groups and infrequent price changes for US manufactured products, 1926–33, 1954–6, and 1957–66*

Product group	Means (1939a)		Riley (1958)		Carlton (1986)	
	NP	APS	NP	APS	NP	APSM
Farm products	64	3	86	4		
Foods	126	30	137	49		
Hides and leather products	39	27	48	27		
Textile products	105	60	190	142		
Fuel and lighting	16	3	40	26	4	5.9
Metal and metal products	111	75	623	577	21	4.2–13
Building materials	96	65	96	53	5	4.7–13.2
Chemicals and drugs	83	64	288	265	23	12.8
Housefurnishing goods	35	31	86	70		
Miscellaneous	70	58	195	179	13	8.1–8.7

Notes:
NP   Number of products.
APS   Number of products whose average length of price stability is three months or longer.
ASPM Average length of price stability (in months).

[20] In Riley's study, frequency of price change for a product was based on how many times its monthly price index changed, a procedure which can lead to over-estimates of the frequency of price changes for the product.

Table 11.4 *Frequency of price changes for UK manufacture products, July 1987–December 1991*

	7/87–6/88	8/88–2/90	4/90–12/91
Average number of products per month	9,906	9,443	10,335
Total possible number of price changes	118,875	179,420	217,035
Total number of actual price changes	17,172	31,194	33,260
Average number of months a product's price remains unchanged	6.9	5.8	6.5

up, normal cost, and target rate of return pricing procedures and which are relatively stable over time and sequences of transactions.[21]

The existence of stable, administered market prices implies that the markets in which they exist are not organized like auction markets or like the early retail markets and oriental bazaars where the retailer engages in individual price negotiation for each transaction. Rather, enterprises which desire to enter these markets must first announce a price for its product and then enter into direct buyer–seller interaction to obtain sales. Since buyer–seller interactions take place both simultaneously and through time, business enterprises have found that stable prices are cost-efficient in terms of selling costs, reduce the threat of price wars, and facilitate the establishment of goodwill relationships with customers.[22] The existence of stable market prices also implies the absence of any determinant inverse price–sales relationship facing the individual business enterprise or for the market as a whole. Where reported (see pricing studies B5, B6, B10, B11, B14, B16, B19, B21, B24, B26, B30, B31, B34, B36, B40, B41, B48, B55, B64), business enterprises stated that variations in their prices within practical limits, given the prices of their competitors, produced virtually no change in their sales and that variations in the market price, especially downward, produced little if any changes in market sales in the short term. Moreover, when the price change is significant enough to result in a non-insignificant change in sales, the impact on profits has been sufficiently negative to persuade enterprises not to try the experiment again (for example, see Bell, 1960).

[21] For additional evidence of the infrequency of price changes, see Blinder (1991), Wilson (1954, vol. II, Appendix 9), and Godley and Gillion (1965).

[22] In the case of price wars, administered prices become more exchange-specific, as are prices in auction markets and before the one-price plan when retail prices were individually negotiated. However, it must be noted that price wars affect only a small part of the transactions and volume of sales in any particular market (see pricing studies B22, B26; see also Learned, 1948; Cassady, 1954).

The absence of any significant market price–sales relationship in the short term has also been noted in various industry studies (for example, see Hirsch, 1950–1; Cassady, 1954; Eisner, 1956; Hazledine, 1979*u*). Consequently, inverse price–sales relationships play a minor, if not an insignificant, role in enterprises' pricing decisions. Enterprises do not set their prices to achieve a specific volume of sales or degree of capacity utilization, but rather set prices which are maintained in face of fluctuations in sales volumes over time.[23] Supporting this pricing policy is the belief that sales are more a function of buyer income, level of aggregate economic activity, government demand for armaments, population growth, service, product design, performance, and reliability, and perhaps advertising then price (see pricing studies B1, B5, B19, B41, B58, B64, B67, B71; Buckner, 1967; Cunningham and White, 1973; Hazledine, 1979*u*).

The existence of stable administered prices does not, however, preclude change. As indicated above, business enterprises utilize pricing periods (or selling seasons) of three months to a year (see pricing studies B1, B6, B9, B16, B24, B26, B30, B33, B36, B37, B40, B42, B43, B44, B45, B48, B52, B55, B61, B65, B69) in which their administered prices remained unchanged; and then at the end of the period, they decide on whether to alter them. The factors which are most important to the enterprises in this regard are changes in labor and material costs (see pricing studies B4, B5, B6, B8, B13, B19, B21, B22, B24, B26, B28, B30, B31, B33, B34, B37, B39, B40, B43, B44, B46, B47, B64, B65, B69), changes in the mark up for profit (see pricing studies B1, B4, B5, B6, B28, B31, B43, B44), and changes in normal output or capacity utilization that are based on budgeted or expected sales (see costing studies A12, A20, A23 and pricing studies B5, B6, B7, B8, B10, B14, B16, B17, B33, B43).[24] Factors prompting the enterprises to alter their mark ups for profit include short-term and long-term competitive pressures (see pricing studies B1, B4, B5, B6, B8, B11, B16, B19, B23, B24, B25, B29, B30, B38, B39, B40, B43, B44, B50, B52, B62, B65), the stage at which the product has reached in its life-cycle (see pricing studies B31, B40, B44, B62), and the need for

---

[23] This necessarily means that administered prices are not market-clearing prices, do not change with each change in sales (or shift in the virtually non-existent market or enterprises "demand curve"), and are not necessarily increased in times of economic booms or shortages (see pricing studies B65, B68, B69). For further discussion, see chapter 12.

[24] The pricing studies in appendix B (see also Choksi, 1979*t*) did not indicate that enterprises based their decisions to alter their prices on the status of their sales. That is, the enterprises did not increase their prices if sales were above normal, and nor did they reduce their prices if sales were below normal.

profit (see pricing studies B1, B22, B43, B46, B50, B62). Consequently, administered prices can change from one pricing period to the next in any direction, irrespective of the state of the business cycle.[25] However, evidence does suggest that within short periods of time (such as two-year intervals), change in costs will dominate the price changes, whereas over longer periods of time changes in the mark up will play a more important role.

The pricing equation

To develop a pricing model that will be a part of the pricing foundations of Post Keynesian price theory, it is necessary to mathematize the mark up, normal cost, and target rate of return pricing procedures formalized above. This will involve delineating the costing and pricing equations at the level of the business enterprise and then at the level of the market. As previously noted, each pricing procedure explicitly takes account of its direct material and labor costs and uses a normal level of output or degree of capacity utilization to determine its normal average direct costs. Normal average direct costs can be mathematized and written as:

$$\sum_{i=1}^{n} md_i p_i + \sum_{v=1}^{z} ld_v w_v \qquad (11.1)$$

where md_i is the ith normal average direct material pricing coefficient
ld_v is the vth normal average direct labor pricing coefficient
p_i is the market price of the ith material input
w_v is the wage rate of the vth labor input.

Overhead costs, which consist of shop and enterprise expenses, are acknowledged in normal cost and target rate of return pricing procedures. In particular, the procedures take account of the material and labor costs and depreciation which make up the two expenses and use a normal level of output to determine normal shop and enterprise expenses.

---

[25] If price administrators decide to increase prices when sales are decreasing or decrease prices when sales are increasing, we then have prices which move in a "perverse" manner. The empirical existence of such prices can be found in Means (1972) and Blair (1972, 1974). The basis for such prices is found in the administratively determined figure for normal output or capacity utilization. That is, if the pricing administrators altered the figure for normal output in a counter-cyclical fashion, then normal average total costs will vary counter-cyclically; and if the profit mark up remains constant, then the pricing administrators would be setting counter-cyclical or "perverse" prices (Blair, 1974; Means, 1983).

It is thus possible to mathematize both normal shop and enterprise expenses, respectively, as

$$\sum_{i=1}^{n} ms_i p_i + \sum_{v=1}^{z} ls_v w_v + ds \qquad (11.2)$$

$$\sum_{i=1}^{n} me_i p_i + \sum_{v=1}^{z} le_v w_v + de \qquad (11.3)$$

where ms_i is the ith normal average shop material pricing coefficient
me_i is the ith normal average enterprise material pricing coefficient
ls_v is the vth normal average shop labor pricing coefficient
le_v is the vth normal average enterprise labor pricing coefficient
ds is the normal average shop depreciation pricing coefficient
de is the normal average enterprise depreciation pricing coefficient.

Normal overhead costs consist of normal shop and enterprise expenses; they can be mathematized as an amalgamation of (11.2) and (11.3):

$$\sum_{i=1}^{n} mo_i p_i + \sum_{v=1}^{z} lo_v w_v + do \qquad (11.4)$$

where mo_i is the ith normal average overhead material pricing coefficient
lo_v is the vth normal average overhead labor pricing coefficient
do is the normal average depreciation pricing coefficient.

Each pricing coefficient represents the average amount of the input needed to produce a unit of output when the level of output is normal. Moreover, as suggested above, since the direct, shop, and enterprise material, labor, and depreciation pricing coefficients are based on a given normal level of output, variations in actual output will leave them unaffected.[26] Hence, with input prices and wage rates taken as known and given, normal average direct costs, shop expenses, enterprise expenses, and overhead costs are not affected by changes in the level of actual output or degree of capacity utilization.

With the various normal cost foundations of the pricing procedures mathematized, it is now possible to complete the process of developing the pricing equations. Working with (11.1), the mark up pricing equation becomes

---

[26] This means that the direct material and labor pricing coefficients will generally differ from the actual direct material and labor production coefficients (see Lee, 1986).

$$\left[\sum_{i=1}^{n} md_i p_i + \sum_{v=1}^{z} ld_v w_v \right] [1 + k] = p \tag{11.5}$$

where k is the mark up for overhead costs and profits
p is the price of the good.

Because normal cost pricing procedure may explicitly take account of only direct costs, of direct costs and shop expenses, or of direct and overhead costs, it is necessary delineate three different normal costs pricing equations. The first consists of a series of shop, enterprise, and profit mark ups on NADC:

$$\left[\sum_{i=1}^{n} md_i p_i + \sum_{v=1}^{z} ld_v w_v \right] [1 + g][1 + h][1 + r] = p \tag{11.6}$$

where g is the mark up for shop expenses
h is the mark up for enterprise expenses
r is the mark up for profit.

The second equation is based on (11.1) and (11.2), which together equal the NAFC. The second normal cost pricing equation consists of enterprise and profit mark ups on NAFC:

$$\left[\sum_{i=1}^{n} md_i p_i + \sum_{v=1}^{z} ld_v w_v \right.$$
$$\left. + \sum_{i=1}^{n} ms_i p_i + \sum_{v=1}^{z} ls_v w_v + ds \right] [1 + h][1 + r] = p. \tag{11.7}$$

The final normal cost pricing equation is based on (11.1), (11.2), and (11.3), which together equal NATC. Thus the pricing equation consists of a profit mark up on NATC:

$$\left[\sum_{i=1}^{n} md_i p_i + \sum_{v=1}^{v} ld_v w_v + \sum_{i=1}^{n} ms_i p_i + \sum_{v=1}^{v} ls_v w_v + ds \right.$$
$$\left. + \sum_{i=1}^{n} me_i p_i + \sum_{v=1}^{v} le_v w_v + de \right] [1 + r] = p. \tag{11.8}$$

Since shop and enterprise expenses comprise overhead costs, (11.8) can with (11.4) be rewritten as

$$\left[\sum_{i=1}^{n} md_i p_i + \sum_{v=1}^{v} ld_v w_v \right.$$

$$\left. + \sum_{i=1}^{n} mo_i p_i + \sum_{v=1}^{v} lo_v w_v + do \right] [1 + r] = p. \quad (11.9)$$

The target rate of return pricing equation is similar to (11.9) except that the mark up for profit, t, is such that it will produce the target rate of return with respect to the value of the enterprise's capital assets:

$$\left[\sum_{i=1}^{n} md_i p_i + \sum_{v=1}^{v} ld_v w_v \right.$$

$$\left. + \sum_{i=1}^{n} mo_i p_i + \sum_{v=1}^{v} lo_v w_v + do \right] [1 + t] = p. \quad (11.10)$$

Being based on pricing coefficients and given input prices, wage rates, and shop, enterprise, and profit mark ups, the above mark up, normal cost, and target rate of return pricing equations and their prices are not affected by changes in the level of actual output or degree of capacity utilization. Moreover, while the above pricing equations are articulated at the level of the business enterprise, their general mathematical form does not change at the level of the market. Whether the market price is determined by a trade association, government agency, or through price leadership arrangements, mark up, normal cost, and target rate of return pricing procedures are always used and, hence, their general mathematical form retained. However, there is a distinction between the enterprise and market pricing equation, in that within the same market they do not have to be identical. For example, in a market where a trade association fixes the market price by taking an average of the average total costs of the member enterprises with the lowest costs adjusted for market share and then applying a profit mark up, the market pricing equation will differ from the pricing equations of the individual enterprises in terms of value for the pricing coefficients and profit mark up. On the other hand, in the case of price-leadership arrangements, the pricing equation of the price leader will also be the market pricing equation, but with the components of the pricing equations of the price followers differing from those of the market pricing equation. Thus, for example, a normal cost market pricing equation can be written as

$$\left[\sum_{i=1}^{n} md_{mi}p_i + \sum_{v=1}^{z} ld_{mv}w_v + \sum_{i=1}^{n} mo_{mi}p_i \right.$$

$$\left. + \sum_{v=1}^{z} lo_{mv}w_v + do_m \right][1 + r_m] = p_m. \qquad (11.11)$$

where md_{mi} is the ith normal average direct material pricing coefficient of the market pricing equation

ld_{mv} is the vth normal average direct labor pricing coefficient of the market pricing equation

mo_{mi} is the ith normal average overhead material pricing coefficient of the market pricing equation

lo_{mv} is the vth normal average overhead labor pricing coefficient of the market pricing equation

do_m is the normal average depreciation pricing coefficient of the market pricing equation

p_i is the market price of the ith material input

w_v is the wage rate of the vth labor input

r_m is the "market" mark up for profit

p_m is the market price of the good.

In comparing the market pricing equation to the enterprise pricing (11.9), md_{mi}, ld_{mv}, mo_{mi}, lo_{mv}, do_m, and r_m will generally differ from md_i, ld_v, mo_i, lo_v, do, and r.

To move from a single market pricing equation to a model of interdependent market pricing equations, it is necessary to first consider the general schema of production that underlies it. Once the schema is outlined, the pricing model can be delineated and the pricing foundations of Post Keynesian price theory set out.

12 The pricing model, the grounded pricing foundation, and Post Keynesian price theory

Any attempt at developing an empirically grounded theoretical pricing model of the economy based on market pricing equations raises a number of conceptual and theoretical issues, the first of which is the model's relationship to the production schema of real capitalist economies. Some Post Keynesian economists take the position that it is not necessary to specify any production schema underlying their pricing models, others take the view that the pricing model need not bear any relationship to the underlying schema, as in the case when production is depicted in terms of a circular flow of produced goods while pricing consists of simply the marking up of labor costs. Since material and labor inputs are explicit components of mark up, normal cost, and target rate of return pricing procedures, the working hypothesis adopted here is, in contrast to the above views, that the foundation of the pricing model must be closely related to the general schema of production of capitalist economies. This decision brings with it a number of further conceptual and theoretical issues which center on the representation of the production schema. Drawing upon a number of input–output studies (see table 12.1), the principal characteristics of the production schema with regard to the flow and use of intermediate inputs and the differentiation between intermediate inputs and final demand products and among final demand products will be set out. Once this has been accomplished and the basic schema of production delineated, the degree of abstract aggregation of the schema with regard to pricing and the structures of consumption and investment will be discussed. The empirically grounded production schema will then be used as a reference point for delineating the pricing model of the economy. After discussion the model's features and properties, the pricing foundations and its implications for a Post Keynesian theory of prices will be outlined and discussed.

Production schema

The production schema of a capitalist economy is reflected in its input–output framework and empirically represented in its input–output tables. One characteristic of the input–output tables surveyed[1] is that they consist of more than one or two products and that the majority of products used more than 40 percent of the products produced in the economy as material and service inputs into their production (see table 12.1, columns (1)–(2)); a second characteristic is that intermediate products made up from 24 to over 50 percent of the total sales of the economy (see table 12.1, column (3)). A third characteristic of the tables is that many of the products produced are used as inputs (and some almost exclusively) while others are used almost exclusively used for consumption or investment (see table 12.1 columns (5)–(8)). The fourth characteristic of the input–output tables is that intermediate inputs are involved directly and indirectly in their own production as well as in the production of all other products – the tables show that intermediate inputs are basic goods and that production in capitalist economies is a circular process in terms of intermediate inputs as opposed to a one-way street. This characteristic is clearly established in those input–output tables in which the Leontief inverse is calculated (see table 12.1, column (4)).[2]

The general characteristics of the production schema of a capitalist economy means that the minimum number of products and markets needed to model it is four – two basic goods for the circular flow of intermediate inputs, one non-basic good to represent a consumption product, and one non-basic good to represent an investment product. As long as there is a continuous demand for the consumption and investment goods, there will be continuous transactions for the intermediate

---

[1] Given the large number of input–output tables in existence, the survey reported in table 12.1 was restricted to the United Kingdom and the United States. The characteristics of the tables for the two countries are not unique to them, but are also found in the tables of all industrialized regions and countries – see, for example, Manne and Rudra (1965); Parker (1965); Cameron (1968); United Nations Statistical Commission (1982); Eurostat (1986); Goudie (1994).

[2] Given that production as a circular process and hence the Sraffian "commodity residual" are inherent characteristics of a capitalist economy, Post Keynesian pricing models which are based on Austrian or Burchardt production models and/or are completely "vertically" integrated production models have no empirical grounding. Further, those Post Keynesian pricing models which do not distinguish between intermediate and final products or between investment and consumption products have little if any correspondence with real capitalist economies. For these reasons, it can be concluded that 26 of the 47 studies in table IA.2 in the appendix to the Introduction (pp. 12–16) have no empirical grounding or correspondence to the real world.

Table 12.1 *Input–output characteristics of capitalist economies, 1919–90*

Country	(1)	(2)	(3)	(4)	(5)	(6)	(7)	(8)
United Kingdom 1935								
(Barna, 1953, table III)	35	69	24	—	4	1	1	5
United Kingdom 1954								
(CSO, 1961, tables B, E)	45	89	54	Yes	3	—	—	6
United Kingdom 1963								
(CSO, 1970, tables D, J)	70	94	34	Yes	10	6	1	10
United Kingdom 1968)								
(CSO, 1973, tables B, L)	90	73	38	Yes	6	5	—	8
United Kingdom 1979								
(CSO, 1983, tables K, L)	99	75	35	Yes	12	4	1	4
United Kingdom 1984								
(CSO, 1988, tables 4, 5)	101	98	39	Yes	6	3	3	22
United Kingdom 1990								
(CSO, 1995, tables 4, 5)	121	98	41	Yes	9	7	1	21
United States 1919 (Leontief, 1951)	41	5	42	—	11	7	—	2
United States 1929 (Leontief, 1951)	41	20	41	—	11	5	—	4
United States 1939 (Leontief, 1951)	35	63	35	—	3	—	—	1
United States 1958								
(NEDS, 1965, tables 1, 3)	82	93	49	Yes	2	1	1	25

Notes:
Column (1) Number of product groups
Column (2) Percentage of product groups which used more than 40 percent of product groups as intermediate inputs
Column (3) Percentage of intermediate products in total sales
Column (4) Leontief inverse
Column (5) Number of product groups in which final demand use comprises 90 percent or more of their total sales
Column (6) Number of product groups in column (5) in which consumer expenditures comprise 80 percent or more of domestic sales
Column (7) Number of product groups in column (5) in which investment expenditures comprise 80 percent or more of domestic sales
Column (8) Number of product groups in which intermediate purchases comprise 90 percent or more of domestic sales.

inputs. Thus a further characteristic of the circular production schema is that all markets are always clogged with sequences of transactions which in turn promote sequences of production followed by further transactions. This continual recursive interaction of production and transactions means that markets in capitalist economies are non-clearable.[3]

---

[3] If transactions ceased to occur in a market, the market itself would disappear.

While capturing the general production characteristics of capitalist economies, the production schema's level of abstract aggregation is too great with regard to pricing, consumption, and investment. The continual development of more sophisticated costing and pricing procedures cited in chapter 11 occurred because enterprises began using a wider range of materials, services, and capital equipment in production. Not only did direct inputs become more varied, they were also different from the overhead inputs which required their own particular procedures in order to be accounted for. The various biological and social needs of workers, capitalists, and their families for housing, food, clothing, transportation, medical care, education, and recreation requires and encourages a multiplicity of consumer goods and services to be produced and priced.[4] Finally, the differentiation of production methods across products and markets combined with technological change requires a multiplicity of investment goods to be produced and priced.[5] The degree of abstract aggregation of the production schema must, therefore, be disaggregated to the extent that all intermediate, consumption, and investment products and market are, in a theoretical sense, explicit.[6] Consequently the general circular production schema will include n "basic" products (markets) which are used as intermediate direct and overhead material (and services) inputs, a "non-basic" intermediate inputs into the final demand products, and f "non-basic" final demand (consumption, investment, government, and export) products (markets). Thus, the schema will have a total of $n + a + f = m$ markets which include both basic and non-basic products as well as v direct and overhead labor inputs, and can be depicted as

---

[4] From the input–output tables it is possible to identify some of the different consumer product groups such as pharmaceuticals, tobacco, confectionery, alcoholic and soft drinks, hosiery and knitted goods, jewelry, clothing, milk and milk products, domestic electrical appliances, hotels, footwear, and housing.

[5] From the input–output tables it is possible to identify some of the different investment product groups such as aerospace, shipbuilding, chemical products, process machinery and contractors, office machinery and computer equipment, and instrument engineering.

[6] This conclusion implies that "vertically" integrated production models must be rejected on the basis that they theoretically "hid" products and markets instead of exposing them. Moreover, such production models make it impossible to deal with vertical price, selling, and buying relationships between enterprises, such as found in resale price maintenance, all of which are issues which a theory of prices would deal with. Finally, such models hid the prices of intermediate products as well as the enterprises which are engaged in the production of intermediate goods. Since the activity associated with intermediate inputs generally constitutes over 40 percent of all economic activity in capitalist economies, the elimination of such activity would give a very distorted picture of what was actually going on.

$$G + V \rightarrow Q_d \tag{12.1}$$

where G is a $m \times n + a$ flow matrix of intermediate inputs
V is a $m \times v$ matrix of labor inputs
Q_d is a $m \times m$ diagonal matrix of output.

The significance of the production schema is that it is empirically grounded and able to handle various degrees of disaggregation as required by the theoretical and empirical issues being dealt with. But in practical terms when considering theoretical issues relating to pricing, prices, and other microeconomic issues, the production schema should have at a minimum 10 products and markets; whereas when dealing with empirical issues or historical investigations, the schema should be disaggregated to at least the number of products and markets found in the input–output tables, if not more. The quantity model corresponding to the production schema consists of three equations determining G, V, and Q:

$$A^T Q_t + F = Q_{t+1}$$
$$Q_{dt} A = G_t \tag{12.2}$$
$$Q_{dt} V^* = V_t$$

where A is a $m \times n + a + f$ matrix of material production coefficients[7]
V^* is a $m \times v$ matrix of labor production coefficients
Q_t is a $m \times 1$ vector of output at time t
F is a $m \times 1$ vector of final demand.[8]

A pricing model of the economy

Given the underlying production schema, the pricing model of the economy, which covers all industrial, wholesale, and retail enterprises and their respective markets, can be delineated in terms of a market pricing equation for each of the basic and non-basic products. Specifying the mark up, normal cost, and target rate of return pricing equations (11.5)–(11.10) as market pricing equations (like (11.11)) and assuming a market pricing equation for each market, the pricing model for the economy takes the form

[7] The material production coefficient matrix A is decomposable and its sub-matrix $A_{n \times n}$ has a maximum eigenvalue that falls between zero and one. Further, the elements of both A and V^* can change as output changes due to the existence of vintage technology (see Lee, 1986).
[8] Although not discussed, both the production schema and the quantity model can be extended to include joint production.

$$[R_d][Mp_t^* + Lw + d] = \begin{bmatrix} p_{t+1}^* \\ p_{t+1}^+ \end{bmatrix} = p_{t+1} \qquad (12.3)$$

where M is a $m \times n + a$ matrix of material pricing coefficients
       L is a $m \times v$ matrix of labor pricing coefficients
       d is a column vector with m depreciation pricing coefficients
       R_d is a $m \times m$ diagonal matrix of overhead and profit mark ups
       w is a column vector with v money-wage rates
       p_t^* is a column vector with $n + a$ material input market prices at time t
       p_{t+1}^+ is a column vector with f market prices at time $t + 1$
       p_{t+1} is a column vector of all market prices at time $t + 1$.

M is a decomposable matrix since it contains both basic and non-basic intermediate inputs.[9] On the other hand, since different products and industrial/competitive environments require different labor skills, the labor matrix L may range from being indecomposable to being largely decomposable punctuated with pockets of quite inter-related groups of markets. Further, depreciation vector d is semi-positive, while wage rate and intermediate input prices vector are strictly positive. Finally, the mth element of R_d consists of $[1 + k][1 + g][1 + h][1 + r][1 + t]$, where k, g, h, r and/or t may be zero depending on the market pricing equation under consideration.

Aside from the formal features of the pricing model, the empirically grounded market pricing equations bring three theoretical features to it. First is that the model is a single-product pricing model, even though the underlying production schema may include joint production. This is due to enterprises using a main product/by-product costing approach when dealing with joint products in which the main product is credited with all the costs minus the recoverable value of the by-product (which is priced at the reigning market price) and then costed and priced using normal cost pricing procedures (see National Association of Accountants, 1957; Slater and Wootton, 1988; and pricing studies B20, B33).[10] The second feature is its correspondence with the underlying production schema on the one hand and its incomplete, imprecise correspondence with the quantity model on the other. The divergence between the two models results from the material pricing coefficient matrix M differing from the

---

[9] The maximum eigenvalue of the sub-matrix $M_{n \times n}$ falls between zero and one.

[10] It should also be noted that in some instances joint products are costed in a manner similar to main products, which would make their pricing indistinguishable from the pricing of main products.

production coefficient matrix A,[11] primarily because many of the market pricing equations do not explicitly include all the material and service inputs actually used in production. Secondary reasons for the two matrices differing include the mismeasurement by the market price-setting administrators of the pricing coefficients *vis-à-vis* the actual production coefficients, the inability of the pricing administrators to actually determine all the pricing coefficients needed for pricing, and, as noted in chapter 11, the possibility that the actual output which determines production coefficients will differ from the normal output which determines the pricing coefficients. The final theoretical feature of the model is that both the wage rates and depreciation pricing coefficients are in money terms, both determined prior to the pricing process, and both determined by social and institutional mechanisms, such as the tax code for the latter.

Together, the formal and theoretical features produce an empirically grounded theoretical pricing model with several important properties. The first is, since M and A differ, the pricing model does not have a "dual" relationship with the quantity model, which suggests that market prices do not carry out the allocation of intermediate, investment, and consumption goods that permit business enterprises to survive and grow and workers to live and attain a socially acceptable standard of living.[12] The absence of labor-based mark up pricing equations coupled with the underlying circular production schema gives the model its second property, that of not being reducible to a labor-based vertically integrated price equation.[13] The third property is that output prices are a function of the pricing model defined for a given set of market pricing equation; hence, pricing models with different compositions of market pricing equations or with different specifications of the pricing coefficients (such as basing the depreciation coefficient on replacement costs as opposed to historical costs) will produce different output prices. For the pricing model to be empirically grounded, its pricing equations must thus be specified as they are in the real world and it must include the pricing

---

[11] The difference between the two matrices may also be indicated by the fact that the maximum eigenvalue of $M_{n \times n}$ will differ from the maximum eigenvalue for $A_{n \times n}$.

[12] The lack of a "dual" relationship also suggests that no substantive meaning can be attached to the term "profit maximization."

[13] Labor-based vertically integrated pricing models have been used by Post Keynesians for macroeconomic theorizing; this property of the pricing model questions the validity and relevance of using such models for that purpose or for any other theoretical or empirical purposes (see Steedman, 1992; Sawyer, 1992b).

equations in the proportions that they actually occur in capitalist economies.[14]

A fourth property of the model is that custom, convention, tradition, reasonableness, and short- and long-term competition are predominate among the determinants of the mark up for profit (see pricing studies B1, B2, B4, B6, B7, B8, B10, B11, B12, B16, B20, B21, B22, B24, B25, B28, B29, B30, B31, B33, B34, B35, B36, B38, B39, B40, B41, B42, B44, B47, B48, B50, B51, B52, B55, B56, B58, B61, B62, B67, B68, B69). On the other hand, the more popular Post Keynesian determinants of the mark up for profit, such as the need to finance investment, maintain and increase market share, barriers to entry, and potential competition,[15] received relatively little support among the pricing studies (see pricing studies B1, B19, B20, B31, B34, B41, B44, B48, B55, B56, B62, B64; see also Smiley, 1988). Consequently, whatever competitive and other factors affect the determination of the profit mark up, the role of custom, fairness, and convention is significant enough to place the motivation of the price administrators outside the simple description of maximizing profits (see costing and pricing studies A18, A19, A23 and B8, B22, B31, B33, B34, B40, B42, B44, B48, B55, B60, B67, B68, B69; see also Shipley, 1981).[16] Since the motivation for profits is historically specific and capitalist societies are beset with varying customs and conventions and cultural lags, the determinants of the profit mark up in the pricing model as well as the mark up itself must necessarily vary from market to market at a single point in time and in a particular market over time (see pricing studies B4, B6, B8, B9, B14, B16, B19, B22, B23, B29, B30, B31, B34, B36, B38, B40, B41, B44, B46, B47, B48, B56, B59, B60, B61, B62, B63, B64).[17] Because the empirically grounded feature of all administratively determined prices is the frequency with which they change, the fifth

---

[14] This property calls into question the tendency of Post Keynesian theory to reduce any and all pricing equations to mark up pricing equations (see Lee, 1996).

[15] 28 of the 47 studies in table IA.2 in the appendix to the Introduction (pp. 12–16) included the need to finance investment, maintain and increase market share, barriers to entry, and/or potential competition as a possible determinant of the profit mark up.

[16] Furthermore, since (as noted in chapter 11) business enterprises do not utilize an inverse price–sales relationship when making pricing decisions, the price elasticity of demand also cannot be a determinant of the profit mark up. Thus the eight Post Keynesian studies in table IA.2 in the appendix to the Introduction which refer to profit maximization and/or price elasticity of demand have no empirical basis or theoretical validity with regard to the pricing model.

[17] The persistent existence of custom, fairness, and convention in the determination of the profit mark up undermines the often stated Post Keynesian cum Sraffian, classical and Marxian view that a tendency towards a uniform rate of profit is a persistent and structural feature of a competitive capitalist economy.

property of the model is that its prices have a range of frequencies with which they change in historical time. Since the time frequency with which some prices change is not significantly different from the frequency with which some pricing coefficients, wage rates, or overhead and profit mark ups change, it is not possible to distinguish within the model between fast- and slow-moving variables. This means that it is inappropriate to place the model in an ahistorical time frame.[18] The last property is that all prices are money prices which means that all market transactions are monetary transactions.

The pricing model and the pricing foundation of Post Keynesian price theory

The empirically grounded pricing model together with the underlying empirically grounded production schema form the pricing foundation for Post Keynesian price theory in that they provide the general production and market framework in which the theory rests and the theoretical foundation on which it is developed. The production component, derived from the circular production schema, consists of an interdependent multi-market economy with inter-industry flows of products while the market transaction component, derived from the pricing model, means that the transactions in the market are money transactions. The pricing foundation thus consists of a monetary circular production schema where money prices determined via the pricing model are the medium in which transactions take place and can be formally depicted as

$$Gp_t^* + Vw \rightarrow Q_d P_{t+1}$$

$$[R_d][Mp_t^* + Lw + d] = p_{t+1}. \tag{12.4}$$

Its principal empirically grounded theoretical components are the market, pricing equations, and prices in that they establish the foundation's theoretical orientation which is transmitted to the theory of prices.

As noted above, a circular production schema means there will be continuous transactions within each market over time and for varying quantities and prices. Thus in the context of the pricing foundation, the market is an abstract concept which collectively denotes all the transactions of a specific product between buyers and sellers irrespective of the

---

[18] This effectively means that there is no convergence of actual market prices via some type of iterative process to short- or long-period "equilibrium" prices. Thus the short-period or long-period "equilibrium" pricing and price models used by Post Keynesians have no empirical grounding and hence are not useful for analyzing and examining real-world capitalist markets. For further discussion of these points, see Lee (1994b, 1996).

quantities and prices involved or the time and place of the transaction. Hence, a market exists simultaneously with the product in the abstract and disappears when the transactions of the product cease. In addition to the production basis there is also a social basis for continual transactions in a market. The business leadership of the enterprises who operate in the market actively create, modify, and recreate rules and market institutions for the purpose of establishing a stable market price which they believe facilities market transactions.[19] The actual rules and market institutions in place at any time depend on the current existing social, legal, and economic factors; and the actual stable market price set depends, in part, on the accounting conventions used by enterprises and market institutions and, in part, on the current customs and conventions regarding the determination of the profit mark up. The market price is consequently set and the market managed for the purpose of ensuring continual transactions for those enterprises in the market, that is for the benefit of the business leaders and their enterprises.[20]

Mark up, normal cost, and target rate of return pricing procedures are used by pricing administrators to establish prices which will cover costs, hopefully produce a profit, and, most importantly, permit the enterprise to engage in sequential acts of production and transactions. The procedures are embodied in the pricing equations, which means that the latter are located in historical time, are unaffected by variations in production and sales, and produce prices that are stable for many sequential transactions and variations in sales. The pricing equations establish prices which ensure that enterprises can continue to engage in sequential acts of production and exchange; and as long as enterprises can do this, the overall result will be continuous transactions in all the markets in the economy. As a result market prices are not market-clearing or profit-maximizing prices, but rather are enterprise-, and hence transaction-reproducing, prices. The pricing equations and their resulting prices are deeply enmeshed in a system of markets and sequential market transactions which are the key to the reproduction of the business enterprise, and hence of the economy as a whole.

The empirical and theoretical nature of markets, pricing equations,

---

[19] At times, the leadership is assisted by external bodies, such as law-makers and government agencies.

[20] Since the management and administration of markets and market prices by business leaders has always existed under capitalism and certainly has existed for the last hundred years under corporate capitalism, the distinction between monopoly capitalism, competitive oligopoly, and competitive capitalism has no firm foundation. There is thus no basis or reason to distinguish between competitive and monopolistic markets.

and prices in conjunction with a monetary circular production schema where money prices, determined via the pricing model, are the medium of transactions creates a pricing foundation which is grounded in time, fact, and history, and hence will vary over time as the historical context changes. It is thus not ahistorical equilibrium, profit maximization, and allocation of resources which the foundation promotes, but an explanation of the historical reproduction and growth of the business enterprise, and through it capitalism. Given this orientation of the foundation, the Post Keynesian price theory for which it is the basis will be historically oriented towards explaining the operation of capitalist economies in the areas of pricing and prices.

The pricing foundation and Post Keynesian price theory

As stated in the Introduction (pp. 3–4), the objective of the book is to move Post Keynesian analysis forward towards a more comprehensive, coherent, and realistic non-neoclassical theory of prices by setting out its non-neoclassical pricing foundation through developing an empirically grounded pricing model in conjunction with an empirically grounded production schema. The pricing model developed above is based on the ideas, arguments, theory, and formal and informal methods of analysis found in the administered prices, normal cost prices, and mark up prices doctrines coupled with their empirical grounding, and thus represents a synthesis of the three doctrines. Similarly, the production schema represents the synthesis of data, theory, and method found in the administered prices and mark up price doctrine. The pricing foundation is an empirically grounded synthesis in which elements of the three doctrines are clearly evident and which is also clearly non-neoclassical in its fundamental characteristics. The process of developing the empirically grounded foundation also requires the discarding of ideas, arguments, and analytical methods which many Post Keynesians have accepted as articles of faith. Hence the pricing foundation is not simply a linear combination of existing ideas (and therefore cannot be called "Kaleckian," "Meansian," or "Andrewsian"); rather, as a synthesis, it has transcended the price doctrines and become Post Keynesian. It can consequently only be judged in terms of its contribution to the development of an empirically grounded Post Keynesian theory of prices.

Given the theoretical orientation of its pricing foundation, Post Keynesian price theory is primarily concerned with issues relevant to understanding the workings of capitalist monetary production economies in which final demand decisions drive the quantities in transactions and the volume of employment, and money prices are the medium of such decisions and market transactions.[21] For example, the co-ordination of economic activity cannot be viewed as simply a function of prices (or relative prices); rather, it emerges from the interaction between the monetary decisions concerning final demand and the role of prices in reproduction of the business enterprise. The relative importance of the two is an issue that will need to be settled in the course of developing the theory of prices in conjunction with developing complementary and commensurable theories of the business enterprise, investment decisions, consumer demand, the state, and international trade. However it can be said that a significant role for market prices in the co-ordination of economic activity is questionable since they can be stable for significant periods of time and the role of prices or profit mark ups in final demand decisions is at best uncertain. In any case, the pricing foundation does not presume any role for market prices, so if such a role exists, then it must be empirically (not just theoretically) established.[22] Another example is the theory's concern with explaining the magnitude of the profit mark up. Given the importance of custom, tradition, and reasonableness in the determination of the profit mark up, any explanation of its magnitude over time will require detailed historical studies covering shifting economic, social, and political environments. Without such an explanation, Post Keynesian price theory will not be in a position to explain the magnitude of the market price and its movement over time, the "iron law of wages," and economic stagnation.

The pricing foundation developed in this chapter will not win the approval of all Post Keynesians, in part because it does not include particular cherished concepts and in part because of its methodological and theoretical orientation. However, if Post Keynesians today are to advance their analysis of capitalism, they must not continue to be constrained in terms of theory and method of analysis accepted by their teachers and mentors and their teachers' teachers and mentors. The

[21] The monetary production economy can be depicted by bringing together the pricing foundation and the quantity model:

$$G_t p_t^* + V_t w \to Q_{dt+1} p_{t+1}$$
$$p_t^{T^*} A^T Q_{dt} + F_d p_t = Q_{dt+1} p_{t+1}$$
$$Q_{dt} A = G_t \qquad\qquad (12.5)$$
$$Q_{dt} V^* = V_t$$
$$[R_d][M p_t^* + L w + d] = p_{t+1}.$$

[22] The questioning of the role of market prices in coordinating economic activity brings some of the core propositions in the administered prices doctrine into doubt.

synthesis of the three doctrines which produced the pricing foundation is an attempt to break with these constraints and, at the same time, suggesting a new empirically grounded theoretical approach for developing Post Keynesian economics.

Appendix A   Studies on cost accounting and costing practices

A1 "Re Cost Accounts," *The Accountant* (March 16, 1906): 351

A2 "Depreciation Policy in Manufacturing Industries," *NACA Bulletin*, 17 (May 1, 1936): 1053–61

A3 Marple, R. P., "Practice in Applying Overhead and Calculating Normal Capacity," *NACA Bulletin*, 19 (April 1, 1938): 917–34

A4 US Congress, Senate, Temporary National Economic Committee, *Industrial wage rates, labor costs and price policies*, by D. V. Brown *et al.*, Senate Committee Monograph 5, Washington, DC: Government Printing Office, 1940; see also Wonson, H. S., "The use of predetermined costs in pricing in the shoe industry," *NACA Bulletin*, 23 (September 1, 1941): 28–40

A5 Black, M. L. and Eversole, H. B., *A Report on Cost Accounting in Industry*, Washington, DC: Government Printing Office, 1946

A6 Keller, I. W., "Standard Manufacturing Costs for Pricing and Budgeting," *NACA Bulletin*, 30 (1948–9): 162–76

A7 Walkden, B., "A Consideration of Some of the Problems Arising in the Investigation of Manufacturers' Costs by the Ministry of Supply from 1939 to 1945 with Particular Reference to Methods of Uniform Costing to Price Determination in the Grey Cloths Section of the Lancashire Cotton Industry and in the Textile Narrow Fabric Industry," College of Technology, Barnsley, Yorkshire, 1957

A8 Langholm, O., "Cost Structure and Costing Method: An Empirical Study," *Journal of Accounting Research*, 3 (1965): 218–27

A9 Sizer, J., "The Accountant's Contribution to the Pricing Decision," *The Journal of Management Studies*, 3 (May 1966): 129–49

A10 Govindarajan, V. and Anthony, R. N., 'How Firms Use Cost Data in Price Decisions," *Management Accounting (USA)* (July 1983): 30–6

A11 National Association of Cost Accountants, Committee on Research, "Direct Costing," *NACA Bulletin*, 34 (April 1953): 1079–128

A12 National Association of Cost Accountants, Committee on Research,

"Product Costs for Pricing," *NACA Bulletin*, 34 (August 1953): 1671–730

A13 Fog, B., *Industrial Pricing Policies: An Analysis of Pricing Policies of Danish Manufacturing*, Amsterdam: North-Holland, 1960

A14 Anglo-American Council on Productivity, *Productivity Report: Management Accounting*, London: Anglo-American Council on Productivity, 1950

A15 Puxty, A. G. and Lyall, D., *Cost Control into the 1990s: A Survey of Standard Costing and Budgeting Practices in the UK*, London: CIMA, 1989

A16 Finnie, J. and Sizer, J., "The Apparent Value Placed upon Product Cost Information in a Sample of Engineering Companies," in D. Cooper, R. Scapens and J. Arnold (eds.), *Management Accounting Research and Practice*, London: The Institute of Cost and Management Accountants, 1983: 307–17

A17 Scapens, R. W., Gameil, M. Y. and Cooper, D. J., "Accounting Information for Pricing Decisions: An Empirical Study," in D. Cooper, R. Scapens and J. Arnold (eds.), *Management Accounting Research and Practice*, London: The Institute of Cost and Management Accountants, 1983: 283–306

A18 Coates, J. B., Smith, J. E. and Stacey, R. J., "Results of a Preliminary Survey into the Structure of Divisionalised Companies, Divisionalised Performance Appraisal and the Associated Role of Management Accounting," in D. Cooper, R. Scapens and J. Arnold (eds.), *Management Accounting Research and Practice*, London: The Institute of Cost and Management Accountants, 1983: 265–82

A19 Innes, J. and Mitchell, F., *Management Accounting: The Challenge of Technological Innovation*, London: CIMA, 1989

A20 Howe, M., "Accounting Information and Product Decisions in the Multi-product Firm," PhD Dissertation, University of Sheffield, 1961

A21 Laudeman, M. and Schaeberle, F. W., "The Cost Accounting Practices of Firms using Standard Costs," *Cost and Management* (Canada) (July–August 1983): 21–5

A22 National Association of Accountants, *Current Practice in Accounting for Depreciation*, Research Report, 33, New York City: National Association of Accountants, 1958

A23 Hart, H. and Prusmann, D. F., *A Report of a Survey of Management Accounting Techniques in the SE Hants Coastal Region*, Southampton: University of Southampton, 1963

A24 Cress, W. P. and Pettijohn, J. B., "A Survey of Budget-Related Planning and Control Policies and Procedures," *Journal of Accounting Education* (Fall 1985): 61–78

A25 Ahmed, M. N. and Scapens, R. W., "The History of Cost Allocation Practices in Britain: Some Illustrations of the Institutional Influence," unpublished, 1992

A26 Drury, C., Braund, S., Osborne, P. and Tayles, M., *A Survey of Management Accounting Practices in UK Manufacturing Companies*, London: Certified Accountants Educational Trust, 1993

Appendix B   Studies on pricing

B1 Brown, Donaldson, "Pricing Policy in Relation to Financial Control," *Management and Administration*, 7 (1924): 195–8, 283–6, 417–22; see also Vanderblue, Homer B., "Pricing Policies in the Automobile Industry," *Harvard Business Review*, 17 (1939): 385–401; Vanderblue, Homer B., "Pricing Policies in the Automobile Industry: Incidence of Demand," *Harvard Business Review*, 18 (1939–40): 64–81; Kaplan, A. D. H., Dirlam, J. B. and Lanzillotti, R. F., *Pricing in Big Business: A Case Approach*, Washington, DC: The Brookings Institution, 1958; Hutton, W. T., "Price Formulation and Price Behavior in Three Heavy Manufacturing Industries," PhD dissertation, Ohio State University, 1959; Johnson, H. T., "Management Accounting in an Early Multidivisional Organization: General Motors in the 1920s," *Business History Review*, 52 (1978): 490–517

B2 Churchill, W. L., *Pricing for Profit*, New York: Macmillan, 1932

B3 Agnew, H. E., "Fundamentals of Price Making," New York University, 1935

B4 Hall, R. L. and Hitch, C. J., 'Price Theory and Business Behaviour," *Oxford Economic Papers*, 2 (May 1939): 12–45

B5 US Congress, Senate, Temporary National Economic Committee, *Industrial Wage Rates, Labor Costs and Price Policies*, by D. V. Brown *et al.*, Senate Committee Print, Monograph no. 5, Washington, DC: Government Printing Office, 1940; US Federal Trade Commission, *Report on the Agricultural Implement and Machinery Industry*, Washington, DC: Government Printing Office, 1938; Conant, M., "Aspects of Monopoly and Price Policies in the Farm Machinery Industry Since 1902," PhD dissertation, University of Chicago, 1949; see also Kaplan, A. D. H., Dirlam, J. B. and Lanzillotti, R. F., *Pricing in Big Business: A Case Approach*, Washington, DC: The Brookings Institution, 1958; and Park, J. C. S., "Value Theory and Oligopolistic Manufacturing Industries," PhD dissertation, University of Nebraska, 1959

B6 Saxton, C. C., *The Economics of Price Determination*, Oxford: Oxford University Press, 1942

B7 Thompson, G. C., "How Industry Prices Its Products," *The Conference Board Business Record*, 4 (1947): 180–2

B8 The Dartnell Report, *Pricing Policies*, Special Investigation Report 572, Chicago: The Dartnell Corporation, 1949

B9 Alt, R. M., "The Internal Organization of the Firm and Price Formation: An Illustrative Case," *Quarterly Journal of Economics*, 63 (1949): 92–110

B10 Hague, D. C., "Economic Theory and Business Behaviour," *The Review of Economic Studies*, 16 (1949–50): 144–57

B11 Saville, L. B., "Price Determination in the Gray-Iron-Foundry Industry," PhD dissertation, Columbia University, 1950

B12 Dean, J. and Yntema, T., National Bureau of Economic Research – Committee of the Conference on Price Research, 1941–51, cited in Dean, J., *Managerial Economics*, Englewood Cliffs, New Jersey: Prentice-Hall, 1951

B13 Woodruff, W., "Early Entrepreneurial Behavior in Relation to Costs and Prices," *Oxford Economic Papers*, 5 (1953): 41–64

B14 Blackwell, R., "The Pricing of Books," *Journal of Industrial Economics*, 2 (1953–4): 174–83

B15 Cook, A. and Jones, E., "Full Cost Pricing in Western Australia," *The Economic Record*, 30 (1954): 272–4

B16 Kohl, M., "The Role of Accounting in Pricing," PhD dissertation, Columbia University, 1954

B17 Shackle, G. L. S., "Business Men on Business Decisions," *Scottish Journal of Political Economy*, 2 (1955): 32–46; Brown, C. V., "Special Seminar – Report," Glasgow University – Management Studies (1967): 1–13

B18 Hinton, B. J., "An Economic Analysis of Selected Factors in Industrial Pricing Techniques," PhD dissertation, Louisiana State University, 1955

B19 Great Britain, The Monopolies and Restrictive Practices Commission, *Report on the Supply and Export of Certain Semi-Manufactures of Copper and Copper-Based Alloys*, 1955

B20 Cook, A. C., Dufty, N. F. and Jones, E. H., "Full Cost Pricing in the Multi-Product Firm," *The Economic Record*, 32 (1956): 142–7

B21 Great Britain, The Monopolies and Restrictive Practices Commission, *Report on the Supply of Hard Fibre Cordage*, 1956

B22 Great Britain, The Monopolies and Restrictive Practices Commission, *Report on the Supply of Standard Metal Windows and Doors*, 1956

B23 Pearce, I. F., "A Study in Price Policy," *Economica*, 23 (1956): 114–27

B24 Pearce, I. F. and Amey, L. R., "Price Policy with a Branded Product," *The Review of Economic Studies*, 24 (1956–7): 49–60

B25 Lazer, W., "Price Determination in the Western Canadian Garment Industry," *The Journal of Industrial Economics*, 5 (1956–7): 124–36

B26 Balkin, N., "Prices in the Clothing Industry," *The Journal of Industrial Economics*, 5 (1956–7): 1–15

B27 Karger, T. and Thompson, G. C., "Pricing Policies and Practices," *The Conference Board Business Record*, 14 (1957): 434–42

B28 Ross, R. B., Eggers, L. H. and staff, *Pricing for Profit in Competitive Markets*, Dartnell Management Report, 606, Chicago: The Dartnell Corporation, 1958

B29 Lydall, H. F., "Aspects of Competition in Manufacturing Industry," *Oxford Institute of Economics and Statistics Bulletin*, 20 (1958): 319–37

B30 Pool, A. G. and Llewellyn, G., *The British Hosiery Industry: A Study in Competition*, Leicester: Leicester University Press, 1958

B31 Brookings Institution Investigation of Pricing Practices: Kaplan, A. D. H., *Big Enterprise in a Competitive System*, Washington, DC: The Brookings Institution, 1954; Kaplan, A. D. H., Dirlam, J. B. and Lanzillotti, R. F., *Pricing in Big Business: A Case Approach*, Washington, DC: The Brookings Institution, 1958; Lanzillotti, R. F., "Pricing Objectives in Large Corporations," *The American Economic Review*, 48 (1958): 921–40

B32 Parks, J. C. S., "Value Theory and Oligopolistic Manufacturing Industries," PhD dissertation, University of Nebraska, 1959

B33 Great Britain, The Monopolies Commission, *Report on the Supply of Chemical Fertilisers*, 1959

B34 Fog, B., *Industrial Pricing Policies: An Analysis of Pricing Policies of Danish Manufacturing*, Amsterdam: North-Holland, 1960; see also, "Price Theory and Reality," *Nordisk Tidsskrift for Teknisk Okonomi* (1948), 12: 89–94

B35 Kempner, T., "Costs and Prices in Launderettes," *The Journal of Industrial Economics*, 8 (June 1960): 216–29

B36 Haynes, W. W., *Pricing Decisions in Small Business*, Lexington: University of Kentucky Press, 1962; Haynes, W. W., "Pricing Practices in Small Firms," *The Southern Economic Journal*, 30 (1964): 315–24

B37 Eliot, G., "Analysis of Small Manufacturers' Pricing Policies in Southern California," PhD dissertation, University of Southern California, 1963

B38 Fitzpatrick, A. A., *Pricing Methods of Industry*, Boulder, Colorado: Pruett Press, 1964

B39 Lanzillotti, R., *Pricing, Production, and Marketing Policies of Small Manufacturers*, Pullman, Washington: Washington State University, 1964

B40 Barback, R. H., *The Pricing of Manufactures*, London: Macmillan, 1964

B41 Knox, R. L., "Competitive Oligopolistic Pricing," *Journal of Marketing*, 30 (1966): 47–51; see also Hutton, W. T., "Price Formulation and Price Behavior in Three Heavy Manufacturing Industries," Ohio State University, 1959; Kaplan, A. D. H., Dirlam, J. B. and Lanzillotti, R. F., *Pricing in Big Business: A Case Approach*, Washington, DC: The Brookings Institution, 1958

B42 Long, W. F. E., "Formula Pricing to Reduce Technological Uncertainty: A Case Study in Computer Transistors," *Antitrust Law & Economics Review*, 1 (1967–8): 131–56

B43 Skinner, R. C., "The Determination of Selling Prices," *Journal of Industrial Economics*, 18 (1969–70): 201–17; see also Sizer, J., "Note on 'The Determination of Selling Prices'," *Journal of Industrial Economics*, 20 (1971–2): 85–9

B44 Howe, M., "Competition and the Multiplication of Products," *Yorkshire Bulletin of Economic and Social Research*, 12 (1960): 57–72; "Accounting Information and Product Decisions in the Multi-Product Firm," PhD dissertation, University of Sheffield, 1961; "The Restrictive Practices Court and the Definition of the Market," *The Manchester School of Economic and Social Studies*, 34 (1966): 41–61; "The Iron and Steel Board and Steel Pricing, 1953–1967," *Scottish Journal of Political Economy*, 15 (1968): 43–67; "A Study of Trade Association Price Fixing," *Journal of Industrial Economics*, 21 (1972–3): 236–56

B45 Rosendale, P. B., "The Short-Run Pricing Policies of Some British Engineering Exporters," *National Institute Economic Review*, 65 (1973): 44–51

B46 Atkin, B. and Skinner, R., 1976, *How British Industry Prices*, London: Industrial Market Research Ltd

B47 Holmes, P. M., *Industrial Pricing Behaviour and Devaluation*, London: Macmillan, 1978

B48 Hankinson, A., *Pricing Behaviour: A Study of Pricing Behaviour of Dorset–Hampshire Small Engineering Firms 1983–1985*, Dorset Institute of Higher Education, 1985; see also *Output Determination: A Study of Output Determination of Dorset–Hampshire Small Engineering Firms 1983–1985*, Dorset Institute of Higher Education, 1985

B49 Jerron, A. M., "Conversion Costs," *The Cost Accountant*, 38 (1960): 56

B50 Gordon, L. A., Cooper, R., Falk, H. and Miller, D., *The Pricing Decision*, New York City: National Association of Accountants, 1981

B51 Raine, G. F. (ed.), *The Woollen and Worsted Industry: An Economic Analysis*, Oxford: Clarendon Press, 1965

B52 Wentz, T., "Realism in Pricing Analyses," *Journal of Marketing*, 30 (1966): 19–26

B53 Likierman, A., "Pricing Policy in the Texturising Industry, 1958–71," *The Journal of Industrial Economics*, 30 (1981): 25–38

B54 Goetz, J. F., "The Pricing Decision: A Service Industry's Experience," *Journal of Small Business Management*, 23 (1985): 61–7

B55 Hague, D. C., *Pricing in Business*, London: George Allen & Unwin, 1971

B56 Wied-Nebbeling, S., *Industrielle Preissetzung*, Tübingen, 1975; Wied-Nebbeling, S., *Das Preisverhalten in der Industrie*, Tübingen, 1985; Wied-Nebbeling, S., Personal communication, January 1, 1992

B57 Mills, R. W. and Sweeting, C., *Pricing Decisions in Practice*, London: CIMA, 1988

B58 Price Commission, *Prices, Costs and Margins in the Distribution of Video Tape Recorders and their Accessories*, London: HMSO, 1979

B59 Price Commission, *Prices, Costs and Margins in the Distribution of Footwear in the United Kingdom*, London: HMSO, 1978

B60 Price Commission, *Prices, Costs and Margins in the Publishing, Printing and Binding, and Distribution of Books*, London: HMSO, 1978

B61 Price Commission, *The Pricing of Beds*, London: HMSO, 1978

B62 Abe, K. and Kometani, M., "Behavioural Style of Modern Japanese Big Business," The Economic Society of Yamaguchi University, 1985, in Japanese, summarized and translated by T. Kanao

B63 Sakurai, M. and Ito, K., "An Empirical Research about Price Determination of Japanese Firms," *Accounting* (1986), in Japanese, summarized and translated by T. Kanao

B64 Hague, D. C., Oakeshott, W. E. F. and Strain, A. A., *Devaluation and Pricing Decisions: A Case Study Approach*, London: George Allen & Unwin, 1977

B65 Hall, S., Walsh, M. and Yates, T., "How do UK Companies Set Prices?," *Bank of England Quarterly Bulletin*, 36 (May, 1996): 180–92

B66 Bruegelmann, T. M. and Haessly, G., "How Variable Costing is Used in Pricing Decisions," *Management Accounting (USA)* (April 1985): 58–61, 65

B67 Thompson, G. C. and MacDonald, M. B., "Pricing New Products," *The Conference Board Record*, 1 (January 1964): 7–14

B68 Curran, J., Jarvis, R., Kitching, J. and Lightfoot, G., "The Pricing

Decision in Small Firms: Complexities and the Deprioritising of Economic Determinants," *International Small Business Journal* (1996)

B69 Katona, G., *Price Control and Business*, Bloomington: The Principia Press, 1945

B70 Sternberg, R. E., "A Study of Full Cost vs. Marginal cost Pricing," PhD dissertation, University of Houston, 1972

B71 Price Commission, *Prices, Costs and Margins in the Manufacture and Distribution of Portable Electric Tools*, London: HMSO, 1979

Bibliography

Note on bibliographical sources

The items in the bibliography are organized according to the type of research source they represent. Each research source is cited in the text by a date or a date/ suffix as follows:
Published material (pp. 241–66 in the bibliography) is cited in the text by a date alone (Acharyya, 1994)
Unpublished material is cited in the text by a date/suffix:
m Unpublished material from a manuscript collection or archive (pp. 266–71) (Andrews, 1939*m*)
t Dissertation/thesis (p. 271–2) (Ahmad, 1956*t*)
i Interview (p. 272) (Means, 1986*i*)
p Personal letter or recollection (pp. 272–3) (Bellamy, 1981*p*)
u Unpublished material (pp. 273–4) (Barna, 1990*u*)
Within each resource source, the items are arranged alphabetically and by date.

Published material

Acharyya, R., 1994. "Principle of Effective Demand and the Vent for Surplus Approach," *Journal of Post Keynesian Economics*, 16 (Spring): 439–51

Adams, W. (ed.), 1961. *The Structure of American Industry: Some Case Studies*, New York: Macmillan

Agliardi, E., 1988. "Microeconomic Foundations of Macroeconomics in the Post-Keynesian Approach," *Metroeconomica*, 38(3): 275–97

Amadeo, E. J., 1994. "Bargaining Power, Mark-up Power, and Wage Differentials in Brazil," *Cambridge Journal of Economics*, 18 (June): 313–22

Andrews, P. W. S., 1944. "Report from the 'Accountancy' side of the Pilot Inquiry into the Relative Efficiency of Small- and Large-Scale Business," in Lee and Earl (1993): 35–72

1948. Letter to Roy Harrod, July 26, in Lee and Earl (1993): 113–15

1949a. *Manufacturing Business*, London: Macmillan

1949b. "A Reconsideration of the Theory of the Individual Business," *Oxford Economic Papers*, 1 (January): 54–89; reprinted in Lee and Earl (1993)

1949c. Letter to D. H. Robertson, February 17, in Lee and Earl (1993): 117–20

1950. "Some Aspects of Competition in Retail Trade," *Oxford Economic Papers*, 2 (June): 137–75; reprinted in Lee and Earl (1993)

1951. "Industrial Analysis in Economics," in T. Wilson and P. W. S. Andrews (eds.), *Oxford Studies in the Price Mechanism*, Oxford: Clarendon Press, 1955: 139–72; reprinted in Lee and Earl (1993)

1952a. "The Netherlands Lectures," in Lee and Earl (1993): 175–219

1952b. "The Legacy of the 1930s in Economics," in Lee and Earl (1993): 159–74

1952c. Letter to E. H. Chamberlin, February 14, in Lee and Earl (1993): 220–1

1952d. Letter to Richard Kahn, April 2, in Lee and Earl (1993): 221–2

1952e. Letter to R. B. Heflebower, June 30, in Lee and Earl (1993): 225–7

1953a. "Some Aspects of Capital Development," *Journal of the Textile Institute*, 44 (September): 687–97; reprinted in Lee and Earl (1993)

1953b. Letter to R. B. Heflebower, January 16, in Lee and Earl (1993): 228–32

1958. "Competition in the Modern Economy," in G. Sell (ed.), *Competitive Aspects of Oil Operations*, London: The Institute of Petroleum: 1–42; reprinted in Lee and Earl (1993)

1961. "The Theory of the Growth of the Firm – Review," *The Oxford Magazine* (November 30): 114–16

1964. *On Competition in Economic Theory*, London: Macmillan

Andrews, P. W. S. and Brunner, E., 1950. "Productivity and the Businessmen," *Oxford Economic Papers*, 2 (June): 197–225

1951. *Capital Development in Steel: A Study of the United Steel Companies Ltd*, New York: Augustus M. Kelley

1962. "Business Profits and the Quiet Life," *The Journal of Industrial Economics*, 11 (November): 72–8

Andrews, P. W. S. and Friday, F. A., 1960. *Fair Trade: Resale Price Maintenance Re-examined*, London: Macmillan

Arestis, P., 1990. "Post-Keynesianism: A New Approach to Economics," *Review of Social Economy*, 48 (Fall): 222–46

1992. *The Post-Keynesian Approach to Economics: An Alternative Analysis of Economic Theory and Policy*, Aldershot: Edward Elgar

1996. "Post-Keynesian Economics: Towards Coherence," *Cambridge Journal of Economics*, 20 (January): 111–35

Arestis, P. and Chick, V., 1992. "The Post-Keynesian Economics Study Group," in P. Arestis and V. Chick (eds.), *Recent Developments in Post-Keynesian Economics*, Aldershot: Edward Elgar: ii

Arestis, P. and Kitromilides, Y. (eds.), *Theory and Policy in Political Economy: Essays in Pricing, Distribution and Growth*, Aldershot: Edward Elgar

Arestis, P. and Sawyer, M., 1993. "Political Economy: An Editorial Manifesto," *International Papers in Political Economy*, 1(1): 1–38

Asimakopulos, A., 1969. "A Robinsonian Growth Model in One-Sector Notation," *Australian Economic Papers*, 8 (June): 41–58

1970. "A Robinsonian Growth Model in One-Sector Notation – An Amendment," *Australian Economic Papers*, 9 (December): 171–6

1975a. "A Kaleckian Theory of Income Distribution," *The Canadian Journal of Economics*, 8 (August): 313–33

1975b. "The Price Policy of Firms, Employment and Distribution: A Comment," *Australian Economic Papers*, 14 (December): 261–2

1977. "Profits and Investment: A Kaleckian Approach," in G. C. Harcourt (ed.), *Microeconomic Foundations of Macroeconomics*, London: Macmillan: 328–42

1978. *An Introduction to Economic Theory: Microeconomics*, Oxford: Oxford University Press

1980–1. "Themes in a Post Keynesian Theory of Income Distribution," *The Journal of Post Keynesian Economics*, 3 (Winter): 158–69

Asimakopulos, A. and Burbidge, J. B. 1974. "The Short-Period Incidence of Taxation," *The Economic Journal*, 84 (June): 267–88

Auerbach, P. and Skott, P., 1988. "Concentration, Competition and Distribution – A Critique of Theories of Monopoly Capital," *The International Review of Applied Economics*, 2: 42–61

Ayres. R and Baird, E., 1935. "Private Price Control and Code Policy," *Investigation of the National Recovery Administration, Part IV. Hearings Before the Committee on Finance on Senate Resolution 79*, Senate, 74th Cong., 1st sess., Washington, DC: Government Printing Office

Baker, G. L., Rasmussen, W. D., Wiser, V. and Porter, J. M., 1963. *Century of Service: The First 100 Years of the United States Department of Agriculture*, Washington, DC: United States Department of Agriculture

Ball, R. J., 1964. *Inflation and the Theory of Money*, London: George Allen & Unwin

Baran, P. A., 1957. *The Political Economy of Growth*, New York: Monthly Review Press

Baran, P. A. and Sweezy, P. M., 1966. *Monopoly Capital: An Essay on the American Economic and Social Order*, New York: Monthly Review Press

Barback, R. H., 1964. *The Pricing of Manufactures*, London: Macmillan

Barna, T., 1945. *Profits During and After the War*, London: Fabian Publications and Victor Gollancz

1953. "Experience with Input–Output in the United Kingdom," in The Netherlands Economic Institute (eds.), *Input–Output Relations*, Leiden: H. E. Stenfert Kroese NV: 123–77

Basile, L. and Salvadori, N., 1984–5. "Kalecki's Pricing Theory," *Journal of Post Keynesian Economics*, 7 (Winter): 249–62

Bell, C. S., 1960. "On the Elasticity of Demand at Retail," *The American Journal of Economics and Sociology*, 20: 63–72

Berle, A. A., 1928. *Studies in the Law of Corporation Finance*, Chicago: Callaghan

1954. *The 20th Century Capitalist Revolution*, New York: Harcourt, Brace

1959. *Power without Property: A New Development in American Political Economy*, New York: Harcourt, Brace & World

1963. *The American Economic Republic*, New York: Harcourt, Brace & World

Berle, A. A. and Means, G. C., 1932. *The Modern Corporation and Private Property*, New York: Macmillan; revised edn, New York: Harcourt, Brace & World, 1967

Bernheim, A. L. (ed.) 1937a. *Big Business: Its Growth and Its Place*, New York: The Twentieth Century Fund

1937b. *How Profitable is Big Business?* New York: The Twentieth Century Fund

Beveridge, W., 1944. *Full Employment in a Free Society*, London: George Allen & Unwin

Bhaduri, A., 1985. *Macroeconomics: The Dynamics of Commodity Production*, Armonk, New York: M. E. Sharpe

Bhagwati, J. N., 1970. "Oligopoly Theory, Entry-prevention, and Growth," *Oxford Economic Papers*, 22 (November): 297–310

Bharadwaj, K. and Schefold, B. (eds.), 1990. *Essays on Piero Sraffa: Critical Perspectives on the Revival of Classical Theory*, London: Unwin Hyman

Blair, J. M. 1959. "Administered Prices: A Phenomenon in Search of a Theory," *The American Economic Review*, 49 (May): 431–50

1964. "Administered Prices and Oligopolistic Inflation: A Reply," *The Journal of Business*, 37 (January): 68–81

1972. *Economic Concentration: Structure, Behavior and Public Policy*, New York: Harcourt Brace Jovanovich

1974. "Market Power and Inflation: A Short-Run Target Return Model," *The Journal of Economic Issues*, 8 (June): 453–77

Blinder, A. S., 1991. "Why are Prices Sticky? Preliminary Results from an Interview Study," *The American Economic Review*, 81 (May): 89–96

Blitch, C. P., 1983. "Allyn A. Young: A Curious Case of Professional Neglect," *History of Political Economy*, 15 (March): 1–24

Bloch, H., 1990. "Price Leadership and the Degree of Monopoly," *Journal of Post Keynesian Economics*, 12 (Spring): 439–51

Bober, S., 1992. *Pricing and Growth: A Neo-Ricardian Approach*, Armonk, New York: M. E. Sharpe

Boggio, L., 1980. "Full Cost and 'Sraffa Prices': Equilibrium and Stability in a System with Fixed Capital," *Economic Notes*, 9: 3–33

Bonbright, J. and Means, G. C., 1932. *The Holding Company*, New York: McGraw-Hill

Braverman, H., 1974. *Labor and Monopoly Capital: The Degradation of Work in the Twentieth Century*, New York: Monthly Review Press

Bronfenbrenner, M., 1971. *Income Distribution Theory*, Chicago: Aldine

Brown, A., 1988. "A Worm's Eye View of the Keynesian Revolution," in J. Hilland (ed.), *J. M. Keynes in Retrospect: The Legacy of the Keynesian Revolution*, Aldershot: Edward Elgar: 18–44

Brunner, E., 1952. "Competition and the Theory of the Firm," *Economia Internazionale*, 5 (August and November): 509–23, 727–45

1975. "Competitive Price, Normal Costs and Industry Stability," in P. W. S. Andrews and E. Brunner (eds.), *Studies in Pricing*, London: Macmillan: 18–34

Buckner, H., 1967. *How British Industry Buys*, London: Hutchinson

Burchardt, F. A., 1931. "Die Schemata des Stationaren Kreislaufs bei Böhm-Barwerk und Marx (part I)," *Weltwirtschaftliches Archiv*, 34: 525–64

1932. "Die Schemata des Stationaren Kreislaufs bei Böhm-Barwerk und Marx (part II)" *Weltwirtschaftliches Archiv*, 35: 116–76

1944. "The Causes of Unemployment," in *The Economics of Full Employment*, Oxford: Basil Blackwell: 1–38

Burns, A. R., 1936. *The Decline of Competition: A Study of the Evolution of American Industry*, New York: McGraw-Hill

Cameron, B., 1968. *Input–Output Analysis and Resource Allocation*, Cambridge: Cambridge University Press

Campbell, P., 1940. *Consumer Representation in the New Deal*, New York: Columbia University Press

Canterberry, E. R., 1992. "An Evolutionary Model of Technical Change with Markup Pricing," in W. Milberg (ed.), *The Megacorp and Macrodynamics: Essays in Memory of Alfred Eichner*, Armonk, New York: M. E. Sharpe: 87–100

Capon, N., Farley, J. U. and Hulbert, J., 1975. "Pricing and Forecasting in an Oligopoly Firm," *The Journal of Management Studies*, 12 (May): 133–56

Carlson, V., 1968. "The Education of an Economist Before the Great Depression," *The American Journal of Economics and Sociology*, 27 (January): 101–12

Carlton, D. W., 1986. "The Rigidity of Prices," *The American Economic Review*, 76 (September): 637–58

Carson, J., 1990. "Kalecki's Pricing Theory Revisited," *The Journal of Post Keynesian Economics*, 13 (Fall): 146–52

1994. "Existence and Uniqueness of Solutions to Kalecki's Pricing Equations," *The Journal of Post Keynesian Economics*, 16 (Spring): 411–34

Carter, J. F. (Unofficial Observer), 1934. *The New Dealers*, New York: Simon & Schuster

Cassady, R., 1954. *Price Making and Price Behavior in the Petroleum Industry*, New Haven: Yale University Press

Cassell, G., 1923. *The Theory of Social Economy*, trans. J. McCabe, London: Unwin

Central Statistical Office (CSO). 1961. *Input–Output Tables for the United Kingdom, 1954*, London: HMSO

1970. *Input–Output Tables for the United Kingdom, 1963*, London: HMSO

1973. *Input–Output Tables for the United Kingdom, 1968*, London: HMSO

1983. *Input–Output Tables for the United Kingdom, 1979*, London: HMSO

1988. *Input–Output Tables for the United Kingdom, 1984*, London: HMSO

1995. *Input–Output Tables for the United Kingdom, 1990*, London: HMSO

Chamberlin, E. H., 1962. *The Theory of Monopolistic Competition: A Re-Orientation of the Theory of Value*, 8th edn, Cambridge, Mass.: Harvard University Press

Chandler, A. D., 1962. *Strategy and Structure: Chapters in the History of the American Industrial Enterprise*, Cambridge, Mass.: MIT Press

1977. *The Visible Hand: The Managerial Revolution in American Business*, Cambridge, Mass.: Harvard University Press

Charmaz, K., 1983. "The Grounded Theory Method: An Explication and Interpretation," in R. M. Emerson (ed.), *Contemporary Field Research: A Collection of Readings*, Boston: Little, Brown: 109–26

Cheek, B. M., 1949. "Economic Theory and Industrial Pricing," *The Economic Record: Supplement*, 25 (August): 140–57

Chernomas, B., 1982. "Keynesian, Monetarist and Post-Keynesian Policy: A Marxist Analysis," *Studies in Political Economy*, 10: 123–42

Chester, N., 1986. *Economics, Politics and Social Studies in Oxford, 1900–85*, London: Macmillan

Chick, V., 1995. "Is There a Case for Post Keynesian Economics?," *Scottish Journal of Political Economy*, 42 (February): 20–36

Clark, D. L., 1984a. "Planning and the Real Origin of Input–Output Analysis," *The Journal of Contemporary Asia*, 14(4): 408–29

1984b. "Confronting the Linear Imperialism of the Austrians," *The Eastern Economic Journal*, 10 (April–June): 107–27

Clifton, J. A., 1977. "Competition and the Evolution of the Capitalist Mode of Production," *The Cambridge Journal of Economics*, 1 (June): 137–51

1983. "Administered Prices in the Context of Capitalist Development," *Contributions to Political Economy*, 2 (March): 23–38

1987. "Competitive Market Process," in J. Eatwell, M. Milgate and P. Newman (eds.), *The New Palgrave: A Dictionary of Economics*, New York: Stockton Press: 553–6

Commons, J. R., 1924. *Legal Foundations of Capitalism*, New York: Macmillan

Coontz, S., 1965. *Productive Labor and Effective Demand*, London: Routledge & Kegan Paul

Cowling, K., 1982. *Monopoly Capitalism*, London: Macmillan

Critchlow, D. T., 1985. *The Brookings Institution, 1916–1952*, De Kalb: Northern Illinois University Press

Crotty, J. R., 1980. "Post-Keynesian Economic Theory: An Overview and Evaluation," *The American Economic Review*, 70 (May): 20–5

Cunningham, M. T. and White, J. G., 1973. "The Determinants of Choice of Supplier: A Study of Purchase Behaviour for Capital Goods," *The European Journal of Marketing*, 7(3): 189–202

Cyert, R. M. and George, K. D., 1969. "Competition, Growth, and Efficiency," *The Economic Journal*, 79 (March): 23–41

Dalziel, P. C., 1990. "Market Power, Inflation, and Income Policies," *The Journal of Post Keynesian Economics*, 12 (Spring): 424–38

Davidson, P., 1960. *Theories of Aggregate Income Distribution*, New Brunswick: Rutgers University Press

1980. "Post Keynesian Economics: Solving the Crisis in Economic Theory," *The Public Interest* (Special Issue): 151–73

Davies, J. E., 1984. *Pricing in the Liner Shipping Industry*, Ottawa and Hull: Canadian Transport Commission

Dean, J., 1976. *Statistical Cost Estimation*, Bloomington, Indiana: Indiana University Press

Dixon, R., 1979–80. "Relative Wages and Employment Theory," *The Journal of Post Keynesian Economics*, 2 (Winter): 181–92

    1981. "The Wage Share and Capital Accumulation," *The Journal of Post Keynesian Economics*, 4 (Fall): 3–9

Dobb, M., 1973. *Theories of Value and Distribution Since Adam Smith*, Cambridge: Cambridge University Press

Dow, S. C., 1985. *Macroeconomic Thought: A Methodological Approach*, Oxford: Basil Blackwell

    1988. "Post Keynesian Economics: Conceptual Underpinnings," *British Review of Economics Issues*, 10 (Autumn): 1–18

    1991. "The Post-Keynesian School," in D. Mair and A. G. Miller (eds.), *A Modern Guide to Economic Thought*, Aldershot: Edward Elgar: 176–206

Downie, J., 1958. *The Competitive Process*, London: Gerland Duckworth

Downward, P. and Reynolds, P., 1996. "Alternative Perspectives on Post-Keynesian Price Theory," *Review of Political Economy*, 8 (January): 67–78

Downward, P., Lavoie, M. and Reynolds, P., 1996. "Realism, Simulations and post-Keynesian Pricing Models," *Review of Political Economy*, 8 (October)

Dugger, W. M., 1992. *Underground Economics: A Decade of Institutionalist Dissent*, Armonk, New York: M. E. Sharpe

Dunlop, J. T., 1944. *Wage Determination Under Trade Unions*, New York: Macmillan

Dutt, A. K., 1984. "Stagnation, Income Distribution and Monopoly Power," *The Cambridge Journal of Economics*, 8 (March): 25–40

    1987. "Alternative Closure Again: A Comment on 'Growth, Distribution and Inflation,'" Cambridge Journal of Economics, 1 (March): 75–82

    1988. "Competition, Monopoly Power and the Prices of Production," *Thames Papers in Political Economy* (Autumn): 1–29

    1990. *Growth, Distribution, and Uneven Development*, Cambridge: Cambridge University Press

    1992. "Rentiers in Post-Keynesian Models," in P. Arestis and V. Chick (eds.), *Recent Development in Post-Keynesian Economics*, Aldershot: Edward Elgar: 98–122

Earl, P. E., 1993. "Epilogue: Whatever Happened to P. W. S. Andrews's Industrial Economics?," in Lee and Earl (1993): 402–27

Edwards, H. R., 1952. "Goodwill and the Normal Cost Theory of Price," *The Economic Record*, 27 (May): 52–74

    1955. "Price Formation in Manufacturing Industry and Excess Capacity," *Oxford Economic Papers*, 7 (February): 94–118

    1962. *Competition and Monopoly in the British Soap Industry*, Oxford: Clarendon Press

Edwards, J. R., 1980. "British Capital Accounting Practices and Business Finance 1852–1919: An Exemplification," *Accounting and Business Research*, 10 (Spring): 241–58

Eichner, A. S., 1969. *The Emergence of Oligopoly: Sugar Refining as a Case Study*, Baltimore: The Johns Hopkins University Press

1973. "A Theory of the Determination of the Mark-Up Under Oligopoly," *The Economic Journal*, 83 (December): 1184–200

1976. *The Megacorp and Oligopoly, Micro Foundations of Macro Dynamics*, New York: Cambridge University Press

1978. "Review of P. W. S. Andrews and E. Brunner, *Studies in Pricing*," *Journal of Economic Literature*, 16 (December): 1436–8

1980. "Gardiner C. Means," *Challenge*, 22 (January–February): 56–9

1983. "The Micro Foundations of the Corporate Economy," *Managerial and Decision Economics*, 4 (November): 136–52

1985. *Towards a New Economics: Essays in Post-Keynesian and Institutional Theory*, Armonk, New York: M. E. Sharpe

1991. *The Macrodynamics of Advanced Market Economies*, Armonk, New York: M. E. Sharpe

Eichner, A. S. and Kregel, J. A., 1975. "An Essay on Post-Keynesian Theory: A New Paradigm in Economics," *Journal of Economic Literature*, 13 (December): 1293–314

Eisner, R., 1956. *Determinants of Capital Expenditures: An Interview Study*, Urbana: The University of Illinois

1963. "Investment: Fact and Fancy," *The American Economic Review*, 53 (May): 237–46

1978. *Factors in Business Investment*, Cambridge, Mass.: Ballinger

Eiteman, W. J., 1945. "The Equilibrium of the Firm in Multi-Process Industries," *The Quarterly Journal of Economics*, 59 (February): 280–6

1947. "Factors Determining the Location of the Least Cost Point," *The American Economic Review*, 37 (December): 910–18

1949. *Price Determination: Business Practice versus Economic Theory*, University of Michigan: Bureau of Business Research, 16, Ann Arbor: University of Michigan

Eurostat, 1986. *National Accounts ESA: Input–Output Tables 1980*, Brussels: ECSC–EEC–EAEC

Farley, J. U., Hulbert, J. M. and Weinstein, D., 1980. "Price Setting and Volume Planning by Two European Industrial Companies: A Study and Comparison of Decision Processes," *The Journal of Marketing*, 44 (Winter): 46–54

Feiwel, G. R., 1975. *The Intellectual Capital of Michal Kalecki*, Knoxville: The University of Tennessee Press

1989. "Towards an Integration of Imperfect Competition and Macrodynamics: Kalecki, Keynes, Joan Robinson," in G. R. Feiwel (ed.), *The Economics of Imperfect Competition and Employment: Joan Robinson and Beyond*, London: Macmillan: 3–145

Ferguson, C. E., 1969. *The Neoclassical Theory of Production and Distribution*, Cambridge: Cambridge University Press

Fickle, J. E., 1980. *The New South and the "New Competition": Trade Association Development in the Southern Pine Industry*, Urbana: The University of Illinois Press

Fisher, W. E. and James, C. M., 1955. *Minimum Price Fixing in the Bituminous Coal Industry*, Princeton: Princeton University

Flanders, A., 1943. "Marxian and Modern Economics," *Socialist Commentary* (January): 20–3

Foster, J. B., 1994. "*Labour and Monopoly Capital* Twenty Years After: An Introduction," *Monthly Review*, 46 (November): 1–13

Foster, J. B. and Szlajfer, H. (eds.), 1984a. *The Faltering Economy: The Problem of Accumulation Under Monopoly Capitalism*, New York: Monthly Review Press

1984b. "Editors' Introduction," in Foster and Szlajfer (1984a): 7–22

Frantzen, D. J., 1985. "The Pricing of Manufacturers in an Open Economy: A Study of Belgium," *The Cambridge Journal of Economics*, 9 (December): 371–82

Gabor, A. and Granger, C. W. J., 1966. "Price as an Indicator of Quality: Report on an Inquiry," *Economica*, 33 (February): 43–70

Gaitskell, H. T. N., 1936. "Notes on the Period of Production – Part I," *Zeitschrift für Nationalökonomie*, 7 (December): 577–95

1938. "Notes on the Period of Production – Part II," *Zeitschrift für Nationalökonomie*, 9 (July): 215–44

Galambos, L., 1966. *Competition and Cooperation*, Baltimore: The Johns Hopkins University Press

Galbraith, J. K., 1952. *American Capitalism: The Concept of Countervailing Power*, Boston: Houghton Mifflin

1967. *The New Industrial State*, Boston: Houghton Mifflin

Gardner, B. M., 1978. "An Alternative Model of Price Determination in Liner Shipping," *Maritime Policy and Management*, 5: 197–218

Gillman, J. M., 1957. *The Falling Rate of Profit: Marx's Law and its Significance to Twentieth-Century Capitalism*, London: Dennis Dobson

1965. *Prosperity in Crisis*, New York: Marzani & Munsell

Glaser, B. G., 1978. *Theoretical Sensitivity*, Mill Valley, California: The Sociology Press

Glaser, B. G. and Strauss, A., 1967. *The Discovery of Grounded Theory: Strategies for Qualitative Research*, Chicago: Aldine

Glick, M. and Ochoa, E. M., 1992. "Competing Microeconomic Theories of Industrial Profits: An Empirical Approach," in W. Milberg (ed.), *The Megacorp and Macrodynamics: Essays in Memory of Alfred Eichner*, Armonk, New York: M. E. Sharpe: 225–47

Godley, W. A. H. and Gillion, C., 1965. "Pricing Behaviour in Manufacturing Industry," *National Institute of Economic and Social Research Review*, 3 (August): 43–7

Goldstein, J. P., 1985. "Pricing, Accumulation, and Crisis in Post Keynesian Theory," *The Journal of Post Keynesian Economics*, 8 (Fall): 121–34

Gordon, R. A., 1945. *Business Leadership in the Large Corporation*, Washington, DC: The Brookings Institution

Goudie, A., 1994. *Scottish Input–Output Tables for 1989*, vol. 1, *Introduction and Detailed Tables*, Edinburgh: HMSO

Grant, A., 1979. "Mergers, Monopoly Power, and Relative Shares," *The Journal of Post Keynesian Economics*, 2 (Fall): 120–34

Grant, J. and Mathews, R., 1957. "Accounting Conventions, Pricing Policies and the Trade Cycle," *Accounting Research*, 8 (April): 145–64

Groenewegen, J. (ed.), 1993. *Dynamics of the Firm*, Aldershot: Edward Elgar

Groenewegen, P., 1986. "In Defence of Post Keynesian Economics," *The 1986 Newcastle Lecture in Political Economy*, New South Wales: University of Newcastle

Halevi, J., 1978. "On the Relationship between Effective Demand and Income Distribution in a Kaleckian Framework," *Banca Nazionale del Lavoro Quarterly Review*, 125: 167–89

Hall, R. L. and Hitch, C. J., 1939. "Price Theory and Business Behaviour," *Oxford Economic Papers*, 2 (May): 12–45; reprinted in T. Wilson and P. W. S. Andrews (eds.), *Oxford Studies in the Price Mechanism*, Oxford: Clarendon Press, 1955: 107–38

Hamilton, W. H., 1957. *The Politics of Industry*, New York: Alfred A. Knopf

Hamouda, O. F., 1991. "Joan Robinson's Post Keynesianism," in I. H. Rima (ed.), *The Joan Robinson Legacy*, Armonk, New York: M. E. Sharpe: 168–84

Hamouda, O. F. and Harcourt, G. C., 1988. "Post Keynesianism: From Criticism to Coherence?," *Bulletin of Economic Research*, 40 (January): 1–33

Hansen, H. L. and Niland, P., 1952. "Esso Standard: A Case Study in Pricing," *Harvard Business Review* (May–June): 114–32

Harcourt, G. C., 1963. "A Critique of Mr. Kaldor's Model of Income Distribution and Economic Growth," *Australian Economic Papers*, 2 (June): 20–36

1965. "A Two-Sector Model of the Distribution of Income and the Level of Employment in the Short-Run," *The Economic Record*, 41 (March): 103–17

1972. *Some Cambridge Controversies in the Theory of Capital*, Cambridge: Cambridge University Press

1982. "Post Keynesianism: Quite Wrong and/or Nothing New?," *Thames Papers in Political Economy* (Summer): 1–19

Harcourt, G. C. and Kenyon, P., 1976. "Pricing and the Investment Decision," *Kyklos*, 29: 449–77

Hargreaves, E. L., 1973. *Memoirs*, Oxford: Bocardo Press

Harris, D. J., 1974. "The Price Policy of Firms, the Level of Employment and Distribution of Income in the Short Run," *Australian Economic Papers*, 13 (June): 144–51

1978. *Capital Accumulation and Income Distribution*, Stanford: Stanford University Press

Harris, J., 1977. *William Beveridge: A Biography*, Oxford: Clarendon Press

Harrod, R. F., 1939. "Price and Cost in Entrepreneurs' Policy," *Oxford Economic Papers*, 2 (May): 1–11

1952. "Theory of Imperfect Competition Revised," in R. F. Harrod (ed.), *Economic Essays*, 2nd edn, London: Macmillan, 1972: 139–87

1953. "The Pre-War Faculty," *Oxford Economic Papers: Supplement Sir Hubert Henderson 1890–1952*, 5: 59–64

1972. *Economic Essays*, 2nd edn, London: Macmillan

Hawley, E. W., 1966. *The New Deal and the Problem of Monopoly*, Princeton: Princeton University Press

Hayek, F. A. von., 1937. "Economics and Knowledge," *Economica*, 4 (February): 33–54

Henderson, H. D., 1931. "The State of Economics," in Sir Henry Clay (ed.), *The Inter-War Years and Other Papers: A Selection From the Writings of Hubert Douglas Henderson*, Oxford: Clarendon Press, 1955: 78–80

Henley, A., 1988. "Political Aspects of Full Employment: A Reassessment of Kalecki," *The Political Quarterly*, 59 (October–December): 437–50

Henry, J., 1993. "Post-Keynesian Methods and the Post-Classical Approach," *International Papers in Political Economy*, 1(2): 1–26

Hicks, J. R., 1954. "The Process of Imperfect Competition," *Oxford Economic Papers*, 6 (February): 41–54

Hieser, R., 1952. "The Degree of Monopoly Power," *The Economic Record*, 28 (May): 1–12

    1954. "Review of J. Steindl, *Maturity and Stagnation in American Capitalism*," *The Economic Record*, 30 (May): 106–9

Hirsch, W. Z., 1950–1. "A Survey of Price Elasticities," *The Review of Economic Studies*, 19(1): 50–9

Howard, M. C. and King, J. E., 1992. *A History of Marxian Economics: Volume 2, 1929–1990*, London: Macmillan

Howson, S. and Winch, D., 1977. *The Economic Advisory Council 1930–1939*, Cambridge: Cambridge University Press

Jarsulic, M., 1981. "Unemployment in a Flexible Price Competitive Model," *The Journal of Post Keynesian Economics*, 4 (Fall): 32–43

Johns, B. L., 1962. "Barriers to Entry in a Dynamic Setting," *The Journal of Industrial Economics*, 11 (November): 48–61

Johnson, H. G., 1973. *The Theory of Income Distribution*, London: Gray–Mills Publishing

Johnston, J., 1960. *Statistical Cost Analysis*, New York: McGraw-Hill

Jones, J., 1988. *Balliol College: A History 1263–1939*, Oxford: Oxford University Press

Jones, K., 1988. "Fifty Years of Economic Research: A Brief History of the National Institute of Economic and Social Research 1938–88," *National Institute Economic Review*, 124 (May): 36–62

Jossa, B., 1989. "Class Struggle and Income Distribution in Kaleckian Theory," in M. Sebastiani (ed.), *Kalecki's Relevance Today*, London: Macmillan: 142–59

Kaldor, N., 1950. "The Economic Aspects of Advertising," *The Review of Economic Studies*, 18: 1–27

    1956. "Alternative Theories of Distribution," *The Review of Economic Studies*, 23(2): 83–100

    1957. "A Model of Economic Growth," in N. Kaldor (ed.), *Essays on Economic Stability and Growth*, London: Gerland Duckworth, 1980: 259–300

    1958. "Capital Accumulation and Economic Growth," in N. Kaldor (ed.),

Further Essays on Economic Theory, London: Gerland Duckworth, 1978: 1–53

1959. "Economic Growth and the Problem of Inflation – Part I," *Economica*, 26 (August): 212–26

1966. "Marginal Productivity and the Macro-Economic Theories of Distribution," *The Review of Economic Studies*, 33 (October): 309–19

1986. "Recollections of an Economist," *Banca Nazionale del Lavoro Quarterly Review*, 156 (March): 3–26

Kaldor, N. and Mirrlees, J. A., 1962. "A New Model of Economic Growth," *The Review of Economic Studies*, 29 (June): 174–92

Kaldor, N. and Silverman, R., 1948. *A Statistical Analysis of Advertising Expenditure and of the Revenue of the Press*, Cambridge: Cambridge University Press

Kalecki, M., 1930. "Influence of a Reduction in the Prices of Industrial Consumer Goods on the Course of the Business Cycle," in Osiatynski (1990): 21–5

1932a. "Reduction of Wages during Crisis," in Osiatynski (1990): 41–4

1932b. "The Influence of Cartelization on the Business Cycle," in Osiatynski (1990): 56–9

1933a. *Essay on the Business Cycle Theory*, in Osiatynski (1990): 65–108

1933b. " 'Critical Remarks on one of the Mathematical Theories of the Business Cycle' by Aleksander Rajchman: A Rejoinder," in Osiatynski (1990): 109–19

1934a. "Three Systems," in Osiatynski (1990): 201–19

1934b. "Rejoinder," in Osiatynski (1990): 492–6

1935. "The Essence of the Business Upswing," in Osiatynski (1990): 187–94

1936. "Some Remarks on Keynes's Theory," in Osiatynski (1990): 223–32

1937a. "A Theory of the Business Cycle," in Osiatynski (1990): 529–57

1937b. "A Theory of Commodity, Income, and Capital Taxation," in Osiatynski (1990): 319–25

1938a. "The Lesson of the Blum Experiment," in Osiatynski (1990): 326–41

1938b. "The Determinants of Distribution of the National Income," in Osiatynski (1991): 3–20

1939a. *Essays in the Theory of Economic Fluctuations*, in Osiatynski (1990): 233–318

1939b. "Money and Real Wages," in Osiatynski (1991): 21–50

1939c. "An Interim Summary of Results," in Osiatynski (1991): 523–4

1940. "The Supply Curve of an Industry under Imperfect Competition," in Osiatynski (1991): 51–78

1941a. "A Theory of Long-Run Distribution of the Product of Industry," in Osiatynski (1991): 79–89

1941b. "A Theorem on Technical Progress," in Osiatynski (1991): 107–16

1942a. "Mr. Whitman on the Concept of 'Degree of Monopoly': A Comment," in Osiatynski (1991): 486–92

1942b. "Excess Profits Tax and Government Contracts," *Oxford Institute of Statistics: Bulletin*, 4 (January 10): 40–3

1943a. *Studies in Economic Dynamics*, in Osiatynski (1991): 117–90

1943b. "Political Aspects of Full Employment," in Osiatynski (1990): 347–56

1944a. "The White Paper on the National Income and Expenditure in the Years 1938–1943," *Oxford Institute of Statistics: Bulletin*, 6 (July 1): 137–44

1944b. "Three Ways to Full Employment," in Osiatynski (1991): 356–76

1945. "Full Employment by Stimulating Private Investment?," in Osiatynski (1991): 377–86

1954. *Theory of Economic Dynamics: An Essay on Cyclical and Long-Run Changes in Capitalist Economy*, in Osiatynski (1991): 205–348

1968a. "The Marxian Equations of Reproduction and Modern Economics," in Osiatynski (1991): 459–66

1968b. "Trend and the Business Cycle," in Osiatynski (1991): 435–50

1968c. "Lectures on Dynamics of Capitalist Economy," in Osiatynski (1991): 607–9

1971. "Class Struggle and Distribution of National Income," in Osiatynski (1991): 96–103

Kaplan, A. D. H., Dirlam, J. B. and Lanzillotti, R. F., 1958. *Pricing in Big Business: A Case Approach*, Washington, DC: The Brookings Institution

Keirstead, B. S., 1953. *An Essay in the Theory of Profits and Income Distribution*, Oxford: Basil Blackwell

Kempner, T., 1960. "Costs and Prices in Launderettes," *The Journal of Industrial Economics*, 8 (June): 216–29

King, J. E., 1995. *Conversations with Post Keynesians*, London: Macmillan

King, J. E. and Regan, P., 1976. *Relative Income Shares*, London: Macmillan

Kirkendall, R. S., 1966. *Social Scientists and Farm Politics in the Age of Roosevelt*, Columbia: The University of Missouri Press

Klein, P. A., 1987. "Power and Economic Performance: The Institutionalist View," *The Journal of Economic Issues*, 21 (September): 1341–77

Knapp, J. G., 1979. *Edwin G. Nourse – Economist for the People*, Danville, Illinois: The Interstate Printers and Publishers

Koot, R. S. and Walker, D. A., 1969–70. "Short-Run Cost Functions of a Multi-Product Firm," *The Journal of Industrial Economics*, 18: 118–28

Kotz, D. M., 1982. "Monopoly, Inflation, and Economic Crisis," *The Review of Radical Political Economics*, 14: 1–17

Kregel, J. A., 1971. *Rate of Profit, Distribution and Growth: Two Views*, Chicago: Aldine & Atherton

1973. *The Reconstruction of Political Economy: An Introduction to Post-Keynesian Economics*, London: Macmillan

Kriesler, P., 1987. *Kalecki's Microanalysis: The Development of Kalecki's Analysis of Pricing and Distribution*, Cambridge: Cambridge University Press

Kurz, H. D. and Salvadori, N., 1995. *Theory of Production: A Long-Period Analysis*, New York: Cambridge University Press

Laffer, K., 1953. "A Note on Some Marginalist and Other Explanations of Full Cost Price Theory," *The Economic Record*, 29 (May): 51–62

Laidler, H. W., 1931. *Concentration of Control in American Industry*, New York: Thomas Y. Crowell

Lamfalussy, A., 1961. *Investment and Growth in Mature Economies: The Case of Belgium*, London: Macmillan

Lancaster, K. J., 1966. "A New Approach to Consumer Theory," *The Journal of Political Economy*, 74 (April): 132–57

Lange, O., 1941. "Review of *Essays in the Theory of Economic Fluctuations* by M. Kalecki," *The Journal of Political Economy*, 49: 279–85

Lanzillotti, R. F., 1958. "Pricing Objectives in Large Corporations," *The American Economic Review*, 48: 921–40

Latham, E., 1957. *Political Theories of Monopoly Power*, College Park: University of Maryland

Lavoie, M., 1986–7. "Systemic Financial Fragility: A Simplified View," *The Journal of Post Keynesian Economics*, 9 (Winter): 258–66

  1992a. "Towards a New Research Programme for Post-Keynesian and Neo-Ricardianism," *The Review of Political Economy*, 4: 37–78

  1992b. *Foundations of Post-Keynesian Economic Analysis*, Aldershot: Edward Elgar

Lavoie, M. and Ramirez-Gaston, P., 1997. "Traverse in a Two-Sector Kaleckian Model of Growth with Target Return Pricing," *The Manchester School of Economic and Social Studies*, 65 (March): 145–69

Learned, E. P., 1948. "Pricing of Gasoline: A Case Study," *Harvard Business Review*, 26 (November): 723–56

Lebowitz, M. A., 1990. "Paul M. Sweezy," in M. Berg (ed.), *Political Economy in the Twentieth Century*, New York: Philip Allan: 131–61

Lee, F. S., 1984a. "Full Cost Pricing: A New Wine in a New Bottle," *Australian Economic Papers*, 24 (June): 151–66

  1984b. "The Marginalist Controversy and the Demise of Full Cost Pricing," *The Journal of Economic Issues*, 18 (December): 1107–32

  1985. "Full Cost Prices, Classical Price Theory, and Long Period Method Analysis: A Critical Evaluation," *Metroeconomica*, 37(2): 199–219

  1986. "Post Keynesian View of Average Direct Costs: A Critical Evaluation of the Theory and the Empirical Evidence," *The Journal of Post Keynesian Economics*, 8 (Spring): 400–24

  1988. "A New Dealer in Agriculture: G. C. Means and the Writing of *Industrial Prices*," *The Review of Social Economy*, 46 (October): 180–202

  1989. "D. H. MacGregor and the Firm: A Neglected Chapter in the History of the Post Keynesian Theory of the Firm," *The British Review of Economic Issues*, 11 (Spring): 21–47

  1990a. "From Multi-Industry Planning to Keynesian Planning: Gardiner Means, the American Keynesians, and National Economic Planning at the National Resources Committee," *The Journal of Policy History*, 2: 186–212

  1990b. "*The Modern Corporation* and Gardiner Means's Critique of Neoclassical Economics," *The Journal of Economic Issues*, 24 (September): 673–93

  1990–1. "Marginalist Controversy and Post Keynesian Price Theory," *The Journal of Post Keynesian Economics*, 13 (Winter): 252–63

  1991. "The History of the Oxford Challenge to Marginalism," *Banca Nazionale del Lavoro Quarterly Review*, 179 (December): 489–511

1993a. "Introduction: Philip Walter Sawford Andrews, 1914–1971," in Lee and Earl (1993): 1–34

(ed.) 1993b. *Oxford Economics and Oxford Economists 1922–1971: Recollections of Students and Economists*, Oxford: Bodleian Library

1994a. "Introduction: Means and the Making of an Anti-Keynesian Monetary Theory of Employment," in G. C. Means, *A Monetary Theory of Employment*, W. J. Samuels and F. S. Lee (eds.), Armonk, New York: M. E. Sharpe: xvii–xxxix

1994b. "From Post-Keynesian to Historical Price Theory, Part I: Facts, Theory and Empirically Grounded Pricing Model," *The Review of Political Economy*, 6(3): 303–36

1995. "From Post-Keynesian to Historical Price Theory, Part II: Facts, Theory and Empirically Grounded Pricing Model," *The Review of Political Economy*, 7(1): 72–124

1996. "Pricing, the Pricing Model and Post-Keynesian Price Theory," *The Review of Political Economy*, 8 (January): 87–99

1997. "Philanthropic Foundations and the Rehabilitation of Big Business, 1934–1977: A Case Study of Directed Economic Research," *Research in the History of Economic Thought and Methodology*, 15

Lee, F. S. and Earl, P. E. (eds.), 1993. *The Economics of Competitive Enterprise: Selected Essays of P. W. S. Andrews: A Collection*, Aldershot: Edward Elgar

Lee, F. S. and Irving-Lessmann, J., 1992. "The Fate of an Errant Hypothesis: The Doctrine of Normal-Cost Prices," *The History of Political Economy*, 24 (Summer): 273–309

Lee, F. S. and Samuels, W. J., 1992a. "Introduction: Gardiner C. Means, 1896–1988," in Lee and Samuels (eds.) (1992b): xv–xxxiii

(eds.), 1992b. *The Heterodox Economics of Gardiner C. Means: A Collection*, Armonk, New York: M. E. Sharpe

Leontief, W. W., 1937. "Implicit Theorizing: A Methodological Criticism of the Neo-Cambridge School," *The Quarterly Journal of Economics*, 51 (February): 337–51

1941. *The Structure of American Economy, 1919–1929*, Cambridge, Mass.: Harvard University Press.

1951. *The Structure of American Economy, 1919–1939*, 2nd edn enlarged, White Plains, New York: International Arts and Sciences Press

1991. "The Economy as a Circular Flow," *Structural Change and Economic Dynamics*, 2(1): 181–212

Levine, D. P., 1975. "The Theory of the Growth of the Capitalist Economy," *Economic Development and Cultural Change*, 23 (October): 47–74

1981. *Economics Theory*, vol. II, *The System of Economic Relations as a Whole*, London: Routledge & Kegan Paul

Levy, H., 1944. *Retail Trade Associations: A New Form of Monopolist Organisation in Britain*, New York: Oxford University Press

Leyland, N. H., 1950. "Review of *Manufacturing Business*, by P. W. S. Andrews," *The Oxford Magazine* (April 27): 422

Lianos, T. P., 1983–4. "A Graphical Exposition of a Post Keynesian Model," *The Journal of Post Keynesian Economics*, 6 (Winter): 313–23

Lowe, A., 1959. "F. A. Burchardt, Part I: Recollections of his Work in Germany," *Oxford Institute of Statistics: Bulletin*, 21 (May): 59–65

1976. *The Path of Economic Growth*, Cambridge: Cambridge University Press

Lydall, H. F., 1955. "Conditions of New Entry and the Theory of Price," *Oxford Economic Papers*, 7 (October): 300–11

Lyon, L. S. and Abramson, V., 1936. *The Economics of Open Price Systems*, Washington, DC: The Brookings Institution

MacGregor, D. H., 1911. *The Evolution of Industry*, London: Williams & Norgate

1934. *Enterprise, Purpose and Profit*, Oxford: Clarendon Press

Macmahon, A. W. and Millett, J. D., 1939. *Federal Administrators*, New York: Columbia University Press

Magdoff, H. and Sweezy, P. M., 1987. *Stagnation and the Financial Explosion*, New York: Monthly Review Press

Mainwaring, L., 1977. "Monopoly Power, Income Distribution and Price Determination," *Kyklos*, 30(4): 674–90

Manne, A. S. and Rudra, A., 1965. "A Consistency Model of India's Fourth Plan," *Sankhya: The Indian Journal of Statistics*, Series B, 27 (September): 57–144

Marris, R. L., 1964. "Incomes Policy and the Rate of Profit in Industry," *Transactions of the Manchester Statistical Society* (December): 1–28

Marshall, A., 1920. *Principles of Economics*, 8th edn, London: Macmillan

Mason, E. S., 1982. "The Harvard Department of Economics from The Beginning to World War II," *The Quarterly Journal of Economics*, 97 (August): 383–433

McFarlane, B., 1973. "Price Rigidity and Excess Capacity in Socialist Economies," *Australian Economic Papers*, 12 (June): 36–41

Means, G. C., 1931a. "Growth in the Relative Importance of the Large Corporation in American Economic Life," *The American Economic Review*, 21 (March): 10–42

1931b. "Stock Dividends, Large Scale Business and Corporate Savings – A Criticism," *The Quarterly Journal of Economics*, 45 (May): 536–40

1931c. "Separation of Ownership and Control in American Industry," *The Quarterly Journal of Economics*, 46 (November): 68–100

1933. "The Corporate Revolution," reprinted in Lee and Samuels (1992b): 6–31

1934a. "The Consumer and the New Deal," *Annals of the American Academy of Political and Social Science*, 173 (May): 7–17

1934b. Letter to the Editor. *The New York Times*, Section IV: 5

1935a. *Industrial Prices and Their Relative Inflexibility*, Senate Document no. 13, 74th Cong., 1st sess., Washington, DC: Government Printing Office; reprinted in Lee and Samuels (1992b)

1935b. "Price Inflexibility and the Requirements of a Stabilizing Monetary Policy," *The Journal of the American Statistical Association*, 30: 401–413

1935c. "The Major Causes of the Depression," reprinted in Lee and Samuels (1992b): 73–92

1938a. *Patterns of Resource Use*, Washington, DC: Government Printing Office

1938b. "Incentives to Capital Creation," reprinted in Lee and Samuels (1992b): 110–12

1939a. *The Structure of the American Economy*, Part I: *Basic Characteristics*, Washington, DC: Government Printing Office

1939b. "Possibilities and Limitations of Antitrust Policy," reprinted in Lee and Samuels (1992b): 113–24

1939–40. "Big Business, Administered Prices, and the Problem of Full Employment," *The Journal of Marketing*, 4: 370–81

1940. "The Controversy Over the Problem of Full Employment," *The Structure of the American Economy*, Part II: *Toward Full Use of Resources*, National Resources Planning Board, Washington, DC: Government Printing Office

1957. "Statement," US Congress, Senate, Committee on the Judiciary, *Administered Prices – Part I: Opening Phase – Economists' Views, Hearings before the Subcommittee on Antitrust and Monopoly*, 85th Cong., Washington, DC: Government Printing Office

1959a. "Discussion," *The American Economic Review*, 49 (May): 451–4

1959b. *Administrative Inflation and Public Policy*, Washington, DC: Anderson Kramer Associates

1962. *Pricing Power & the Public Interest*, New York: Harper

1964. "Letter to Jerry Cohen," reprinted in Lee and Samuels (1992b): 170–9

1972. "The Administered-Price Thesis Reconfirmed," *The American Economic Review*, 62 (June): 292–306

1974. "Prepared Statement of Gardiner C. Means," US Congress, *Market Power, The Federal Trade Commission, and Inflation, Hearings before the Joint Economic Committee*, 93rd Cong., 2nd sess., Washington, DC: Government Printing Office

1975a. "Simultaneous Inflation and Unemployment: A Challenge to Theory and Policy," in *The Roots of Inflation*, New York: Burt Franklin: 1–31; reprinted in Lee and Samuels (1992b)

1975b. "How to Control Inflation in the United States: An Alternative to 'Planned Stagnation,'" *Wage–Price Law & Economic Review*, 1: 47–74; reprinted in Lee and Samuels (1992b)

1975c. "Prepared Statement of Gardiner C. Means, Economic Consultant," US Congress House, *Incomes Policy Legislation – 1975, Hearings before the Committee on Banking, Currency and Housing on HR 4594, HR 6577, HR 4214, and HR 5142*, 94th Cong., 1st sess., Washington, DC: Government Printing Office

1975d. "Remarks Upon Receipt of the Veblen–Commons Award," *Journal of Economic Issues*, 9 (June): 149–57

1983. "Corporate Power in the Marketplace," *The Journal of Law and Economics*, 26 (June): 467–85; reprinted in Lee and Samuels (1992b)

1994. *A Monetary Theory of Employment*, W. J. Samuels and F. S. Lee (eds.), Armonk, New York: M. E. Sharpe

Mercer, H., 1995. *Constructing a Competitive Order: The Hidden History of British Antitrust Policies*, Cambridge: Cambridge University Press

Mills, F. C., 1935. "On the Changing Structure of Economic Life," in *Economic Essays in Honor of Wesley Clair Mitchell*, New York: Columbia University Press: 353–91

Minsky, H. P. and Ferri, P., 1984. "Prices, Employment, and Profits," *The Journal of Post Keynesian Economics*, 6 (Summer): 489–99

Mitchell, D. W., 1981. "Deficit and Inflation in a Post Keynesian Model," *The Journal of Post Keynesian Economics*, 3 (Summer): 560–7

Mitra, A., 1954. *The Share of Wages in National Income*, The Hague: Planbureau; reprinted, Calcutta: Oxford University Press, 1980

Moss, S. J., 1976. "The Firm, Finance and Equilibrium in Economic Theory," in M. J. Artis and A. R. Nobay (eds.), *Essays in Economic Analysis*, Cambridge: Cambridge University Press: 261–76

1978. "The Post Keynesian Theory of Income Distribution in the Corporate Economy," *Australian Economic Papers*, 17 (December): 303–22

1981. *An Economic Theory of Business Strategy*, New York: John Wiley

Mott, T. and Slattery, E., 1994. "Tax Incidence and Macroeconomic Effects in a Kaleckian Model," *The Journal of Post Keynesian Economics*, 16 (Spring): 391–409

Moulton, H. G., 1935. *Income and Economic Progress*, Washington, DC: The Brookings Institution

Myatt, A., 1986. "On the Non-existence of a Natural Rate of Unemployment and Kaleckian Micro Underpinnings to the Phillips Curve," *The Journal of Post Keynesian Economics*, 8 (Spring): 447–62

National Association of Accountants, 1957. *Costing Joint Products*, Research Report, 31, New York: National Association of Accountants

National Economics Division Staff (NEDS), 1965. "The Transactions Table of the 1958 Input–Output Study and Revised Direct and Total Requirements," *Survey of Current Business*, 45 (September): 33–56

Nelson, M. N., 1922. *Open Price Associations*, Urbana: The University of Illinois

Nightingale, J., 1978. "On the Definition of 'Industry' and 'Market,'" *Journal of Industrial Economics*, 27 (September): 31–40

Nikaido, H. and Kobayashi, S., 1978. "Dynamics of Wage–Price Spirals and Stagflation in the Leontief–Sraffa Syatem," *The International Economic Review*, 19 (February): 83–102

Norton, B., 1986. "Steindl, Levine, and the Inner Logic of Accumulation: A Marxian Critique," *Social Concept*, 3 (December): 43–66

1988. "Epochs and Essences: A Review of Marxist Long-Wave and Stagnation Theories," *Cambridge Journal of Economics*, 12 (June): 203–24

Nourse, E. G., 1941. "The Meaning of 'Price Policy,'" *The Quarterly Journal of Economics*, 55 (February): 175–209

1944. *Price Making in a Democracy*, Washington, DC: The Brookings Institution

1945. "Prefatory Note," in R. A. Gordon (ed.), *Business Leadership in the Large Corporation*, Washington, DC: The Brookings Institution: v–viii

Nourse, E. G. and Drury, H. B., 1938. *Industrial Price Policies and Economics Progress*, Washington, DC: The Brookings Institution

Nurske, R., 1935. "The Schematic Representation of the Structure of Production," *Review of Economic Studies*, 2 (June): 232–44

Nuti, D. M., 1970. " 'Vulgar Economy' in the Theory of Income Distribution," *De Economist*, 118: 363–9

Ohl, J. K., 1985. *Hugh S. Johnson and the New Deal*, Dekalb: Northern Illinois University Press

Ong, N.-P., 1981. "Target Pricing, Competition, and Growth," *Journal of Post Keynesian Economics*, 4 (Fall): 101–16

Osiatynski, J. (ed.), 1990. *Collected Works of Michal Kalecki*, vol. I, *Capitalism: Business Cycles and Full Employment*, Oxford: Clarendon Press

1991. *Collected Works of Michal Kalecki*, vol. II, *Capitalism: Economic Dynamics*, Oxford: Clarendon Press

Oxenfeldt, A. R., 1951. *Industrial Pricing and Market Practices*, New York: Prentice-Hall

Oxford Institute of Statistics, 1945. *Annual Report for the Academic Year 1944–45*, Oxford: Oxford University Press

1947. *Annual Report for the Academic Year 1946–47*, Oxford: Oxford University Press

1948. *Annual Report for the Academic Year 1947–48*, Oxford: Oxford University Press

1949. *Annual Report for the Academic Year 1948–49*, Oxford: Oxford University Press

1950. *Annual Report for the Academic Year 1949–50*, Oxford: Oxford University Press

Oxford University Gazette, 1938–45

Park, M.-S., 1995. "A Note on the 'Kalecki–Steindl' Steady-State Approach to Growth and Income Distribution," *The Manchester School of Economic and Social Studies*, 63 (September): 297–310

Parker, M. L., 1965. "Input–Output Analysis in Western Australia," *The Economic Record*, 41 (December): 626–8

Pasinetti, L. L., 1977. *Lecturers on the Theory of Production*, New York: Columbia University Press

Penrose, E., 1959. *The Theory of the Growth of the Firm*, Oxford: Basil Blackwell

Phelps Brown, E. H. and Hart, P. E., 1952. "The Share of Wages in National Income," *The Economic Journal*, 62 (June): 253–77

Political and Economic Planning, 1957. *Industrial Trade Associations: Activities and Organisation*, London: George Allen & Unwin

Reder, M. W., 1959. "Alternative Theories of Labor's Share," in P. A. Baran, T. Scitovsky and E. S. Shaw (eds.), *The Allocation of Economic Resources*, Stanford: Stanford University Press: 180–206

Reynolds, P. J., 1983. "Kalecki's Degree of Monopoly," *The Journal of Post Keynesian Economics*, 5 (Spring): 493–503

1984a. "An Empirical Analysis of the Degree of Monopoly Theory of Distribution," *The Bulletin of Economic Research*, 36(1): 59–84

1984b. "Toward a Kaleckian Alternative Economics," *The British Review of Economic Issues*, 6 (Autumn): 121–4

1987. *Political Economy: A Synthesis of Kaleckian and Post Keynesian Economics*, New York: St. Martin's Press

1989. "Kaleckian and Post-Keynesian Theories of Pricing: Some Extensions and Implications," *Thames Papers in Political Economy* (Autumn): 1–31

Riach, P. A., 1969. "A Framework for Macro-Distribution Analysis," *Kyklos*, 22(3): 542–65

1971. "Kalecki's Degree of Monopoly Reconsidered," *Australian Economic Papers*, 10 (June): 50–60

Richardson, G. B., 1960. *Information and Investment: A Study in the Working of the Competitive Economy*, Oxford: Oxford University Press

1965. "The Theory of Restrictive Trade Practices," *Oxford Economic Papers*, 17 (November): 432–49

1966. "The Pricing of Heavy Electrical Equipment: Competition or Agreement?," *The Bulletin of the Oxford University of Economics and Statistics*, 28: 73–92

1967. "Price Notification Schemes," *Oxford Economic Papers*, 19: 359–69

1969. *The Future of the Heavy Electrical Plant Industry*, London: BEAMA

Riley, H. E., 1958. *Frequency of Change in Wholesale Prices: A Study of Price Flexibility*, report 142, Washington: US Department of Labor, Bureau of Labor Statistics

Rimmer, R., 1993. *Income Distribution in a Corporate Economy*, Aldershot: Edward Elgar

Ripley, W. Z. (ed.), 1905. *Trusts, Pools and Corporations*, Boston: Ginn

1927. *Main Street and Wall Street*, Boston: Little, Brown

Robertson, D. H., 1949. Letter to P. W. S. Andrews, February 14, in Lee and Earl (1993): 116–17

Robinson, E. A. G., 1950. "The Pricing of Manufactured Products," *The Economic Journal*, 60 (December): 771–80

Robinson, J., 1942. *An Essay on Marxian Economics*, London: Macmillan

1943a. "Abolishing Unnecessary Poverty," in *Planning for Abundance*, London: National Peace Council: 3–7

1943b. *The Problem of Full Employment*, London: Workers' Educational Association

1943c. "Planning Full Employment," in J. Robinson, *Collected Economic Papers*, vol. I, Oxford: Basil Blackwell, 1966: 81–8

1943d. *The Future of Industry*, London: Commonwealth

1952. *The Rate of Interest and Other Essays*, London: Macmillan

1956. *The Accumulation of Capital*, London: Macmillan

1957. "The Theory of Distribution," in J. Robinson, *Collected Economic Papers*, vol. III, Oxford: Basil Blackwell, 1975: 145–58

1960. *Exercises in Economic Analysis*, London: Macmillan

1962. *Essays in the Theory of Economic Growth*, London: Macmillan

1965. "A Reconsideration of the Theory of Value," in J. Robinson, *Collected Economic Papers*, vol. III, Oxford: Basil Blackwell, 1975: 173–81

1969a. "A Further Note," *Review of Economic Studies*, 36 (April): 260–2

1969b. "The Theory of Value Reconsidered," *Australian Economic Papers*, 8 (June): 13–19

1970. "Harrod after Twenty-one Years," *The Economic Journal*, 80 (September): 731–7

1971. *Economic Heresies: Some Old-Fashioned Questions in Economic Theory*, New York: Basic Books

1977. "Michal Kalecki on the Economics of Capitalism," *Oxford Bulletin of Economics and Statistics*, 39 (February): 7–17

1961. "The Economics of Disequilibrium Price," *The Quarterly Journal of Economics*, 75 (May): 199–233

1978. "The Theory of Imperfect Markets Reconsidered," *The Journal of Economic Issues*, 12 (December): 871–90

Rockoff, H., 1984. *Drastic Measures: A History of Wage and Price Controls in the United States*, Cambridge: Cambridge University Press

Roncaglia, A., 1978. *Sraffa and the Theory of Prices*, New York: John Wiley

1994. "Josef Steindl's Relations to Italian Economics," *The Review of Political Economy*, 6(4): 450–8

Roos, C. F., 1937. *NRA Economic Planning*, Bloomington: The Principia Press

Ros, J., 1980. "Pricing in the Mexican Manufacturing Sector," *The Cambridge Journal of Economics*, 4 (September): 211–31

Rosenof, T., 1975. *Dogma, Depression, and the New Deal*, Washington, New York: Kennikat Press

1983. *Patterns of Political Economy in America*, New York: Garland Publishing

Rostas, L., 1948. *Productivity, Prices and Distribution in Selected British Industries*, Cambridge: Cambridge University Press

Rostow, W. W., 1948. *British Economy of the Nineteenth Century*, Oxford: Clarendon Press

Rothschild, K. W., 1947. "Price Theory and Oligopoly," *The Economic Journal*, 57 (September): 299–320

1961. "Some Recent Contributions to a Macroeconomic Theory of Income Distribution," *The Scottish Journal of Political Economy*, 8 (October): 173–99

Rowthorn, R. E., 1977. "Conflict, Inflation and Money," *The Cambridge Journal of Economics*, 1 (September): 215–39

1981. "Demand, Real Wages and Economic Growth," *Thames Papers in Political Economy* (Autumn): 1–39

Saloutos, T., 1982. *The American Farmer and the New Deal*, Ames: The Iowa State University Press

Sawyer, M. C., 1982a. *Macro-Economics in Question: The Keynesian-Monetarist Orthodoxies and the Kaleckian Alternatives*, Armonk, New York: M. E. Sharpe

1982b. "Towards a Post-Kaleckian Macroeconomics," *Thames Papers in Political Economy* (Autumn): 1–28

1985. *The Economics of Michal Kalecki*, London: Macmillan

1988. "Theories of Monopoly Capitalism," *The Journal of Economic Surveys*, 2: 47–76

1990. "On the post-Keynesian Tradition and Industrial Economics," *The Review of Political Economy*, 2 (March): 43–68

1991. "Post Keynesian Economics: The State of the Art," in W. L. M. Adriaansen and J. T. J. M. van der Linden (eds.), *Post-Keynesian Thought in Perspective*, Gronigen: Wolters-Noordhof: 31–56

1992a. "On the Origins of Post-Keynesian Pricing Theory and Macro-economics," in P. Arestis and V. Chick (eds.), *Recent Developments in Post-Keynesian Economics*, Aldershot: Edward Elgar: 64–81

1992b. "Questions for Kaleckians: A Response," *The Review of Political Economy*, 4: 152–62

1993. "Prices and Pricing in the Post-Keynesian and Kaleckian Traditions in the Short Run and the Long Run," in G. Mongiovi and C. Ruhl (eds.), *Macroeconomics Theory: Diversity and Convergence*, Aldershot: Edward Elgar: 22–36

1995. "Prices, Pricing, Capacity Utilisation and Unemployment in the Post Keynesian Tradition," in M. C. Sawyer (ed.), *Unemployment, Imperfect Competition and Macroeconomics: Essays in the Post Keynesian Tradition*, Aldershot: Edward Elgar

Schumacher, E. F., 1944a. "Public Finance – Its Relation to Full Employment," in *The Economics of Full Employment*, Oxford: Basil Blackwell: 85–125

1944b. "An Essay on State Control of Business," *Agenda*, 3(1): 42–60

Screpanti, E., 1993. "Sraffa after Marx: A New Interpretation," *The Review of Political Economy*, 5 (January): 1–21

Seccareccia, M. S., 1984. "The Fundamental Macroeconomic Link Between Investment Activity, the Structure of Employment and Price Changes: A Theoretical and Empirical Analysis," *Economies et Sociétés*, 18 (April): 165–219

Select Committee on National Expenditure, 1941. *Fourth Report*, The House of Commons, Session 1940–41, London: HMSO

Semmler, W., 1984. *Competition, Monopoly, and Differential Profit Rates*, New York: Columbia University Press

Sen, K. and Vaidya, R. R., 1995. "The Determination of Industrial Prices in India: A Post Keynesian Approach," *The Journal of Post Keynesian Economics*, 18 (Fall): 29–52

Shapiro, N., 1977. "The Revolutionary Character of Post-Keynesian Economics," *The Journal of Economic Issues*, 11 (September): 541–60

1981. "Pricing and the Growth of the Firm," *The Journal of Post Keynesian Economics*, 4 (Fall): 85–100

1988. "Market Structure and Economic Growth: Steindl's Contribution," *Social Concept*, 4 (June): 72-83

Shipley, D. D., 1981. "Pricing Objectives in British Manufacturing Industry," *The Journal of Industrial Economics*, 29: 429–43

Simon, H. A., Guetzkow, H., Kozmetsky, G. and Tyndall, G., 1954. *Centralization vs. Decentralization in Organizing the Controller's Department*, New York: Controllership Foundation

Slater, K. and Wootton, C., 1988. *A Study of Joint and By-Product Costing in the UK*, London: The Chartered Institute of Management Accountants

Smiley, R., 1988. "Empirical Evidence on Strategic Entry Deterrence," *The International Journal of Industrial Organization*, 6: 167–80

Sraffa, P., 1951. "Introduction," in P. Sraffa (ed.), *The Works and Correspondence of David Ricardo*, vol. I, *On the Principles of Political Economy and Taxation*, Cambridge: Cambridge University Press: xiii–lxii

1960. *Production of Commodities by Means of Commodities*, Cambridge: Cambridge University Press

Steedman, I., 1977. *Marx after Sraffa*, London: NLB

1992. "Questions for Kaleckians," *The Review of Political Economy*, 4: 125–51

Steindl, J., 1941a. "Economic Incentive and Efficiency in War Industry," *Oxford Institute of Statistics: Bulletin*, 3 (June 7): 164–9

1941b. "On Risk," *Oxford Economic Papers*, 5 (June): 43–53; reprinted in Steindl (1990b)

1942. "The Problem of Price and Wage Control," *Oxford Institute of Statistics: Bulletin*, 4 (October 10): 269–74

1945a. "Capitalist Enterprise and Risk," *Oxford Economic Papers*, 7 (March): 21–45; reprinted in Steindl (1990b)

1945b. *Small and Big Business: Economic Problems of the Size of Firms*, Oxford: Basil Blackwell

1952. *Maturity and Stagnation in American Capitalism*, Oxford: Basil Blackwell

1976. *Maturity and Stagnation in American Capitalism*, 2nd edn, New York: Monthly Review Press

1979. "Stagnation Theory and Stagnation Policy," *Cambridge Journal of Economics*, 3 (March): 1–14

1984. "Reflections on the Present State of Economics," *Banca Nazionale del Lavoro Quarterly Review*, 148 (March): 3–14; reprinted in Steindl (1990b)

1987. "Kalecki's Theory of Pricing: Notes on the Margin," in G. Fink, G. Poll and M. Riese (eds.), *Economic Theory, Political Power and Social Justice*, New York: Springer-Verlag: 1–17; reprinted in Steindl (1990b)

1990a. "From Stagnation in the 1930s to Slow Growth in the 1970s," in M. Berg (ed.), *Political Economy in the Twentieth Century*, London: Philip Allan: 97–115

1990b. *Economic Papers, 1941–88*, London: Macmillan

Stocking, G. W. and Watkins, M. W., 1951. *Monopoly and Free Enterprise*, New York: The Twentieth Century Fund

Strauss, A., 1987. *Qualitative Analysis for Social Scientists*, Cambridge: Cambridge University Press

Strauss, A. and Corbin, J., 1990. *Basics of Qualitative Research: Grounded Theory Procedures and Techniques*, London: Sage

Streeten, P., 1949. "The Theory of Pricing," *Jahrbücher für Nationalökonomie und Statistik*, 161 (October): 161–87

Strotz, R. H., 1957. "The Empirical Implications of a Utility Tree," *Econometrica*, 25 (April): 269–80

Swann, D., O'Brien, D. P., Maunder, W. P. J. and Howe, W. S., 1974. *Competition in British Industry: Restrictive Practices Legislation in Theory and Practice*, London: George Allen & Unwin

Sweezy, P. M., 1972. *Modern Capitalism and Other Essays*, New York: Monthly Review Press

1979. "Marxian Value Theory and Crisis," in Foster and Szlajfer (1984a): 236–50

1981. "Competition and Monopoly," in Foster and Szlajfer (1984a): 27–40

1991. "*Monopoly Capital* After Twenty-Five Years," *Monthly Review*, 43 (December): 52–7

Sweezy, P. M. and Magdoff, H., 1972. *The Dynamics of US Capitalism: Corporate Structure, Inflation, Credit, Gold, and the Dollar*, New York: Monthly Review Press

1988. *The Irreversible Crisis*, New York: Monthly Review Press

Sylos-Labini, P., 1962. *Oligopoly and Technical Progress*, revised edn, 1969, Cambridge, Mass.: Harvard University Press

1967. "Prices and Wages: A Theoretical and Statistical Interpretation of Italian Experience," *The Journal of Industrial Economics*, 15 (April): 109–27

1971. "The Theory of Prices in Oligopoly and the Theory of Growth," in P. Sylos-Labini, *The Forces of Economic Growth and Decline*, Cambridge, Mass.: MIT Press, 1984: 123–45

1974. *Trade Unions, Inflation and Productivity*, Lexington, Mass.: D.C. Heath

1979. "Prices and Income Distribution in Manufacturing Industry," *The Journal of Post Keynesian Economics*, 2 (Fall): 3–25

1983–4. "Factors Affecting Changes in Productivity," *The Journal of Post Keynesian Economics*, 6 (Winter): 161–79

Tarling, R. and Wilkinson, F., 1985. "Mark-up Pricing, Inflation and Distributional Shares: A Note," *The Cambridge Journal of Economics*, 9 (June): 179–85

Tarshis, L., 1980. "Post-Keynesian Economics: A Promise that Bounced?," *The American Economic Review*, 70 (May): 10–14

Taylor, L., 1985. "A Stagnationist Model of Economic Growth," *The Cambridge Journal of Economics*, 9 (December): 383–403

Terborgh, G., 1934. *Price Control Devices in NRA Codes*, Washington, DC: The Brookings Institution

The New York Times, 1933. "Means on Consumer Board," (September 29): 3

1935. "Wallace To Urge Monopoly Curbs," (January 9): 2

Thompson, A. M., 1992. "Unproductive Expenditure in Manufacturing," *The Cambridge Journal of Economics*, 16 (June): 147–68

Tsiang, S. C., 1947. *The Variations of Real Wages and Profit Margins in Relation to the Trade Cycle*, London: Pitman

Tucker, R., 1938a. "The Essential Historical Facts About 'Sensitive' and 'Administered' Prices," *The Annalist* (February 4): 195–6

1938b. "Reasons for Price Rigidity," *The American Economic Review*, 28 (March): 41–54

1940. "Concentration and Competition," *The Journal of Marketing*, 4 (April): 354–61

United Nations Statistical Commission, 1982. *Standardized Input–Output Tables of ECE Countries for Years Around 1970*, Conference of European Statisticians Statistical Standards and Studies, 33, New York: United Nations

US Congress, 1935. Senate, Senator Borah speaking on Monopolistic Influence Upon Industrial Prices; S. Res. 17, 74th Cong., 1st sess., January 7, *Congressional Record*, 79 (Part 1), Washington, DC: Government Printing Office: 141

Vicarelli, F., 1984. "Stagflation in the Seventies: A Relative Prices Theoretical Approach," *Metroeconomica*, 36 (June–October): 127–41

Wale, J., 1990. "The Reliability of Reported Profits and Asset Values, 1890–1914: Case Studies from the British Coal Industry," *Accounting and Business Research*, 20 (Summer): 253–67

Ware, C. F., Means, G. C. and Blaisdell, T. C., Jr., 1982. "Consumer Participation at the Federal Level," in E. Angevine (ed.), *Consumer Activists*, Mount Vernon, New York: Consumers Union Foundation: 171–97

Washington Post, 1935. "NRA Launches Hearing Today On Price Fixing" (January 9): 7

Watanabe, K., 1982–3. "An Adaptation of Weintraub's Model," *Journal of Post Keynesian Economics*, 5 (Winter): 228–44

Weintraub, E. R., 1983. "On the Existence of a Competitive Equilibrium: 1930–1954," *The Journal of Economic Literature*, 21 (March): 1–39

Weintraub, S., 1978. *Keynes, Keynesians, and Monetarists*, Philadelphia: The University of Pennsylvania Press

1979. "Generalizing Kalecki and Simplifying Macroeconomics," *The Journal of Post Keynesian Economics*, 1 (Spring): 101–6

1981. "An Eclectic Theory of Income Shares," *The Journal of Post Keynesian Economics*, 4 (Fall): 10–24

White, A. P., 1980. *The Dominant Firm: A Study of Market Power*, Ann Arbor: UMI Research Press

Wilberforce, Lord, Campbell, A. and Elles, N., 1966. *The Law of Restrictive Trade Practices and Monopolies*, 2nd edn, London: Sweet & Maxwell

Wilcox, C., 1940. *Competition and Monopoly in American Industry*, Washington, DC: Government Printing Office

Williams, J. B., 1967. "The Path to Equilibrium," *The Quarterly Journal of Economics*, 81 (May): 241–55

1979. *Fifty Years of Investment Analysis*, Charlottesville, Virginia: The Financial Analysts Research Foundation

Wilson, C., 1954. *The History of Unilever*, London: Cassell

Wilson, T., 1948. "Private Enterprise and the Theory of Value," *The Manchester School of Economic and Social Studies*, 16 (May): 165–91

Wilson, T. and Andrews, P. W. S. (eds.), 1955. *Oxford Studies in the Price Mechanism*, Oxford: Clarendon Press

Wolfe, J. N., 1954. "The Problem of Oligopoly," *The Review of Economic Studies*, 21: 181–92

Wood, A., 1975. *A Theory of Profits*, London: Cambridge University Press

Worswick, G. D. N., 1944. "The Stability and Flexibility of Full Employment," in *The Full Employment of Full Employment*, Oxford: Basil Blackwell: 59–84

   1945. "A Survey of War Contract Procedure," *Oxford Institute of Statistics: Bulletin*, 7 (April 7): 79–90

   1977. "Kalecki at Oxford, 1940–44," *Oxford Institute of Economics and Statistics: Bulletin*, 39 (February): 19–29

Yamazaki, H. and Miyamoto, M., 1988. *Trade Associations in Business History*, Tokyo: University of Tokyo Press

Yellen, J. L., 1980. "On Keynesian Economics and the Economics of the Post-Keynesians," *The American Economic Review*, 70 (May): 15–19

Young, W., 1987. *Interpreting Mr. Keynes: The IS–LM Enigma*, Boulder: Westview Press

   1989. *Harrod and his Trade Cycle Group*, London: Macmillan

Young, W. and Lee, F. S., 1993. *Oxford Economics and Oxford Economists*, London: Macmillan

Unpublished material

Manuscript collections and archives

Manuscript Collections

Andrews, P. W. S., 1939. Letter to J. Willits, June 3, Rockefeller Foundation Archives, Record Group 1.1, Series 401S, Business Cycle File

   1946. Letter to D. H. MacGregor, April 18, P. W. S. Andrews Papers

   1951. Letter to Roy Harrod, October 15, P. W. S. Andrews Papers

   1966. Letter to Paolo Sylos-Labini, September 6, P. W. S. Andrews Papers

Bean, L. H., 1935. "The Need for a Flexible Industrial Price Policy," January 10, L. H. Bean Papers

   1952. "Reminiscences," Columbia Oral History Collection

Berle, A. A., 1929. Letter to Stephen G. Williams, April 24, A. A. Berle Papers, Box 12, Folder Wi–Wr

Borts, G. H., 1972. Letter to Alfred Eichner, August 23, J. V. Robinson Papers

"Cambridge Research Scheme," 1938. December, R. F. Kahn Papers, 5.1: Cambridge Research Scheme

Clague, E., 1934. Letter to Gardiner C. Means, September 27, G. C. Means Papers, Series I, Correspondence

Dobb, M., 1941a. Letter to Joan Robinson, March 7, J. V. Robinson Papers, VII: Maurice Dobb

   1941b. Letter to Joan Robinson, March 14, J. V. Robinson Papers, VII: Maurice Dobb

DeBrul, S. M., 1934a. Letter to Gardiner C. Means, November 30, G. C. Means Papers, Series I, Correspondence

1934b. Letter to Gardiner C. Means, November 30, G. C. Means Papers, Series I, Correspondence

Eichner, A. S., 1969a. Letter to Joan Robinson, February 12, J. V. Robinson Papers

1969b. Letter to Joan Robinson, March, J. V. Robinson Papers

1969c. Letter to Joan Robinson, April, J. V. Robinson Papers

1969d. Letter to Joan Robinson, August 13, J. V. Robinson Papers

1970a. Letter to Joan Robinson, March, J. V. Robinson Papers

1970b. Letter to Joan Robinson, April, J. V. Robinson Papers

1971a. Letter to Joan Robinson, April, J. V. Robinson Papers

1971b. Letter to Joan Robinson, July 13, J. V. Robinson Papers

1971c. Letter to Joan Robinson, August 9, J. V. Robinson Papers

1972a. Letter to Joan Robinson, February 1, J. V. Robinson Papers

1972b. Letter to Joan Robinson, February 28, J. V. Robinson Papers

1974. Letter to Joan Robinson, July 23, J. V. Robinson Papers

1978a. Letter to Gardiner C. Means, November 2, G. C. Means Papers, Series V, Correspondence: Alfred S. Eichner

1978b. Letter to Caroline Ware [Means], December 6, G. C. Means Papers, Series V, Correspondence: Alfred S. Eichner

1978c. Letter to Gardiner C. Means, October 5, G. C. Means Papers, Series V, Correspondence: Alfred S. Eichner

Frank, J., 1935. Letter to Gardiner C. Means, April 22, J. Frank Papers, Box 14, Folder 162

1938a. Letter to Gardiner C. Means, June 30, J. Frank Papers, Box 33, Folder 472

1938b. Letter to Gardiner C. Means, August 11, J. Frank Papers, Box 33, Folder 472

Galbraith, J. K., 1970. Letter to Gardiner C. Means, August 19, G. C. Means Papers, Series VIA, Stigler on Industrial Prices

Hall, R. L., 1937. "Notes on the Behaviour of Entrepreneurs During Trade Depression," P. W. S. Andrews Papers

1938. "The Business View of the Relation Between Price and Cost," P. W. S. Andrews Papers

Hamilton, W. H., 1934. "Study of Price Policy," October 8, L. Henderson Papers, NRA Papers, Price, Cabinet Committee on

Harriman, H. I., 1934. Letter to Gardiner C. Means, October 19, G. C. Means Papers, Series I, Correspondence

Harrod, R. F., 1936. Letter to Hubert Henderson, March 4, H. D. Henderson Papers

1937. "Notes on Interviews with Entrepreneurs," P. W. S. Andrews Papers

Henderson, H. D., 1936. Letter to Sir Malcolm McAlpine, December 18, H. D. Henderson Papers

1937. Letter to R. H. Brand, March 31, H. D. Henderson Papers

1938a. Letter to Tracy Kittredge, January 26, H. D. Henderson Papers

1938b. Letter to Sir Henry Price, April 26, H. D. Henderson Papers

Henderson, L., 1934. "Price Conference in Secretary Perkins' Office Today," May 11, L. Henderson Papers, NRA Papers, Price, Cabinet Committee on

Hitch, C. J., 1937. "Notes on Imperfect Competition and the Trade Cycle," P. W. S. Andrews Papers

Homan, P. T., 1934. Letter to Gardiner C. Means, October 24, G. C. Means Papers, Series I, Correspondence

Kahn, R. F., 1939a. Letter to M. Kalecki, July 10, R. F. Kahn Papers, 5.1: Cambridge Research Scheme

   1939b. Letter to M. Kalecki, July 11, R. F. Kahn Papers, 5.1: Cambridge Research Scheme

Kalecki, M., 1939a. Letter to R. F. Kahn, June 9, R. F. Kahn Papers, 5.1: Cambridge Research Scheme

   1939b. Letter to R. F. Kahn, July 27, R. F. Kahn Papers, 5.1: Cambridge Research Scheme

Keynes, J. M., 1939a. "Mr. Rothbart's Interim Report on Retail Sales in Great Britain," May 22, R. F. Kahn Papers, 5.1: Cambridge Research Scheme

   1939b. Undated Letter to R. F. Kahn, R. F. Kahn Papers, 5.1: Cambridge Research Scheme

Kittredge, T. B., 1936. "Research Project at Oxford Relating to Business Cycle Problems," November 16, Rockefeller Foundation Archives, Record Group 1.1, Series 401S, Trade and Business Cycle Files

   1937. "Application for Appropriation for Business Cycle Research Program, University of Oxford," January 5, Rockefeller Foundation Archives, Record Group 1.1, Series 401S, Trade and Business Cycle Files

Lanzillotti, R. F., 1960. Letter to Gardiner C. Means, September 12, G. C. Means Papers, Series V, Folder: Correspondence

Lester, R. A., 1949. Letter to P. W. S. Andrews, June 2, P. W. S. Andrews Papers

Lubin, I., 1935. "Cabinet Committee on Prices," September 5, Franklin D. Roosevelt Papers, Official File 327, Price Fixing 1936

Means, G. C., 1934a. "Research on Prices," G. C. Means Papers, Series I: Price, Cabinet Committee on

   1934b. Letter to Victor von Szeliski, September 14, National Recovery Administration, Office Files of Victor Sparton von Szeliski, Box 7416, Folder M

   1934c. Letter to H. I. Harriman, October 27, G. C. Means Papers, Series I, Correspondence

   1934d. Letter to H. L. Shepherd, December 21, G. C. Means Papers, Series I, Correspondence

   1934e. "NRA and AAA and the Reorganization of Industrial Policy Making," October 15, C. E. Merriam Papers, Box 172, Folder 9

   1934f. "Price Fixing," March 14, G. C. Means Papers, Series I, Price Fixing

   1934g. "The Price Problem," May 3, G. C. Means Papers, Series I, Price Problem

   1935a. Letter to John R. Commons, February 5, G. C. Means Papers, Series I, Correspondence

1935b. Letter to Willford I. King, May 10, G. C. Means Papers, Series I, Senate Document 13

1938a. Letter to Jerome Frank, June 27, J. Frank Papers, Box 33, Folder 472

1938b. Letter to Jerome Frank, July 16, J. Frank Papers, Box 33, Folder 472

1938c. Letter to Jerome Frank, October 20, J. Frank Papers, Box 33, Folder 472

1939. "Chapter X: Conclusion," National Resources Planning Board, 751

1944. Letter to William Benton, January 21, G. C. Means Papers, Series IV, Benton

1946. "Marginality and Empiricism," G. C. Means Papers, Series VIA, dr-11

1949. Letter to Herbert Elliston, November 28, G. C. Means Papers, Series IV, Correspondence: D–F

1952a. Letter to Richard A. Lester, November 14, G. C. Means Papers, Series IV, Correspondence: L–M

1952b. Letter to Richard Heflebower, December 10, G. C. Means Papers, Series IV, Correspondence: G–H

1953a. Letter to Martin Bronfenbrenner, October 5, G. C. Means Papers, Series IV, Correspondence: A–B

1953b. "Price Administration by a Monopolist," G. C. Means Papers, Series IV, Price Administration – General

1953c. "Administered Prices and Individual Firm Theory," G. C. Means Papers, Series IV, Prices, Administered and Individual Firm Theory

1953d. Letter to Rexford G. Tugwell, March 17, G. C. Means Papers, Series IV, Correspondence: T–V

1957. Letter to Richard Ruggles, August 6, G. C. Means Papers, Series IV, Correspondence: R–S

1960. Letter to James C. Bonbright, August 14, J. C. Bonbright Papers, Box 3, Folder Me

1963. Letter to Estes Kefauver, May 31, J. M. Blair Papers

1964. Letter to Howard Ross, G. C. Means Papers, Series V, Correspondence: Howard N. Ross

1971. Letter to Abba Lerner, February 17, G. C. Means Papers, Series V, Correspondence: Abba P. Lerner

1972. Letter to Dan Boorstin, February 9, G. C. Means Papers, Series V, Correspondence: B

1978a. Letter to John H. Hotson, March 30, G. C. Means Papers, Series V, Correspondence: H

1978b. Letter to Alfred S. Eichner, September 22, G. C. Means Papers, Series V, Correspondence: Alfred S. Eichner

1980. Letter to Yakov Amihud, July 17, G. C. Means Papers, Series V, Correspondence: A

Minutes of Cabinet Committee on Prices, May 23, 1934, L. Henderson Papers, NRA Papers, Price, Cabinet Committee on

Minutes of Committee on Prices, September 16, 1933, G. C. Means Papers, Series I, Price Policy Committee

Minutes of Consumer Advisory Board, September 26, 1933, G. C. Means Papers, Series I, Consumers' Advisory Board (2)

Phelps Brown, E. H., 1936a. Letter to Hubert Henderson, July 17, H. D. Henderson Papers

1936b. Letter to Hubert Henderson, November 31, H. D. Henderson Papers

1937. Letter to Wesley Mitchell, October 24, W. C. Mitchell Papers

Robinson, A., Sraffa, P. and Champernowne, D., 1938. "Report of Committee Appointed to Consider Projects of Research," August 11, R. F. Kahn Papers, 5.1: Cambridge Research Scheme

Robinson, J., 1939. Untitled Memo on the Degree of Monopoly, R. F. Kahn Papers, 5.1: Cambridge Research Scheme

1943. "Control of Monopoly," March 15, J. V. Robinson Papers, IV.6

1945. "Are Cartels Either Desirable or Necessary?," January 19, BBC Written Archives Centre

1969a. Letter to Alfred S. Eichner, June 19, J. V. Robinson Papers

1969b. Letter to Alfred S. Eichner, September 5, J. V. Robinson Papers

1970a. Letter to Alfred S. Eichner, June 9, J. V. Robinson Papers

1970b. Letter to Alfred S. Eichner, June 12, J. V. Robinson Papers

1971a. Letter to Alfred S. Eichner, April 1, J. V. Robinson Papers

1971b. Letter to Alfred S. Eichner, April 24, J. V. Robinson Papers

1971c. Letter to Alfred S. Eichner, May 19, J. V. Robinson Papers

1974. Letter to Alfred S. Eichner, July 31, J. V. Robinson Papers

Roos, C. F., 1934. "NRA and AAA and the Reorganization of Industrial Policy Making by Gardiner C. Means," September 6, L. Henderson Papers, NRA Papers, Means, Gardiner

Steindl, J., 1943. "Investigation on Small Firms," October, G. D. H. Cole Papers

1944. "Inquiry into the Size of Firms," May, G. D. H. Cole Papers

Stocking, C., 1934. Letter to Gardiner C. Means, November 22, G. C. Means Papers, Series I, Correspondence

Sylos-Labini, P., 1966. Letter to P. W. S. Andrews, September 3, P. W. S. Andrews Papers

Technical Committee, 1943–4. Minutes, W. Beveridge Papers, V.IXa, Folder 13: Minutes

Tucker, R., 1934–5. "Progress of Corporation Study," in the 1934–5 Director's Report, Appendix I, The Twentieth Century Fund Archives

1938a. "Competition, Prices, and Profits," A. D. H. Kaplan Papers, Box 82, Tucker, Rufus S.

1938b. "Price Rigidity and Oligopoly," A. D. H. Kaplan Papers, Box 82, Tucker, Rufus S.

The Twentieth Century Fund, 1934. Minutes of the Board of Trustees Meeting, May, The Twentieth Century Fund Archives

1934–5. Director's Report, The Twentieth Century Fund Archives

Washington Herald, January 8, 1935. G. C. Means Papers, Series I, Clippings

Whitney, S., 1934. "Gardiner Means, Paper on 'NRA and AAA and the Reorganization of Industrial Policy Making,'" September 26, L. Henderson Papers, NRA Papers, Means, Gardiner

Ware, C., 1982. "Reminiscences," Women in Federal Government Project

Archives
Philip W. S. Andrews Papers, London School of Economics, London, England
BBC Written Archives Centre, Reading, England
Louis H. Bean Papers, Franklin D. Roosevelt Library, Hyde Park, New York
Adolf A. Berle Papers, Franklin D. Roosevelt Library, Hyde Park, New York
William Beveridge Papers, London School of Economics, London, England
John M. Blair Papers, National Archives, Washington, DC
James C. Bonbright Papers, Columbia University, New York City, New York
G. D. H. Cole Papers, Nuffield College, Oxford, England
Columbia Oral History Collection, Columbia University, New York City, New York
Jerome Frank Papers, Yale University, New Haven, Connecticut
Hubert D. Henderson Papers, Nuffield College, University of Oxford, Oxford, England
Leon Henderson Papers, Franklin D. Roosevelt Library, Hyde Park, New York
Richard F. Kahn Papers, King's College, Cambridge, England
Abraham D. H. Kaplan Papers, University of Wyoming, Laramie, Wyoming
Gardiner C. Means Papers, Franklin D. Roosevelt Library, Hyde Park, New York
Charles E. Merriam Papers, University of Chicago, Chicago, Illinois
Wesley C. Mitchell Papers, Columbia University, New York City, New York
National Recovery Administration (Record Group 9), National Archives, Washington, DC
National Resources Planning Board (Record Group 187), National Archives, Washington, DC
Joan V. Robinson Papers, King's College, Cambridge, England
Rockefeller Foundation Archives, Rockefeller Archive Center, North Tarrytown, New York
Franklin D. Roosevelt Papers, Franklin D. Roosevelt Library, Hyde Park, New York
The Twentieth Century Fund Archives, The Twentieth Century Fund, New York City, New York
Women in Federal Government Project, Schlesinger Library, Radcliffe College, Cambridge, Massachusetts

Dissertations

Ahmad, S., 1956. "Marginal Analysis and the Theory of Full-Cost Pricing," MSc thesis, London School of Economics and Political Science
Burrowes, R. D., 1966. "Adolf Augustus Berle, Jr.: Brandeis of the Future," PhD dissertation, Princeton University
Carson, J., 1991. "Kalecki's Pricing Theory," PhD dissertation, University of Sydney
Choksi, S., 1979. "Pricing Policies in the Canadian Copper, Aluminium, Nickel, and Steel Industries," PhD dissertation, McGill University

Conant, M., 1949. "Aspects of Monopoly and Price Policies in the Farm Machinery Industry Since 1902," PhD dissertation, University of Chicago

Edwards, H. R., 1957. "Aspects of the Formation of the Prices of Manufactured Commodities," PhD dissertation, University of Oxford

Irving, J., 1978. "P. W. S. Andrews and the Unsuccessful Revolution," DPhil thesis, University of Wollongong

Norton, B., 1983. "The Accumulation of Capital and Market Structure: A Critique of the Theory of Monopoly Capitalism," PhD dissertation, University of Massachusetts

Interviews

Means, G. C., 1986. Interview, December 31
Phelps Brown, 1980. Interview, Oxford, May 19, in Lee (1993b)
Richardson, G. B., 1986. Interview, August 6, Oxford, in Lee (1993b)
Roberthall, Lord Robert, 1980. Interview, London, May 15, in Lee (1993b)
Steindl, J., 1981. Interview, September 2, in Lee (1993b)
Williams, J. B., 1986. Interview, Wellesley Hills, Mass., August
Worswick, 1986. Interview, August 5, in Lee (1993b)

Personal communications and recollections

   Personal communications
Barna, T., 1990. Personal communication, November 17
Bellamy, R., 1981. Personal communication, September 10, in Lee (1993b)
Bretherton, R. F., 1980. Personal communication, May 20, in Lee (1993b)
Brown, A. J., 1979. Personal communication, August 22, in Lee (1993b)
Edwards, H. R., 1982. Personal communication, August 2, in Lee (1993b)
Eiteman, W. J., 1982. Personal communication, February 9, in Lee (1995u)
   1985. Personal communication, June 27, in Lee (1995u)
Green, J., 1986. Personal communication, November 13
Hon, R. C., 1987. Personal communication, September 8, in Lee (1995u)
Jennings, M. J., 1991. Personal communication, September 6
Law, M. E., 1986. Personal communication, October 8
Phelps Brown, E. H., 1979. Personal communication, August 29, in Lee (1993b)
Reddaway, B. R., 1994. Personal communication, November 11
Richardson, G. B., 1981. Personal communication, September 3, in Lee (1993b)
Roberthall, Lord Robert, 1979. Personal communication, October 3, in Lee (1993b)
   1982. Personal communication, February 17, in Lee (1993b)
Robinson, E. A. G., 1980. Personal communication, May 31, in Lee (1993b)
Robinson, R., 1981. Personal communication, June 18, in Lee (1995u)
   1982. Personal communication, February 9, in Lee (1995u)
   1989. Personal communication, November 19
Shackle, G. L. S., 1979. Personal communication, July 11, in Lee (1993b)
   1980. Personal communication, April 16, in Lee (1993b)

Sylos-Labini, P., 1982. Personal communication, January 10, in Lee (1995*u*)
Thorp, W. L., 1987. Personal communication, February 10, in Lee (1995*u*)
Williams, J. B., 1983. Personal communication, October 14, in Lee (1995*u*)
Wilson, T., 1982. Personal communication, April 22, in Lee (1993b)

Recollections
Beginning in 1979, the author began collecting recollections from economists who were some way connected with the doctrines of administered prices, normal cost pricing, and mark up pricing. The recollections consist of letters and interviews in which answers were given to specific questions. A compilation of all the interviews and letters may be found in Lee (1993b, 1995*u*).

Unpublished material

Andrews, P. W. S., 1953. Letter to A. Silberston, March 23, a copy of the letter in the author's possession; the original in A. Silberston's possession
    1966. Letter to R. Robinson, March 3, in possession of the author
Carson, J., 1993. "Kalecki's Pricing Theory: Marginalist to the End?"
Deprez, J., 1990. "Markup Pricing and Effective Demand Changes in a Post Keynesian Model"
Eichner, A. S., 1972. Letter to Adrian Wood, June 7, in possession of the author
Foss, N. J., 1994. "G. B. Richardson, Austrian Economics, and the Post-Marshallians," *Working Paper*, 94-3, Institute of Industrial Economics and Strategy, Copenhagen Business School
Hazeldine, T., 1979. "Generalizing from Case Studies: The First 46 Reports of the UK Price Commission," *Warwick Economic Research Papers*, 147
King, J. E. and Rimmer, R. J., 1994. "Industrial Structure, Pricing and Stagnation: a Model in the Spirit of Kaldor, Kalecki and Steindl"
Lavoie, M., 1990. "Money in a Common Research Programme for Post-Keynesianism and Neo-Ricardianism"
Lee, F. S., 1995. "Grounding Post Keynesian Price Theory: Recollections of Economists"
    1997. "Gunpowder Trade Association and Market Stability, 1872–1902"
Ludlow-Wiechers, J., 1990. "Second Thoughts on First Questions"
Means, G. C., 1934. "NRA and AAA reorganization of Industrial Policy Making," Washington, DC, August 29
    1988. "The New Non-Monetary Source of Inflation and Its Elimination"
Nightingale, J., 1995. "Contrasts and Common Threads in the Work of Two Oxford Economists: G. B. Richardson and Jack Downie try to reverse the tide of Cambridge orthodoxy in the 1950s"
    1988. "The Marxian New Classicism: Accumulation and Society in Marx and the Theory of Monopoly Capitalism"
Park, M.-P., 1993. "Mark-up Pricing and the Prices of Production"
Reynolds, P. J., 1980. "Kalecki and the Post-Keynesians: A Reinterpretation," North Staffordshire Polytechnic, Department of Economics, *Working Paper*, 4

Robinson, R., 1980. "Pricing in Oligopolistic Markets"

Sawyer, M. C., 1990. "Prices, Pricing and Growth: An Attempted Synthesis"

Skott, P., 1988. "Dynamics of a Keynesian Economy under Different Monetary Regimes," University of Aarhus, Institute of Economics, *Working Paper*, 16

Slattery, E. M. and Slattery, S. P., 1993. "Tax Incidence and Conflict Inflation"

Thorp, W. L., 1934. "Recent Price Behavior," Washington, DC

Toporowski, J., 1990. "Profits, Wages and Industrial Structure: An Essay on Kalecki and Maturity and Stagflation in British Capitalism"

1993. "Methodology and Industrial Maturity in Steindl's Capitalism," *Research Papers in International Business*, 21, South Bank University, London

University of Lowell, n.d. Registrar, Permanent Record Card of Gardiner Coit Means, University of Lowell, Massachusetts

Ware, C. F., 1988. "Some Notes on Gardiner C. Means"

Williams, J. B., 1949. "The Current Assets Theory of Value"

1964. *The Current Assets Mechanism: A Financial Theory of the Firm*

Wood, A., 1973. Letter to Brian Reddaway, January 3, in possession of the author

Index